Reference Guides in Literature
Number 17
Ronald Gottesman, *Editor*
Joseph Katz, *Consulting Editor*

William James: A Reference Guide

Ignas K. Skrupskelis

G. K. HALL & CO., 70 LINCOLN STREET, BOSTON, MASS.

Library of Congress Cataloging in Publication Data

Skrupskelis, Ignas K   1938-
    William James : a reference guide.

    (Reference guides in literature ; no. 17)
    Includes index.
    1.   James, William, 1842-1910--Bibliography.
Z8447.5.S57   [B945.J24]   016.191   76-25166
ISBN 0-8161-7805-4

This publication is printed on permanent/durable acid-free paper
MANUFACTURED IN THE UNITED STATES OF AMERICA

Contents

Introduction

There is no room in the present volume for a detailed study of
the ebb and flow of James's reputation. However, some of its major
aspects should be indicated. For references to actual writings,
omitted from the present survey, the reader should consult the index.

During his lifetime, James was involved in a number of controver-
sies in which he was a central figure but which were not restricted
to a discussion of his work. James's theory of emotion evoked much
comment in the 1890's and brought him considerable fame. In time,
it led to numerous experimental investigations. However, the theory
was shortly joined to similar views being expressed by Carl Lange,
a Danish physiologist, christened the James-Lange theory, and given
a life of its own, largely independent of James's formulation. Many
treatments of the James-Lange theory make few references to the work
of James himself. This raises a difficult problem of selection.
Every effort was made to include only those treatments of the James-
Lange theory which contain extended discussions of James's views. As
a result, some writings with experimental results bearing on the
theory are not included. The theory is still being actively discussed
and there are several survey articles to guide the reader to further
literature on the subject.

The pragmatism controversy also went beyond the limits of James's
own work. Especially before the publication of James's Pragmatism
(1907), books and articles on pragmatism often made no mention of
James, but dealt with Henri Bergson, Edouard Le Roy, and other writers. Furthermore, pragmatism was often treated as a philosophical
position and discussed entirely independently of the writings of any
particular author. This is true of some articles published in the
Journal of Philosophy which in 1906-1908 was devoting many pages to
the controversy, but also holds for other journals. James followed
the controversy intently. His vast network of correspondents sent
him clippings so that it is safe to assume that he was aware of much
of the discussion. Often, he did not distinguish between attacks on
himself, on other pragmatists, or on pragmatism in general. The
present reference guide is a guide to William James and not to the
pragmatism controversy. The inclusion only of those articles which
discuss James at some length means that important items, articles
which affected James's own statement of his views, are omitted.

Introduction

What has been said of pragmatism can be said of radical empiricism, except that the latter controversy was confined to the philosophical profession and did not reach the general public. Many discussions of radical empiricism deal with John Dewey rather than James or with a philosophical doctrine simply identified by that label.

Even such a Jamesian phrase as "the will to believe" came to be used with no reference to James himself. For example, Eleanor Harris Rowland does not mention James in her The Right to Believe (Boston: Houghton, Mifflin, 1909), while Marcus Bach in The Will to Believe (Englewood Cliffs, N. J.: Prentice-Hall, 1956) mentions James briefly, but not in connection with the will to believe.

James was already a public figure before the pragmatism controversy; the general outcry made his comings and goings even more a matter of interest to the general public. Pragmatism was discussed in the popular press at least as much as it was discussed in the learned journals. James was hailed as a revealer of a new gospel, either of light or of darkness. There is little question that this public outcry influenced James's own stance. He often commented on the size of his audiences and exulted when they grew from lecture to lecture. The entries for 1907 and neighboring years give some indication of the scope of the controversy. However, it should be remembered that newspapers and more casual references are excluded from the present volume.

Popular interest in James survived his death. The popular tradition agrees that James was a remarkable human being and, in a sense which is rarely explained, that his philosophy is especially applicable to the needs of the common man. This is often said not in reference to James's inspirational writings, but in reference to the more theoretical ones. Charles H. Compton's survey of James's readers, Who Reads What? (1934), found considerable interest in Some Problems of Philosophy among lay readers.

An aspect of James's popular reputation is his Americanism. He is often viewed as distinctively an expression of American culture, as embodying distinctively American virtues or vices. His openness to ideas regardless of their origin is often said to reflect the American repudiation of aristocracy. His pluralism, impatience with abstractions, intellectual adventurousness, have been held up as expressions of American traits. In a similar way, James's critics find in him a businessman's mentality, pre-occupation with cash-values, rather than a concern for things of the spirit. After all, does not pragmatism declare that truth is what works?

James's Americanism is not only a part of his popular reputation but is of concern to more scholarly commentators. One of James's closest friends, the philosopher Josiah Royce, finds that James expresses and purifies American ideals, while another Harvard colleague, George Santayana, depicts James against the background of the

INTRODUCTION

genteel tradition. Marxist writers follow the popular critics and
see in James an apologist for capitalism and American imperialism.

Among psychologists, it is a matter of general agreement that,
with one or two exceptions, James has no facts or theories to contribute to psychology. It is agreed, however, that he was a very
important psychologist. James represents an attitude: he was one of
the pioneers in turning psychology into a natural science. He is
important historically, for he turned psychology away from the older
introspectionism. The theory of emotion is an exception here. Another exception is James's instinct theory which, although not as
often as the theory of emotion, is sometimes held to be a contribution
to the body of psychology.

In connection with religion, there is widespread disagreement
about James's intentions in the Varieties. For some, James is a
polytheist and his work is primarily an apology for this rather pecu-
liar theology. Others treat him as a descriptive psychologist whose
primary aim is to sort out the varieties of religious experience.

In philosophy, a number of developments in James scholarship have
occurred during the last several decades. There has arisen a body of
interpretative scholarship centered around The Will to Believe pro-
viding conceptual frameworks for interpretations of James. The idea
of rationality, distinctions between the right and the will to believe,
have been introduced to show that even in The Will to Believe James
is more rigorous than at first sight appears. Another recent tendency,
represented by several books and some articles, is to search in James
for the roots, or at least traces, of the phenomenological tradition.
This tendency agrees with older interpreters such as Schiller and
Howard V. Knox in holding that The Principles of Psychology is
James's major philosophical work.

The Journal of the History of Ideas and other journals have over
the years published a number of articles studying in detail James's
sources based on James's marginalia and unpublished notes. Much in
this area remains untouched, although the critical edition now being
published should considerably advance this research.

There are many writings on James and the subject of truth, far
fewer on the pragmatic criterion of meaning and the pragmatic method.
Much of this is critical rather than expository. Commentators are
more concerned to extract the pragmatic conception of truth, and then
defend or refute it, than explain what James's own views were.

Philosophical commentators disagree about James's devotion to
rigor in philosophy. Most find him a loose, untechnical thinker.
However, there are dissenting voices who claim that James was a
rigorous thinker, the appearance of his works notwithstanding. It
is perhaps here that a critical edition can make its most important
contribution. A study of the development of James's text should show
how much attention he paid to philosophical form. The evidence is

overwhelming that he was very careful concerning points of style, even such things as capitalization and the use of italics.

This reference guide attempts to list and abstract all books and articles about William James published not later than 1974 in English, French, and German. There is a supplementary and much shorter list, without abstracts, of writings in other languages. The exclusion of Italian scholarship from the main list, made necessary by language barriers, is a matter of regret, since the Italian tradition appears rich and through Giovanni Papini and others traceable to James himself.

The supplementary list, with a few Russian exceptions, includes only languages written in the Roman alphabet. The catalogues of the Library of Congress list several Japanese works on American philosophy and about James. But in their case, the judgment of a librarian about the content of the work, as well as the rules of transliteration, would simply have to be accepted. These reference guides require that the compiler be responsible for all items listed. As a result, material of this kind had to be omitted.

The list of books was compiled from the catalogues of several libraries and bibliographies in writings about James as well as in histories of philosophy, psychology, and other relevant fields. The number of books in German is exaggerated by the fact that German dissertations were often published, while those in French and English were published infrequently. Some German dissertations are slight both in content and size, but these nevertheless appear as books. American dissertations, except the few which have been published, are relegated to a special list.

The list of articles was compiled from periodical indexes and bibliographies in works about James. Almost all of the items mentioned were themselves examined for further references. While no claims to completeness can be made, the reader can be reasonably confident that articles which have entered the main tradition of James study are listed. The use of periodical indexes results in a bias in favor of articles in which James's name is part of the title, since most periodical indexing seems to proceed in this way. In a very few cases, the compiler exercised editorial discretion and excluded short articles in practically inaccessible periodicals when their content was found to be too trivial. This was done rarely, because these guides are intended to reflect the whole range of writings about an author and not hide the fact of their triviality. Thus, something in Reader's Digest, of no interest to a scholarly interpreter, provides evidence for a certain kind of interest in James and would be listed. But a few short articles were excluded in view of the quantity of similar material.

An attempt was made to include introductions and prefaces to republications of James's works and to translations. In the case of translations, only those located in American libraries could be considered, since only such are available through inter-library loan.

Introduction

Book reviews presented a special problem. Reviews of books about James were, with a few exceptions, excluded. Reviews of books by James were selected. Several hundred reviews, especially German ones, were excluded in order to keep the project within bounds. There are numerous periodicals in which books are given brief notices, often by people with little knowledge of the author being reviewed. The bare fact that a book is mentioned in such a publication is of little significance, since most books are similarly mentioned, and does not even provide evidence of interest in a book. Even professional journals are often content with capsule notices. The compiler tried to make a selection of the longer reviews, keeping in mind the status of the reviewer and the content of the review. Thus, a brief notice by W. Ostwald was included, while a somewhat longer piece by an unknown author was not. The compiler was especially interested in criticisms and expressions of attitudes. Anyone wishing to make a more thorough study of the reception of James's books can assume that just about any periodical and newspaper took some kind of notice of a book by James, certainly after The Will to Believe (1897).

Chapters or extended references in histories of philosophy, psychology, education, religion, American culture are much more difficult to locate and often of no apparent importance. A selection was made. General histories of philosophy were excluded entirely, while histories of American philosophy were generally included. One of the issues in James scholarship is the extent of his Americanism and histories of American philosophy often contribute to this debate.

Many of James's contemporaries were posthumously honored with a "life and letters" containing anecdotes about prominent friends and letters. Such lives often include letters by James. With the addition of autobiographies, these constitute a considerable body of writing, often of interest and importance. However, such items are very difficult to locate. As many as were discovered were listed, but there is little question that many could have evaded detection.

Articles in dictionaries, encyclopedias, articles and reviews in newspapers, with rare exceptions, were excluded. The user should be warned, however, that many prominent figures contributed to newspapers, for example the Boston Evening Transcript and the New York Times, and such items could be sources of interesting opinion and information.

A major puzzle for a James bibliographer is posed by his posthumous writings. Since James's death, many have claimed to have received communications from him. Apparently, as did many psychical researchers, James had promised to try to communicate after his death. Where should such writings be listed, without committing oneself to some definite view about their origin? A compromise solution is offered by a special appendix. No attempt was made to locate these, but the items which were noticed were listed.

Introduction

A James bibliographer has to come to terms with the fact that James worked in many different fields and has been studied from many different angles. Furthermore, he never was primarily a local American figure. Thus, he is very difficult to treat bibliographically, since various fields and languages are quite unequal in the availability of bibliographic aids. Very early in the course of the project, the attempt to achieve completeness was abandoned. Not enough had been done previously to support such an ambition. Rather, the goal of the study is to reflect the different ways in which James's work has been approached and studied.

No previous published attempts at an exhaustive listing have been located. Charles H. Compton, in William James: Philosopher and Man (1957), lists references to James in 652 books. Compton was not interested in scholarly work about James. His concern was to demonstrate the extent of James's influence by finding traces of his thought in the works of others. This reference guide, however, is primarily concerned with work about James. As a result, little use of Compton's work was made here and there is little overlap between Compton's list and the present one. More helpful were bibliographies in Gilbert Maire's William James et le pragmatisme religieux (1933) and Herbert W. Schneider's A History of American Philosophy (1946). As has been said, most of the items listed were examined for further references and this process yielded numerous entries.

In the end, the quality of the coverage reflects the availability of periodical indexes. It was impossible to examine many periodicals directly, although this was done for some of the more important philosophical and psychological journals.

James was a popular figure and the publication of works such as Pragmatism (1907) were events noted by most cultural periodicals in the United States and in Europe. James's non-professional reputation is reflected in indexes to general literature, The Reader's Guide (coverage from 1890), International Index to Periodicals (begun in 1907), Essay and General Literature Index (begun in 1900), and the Biography Index (begun in 1946). These four indexes give access to hundreds of items about James. In this context, one should mention Poole's Index. This work would have provided the broadest and most exhaustive coverage. Unfortunately, Poole's is a subject index which rarely treats persons as subjects. Furthermore, it ceased publication in 1907. Also in this category should be placed the Internationale Bibliographie der Zeitschriftenliteratur, in three series, reaching into the nineteenth century. Especially extensive is the coverage of reviews and notices of books, not only German ones. This index, however, uses a system of abbreviations at times difficult to decode. The entries often are incomplete and inaccurate.

Academic fields suffer from much poorer indexing. For psychology, there is the Psychology Index (begun in 1894), but it is a subject index and persons are not treated as subjects. In philosophy, there is the Philosopher's Index (begun in 1967), an excellent index which,

unfortunately, does not cover most of our period. Philosophy also
has the Repertoire Bibliographique de Philosophie, which in various
forms goes back to James's lifetime. Not all these forms are equally
helpful. The Bulletin Signaletique 519 was also used.

Also consulted were the Education Index (begun in 1929), and the
Index to Religious Periodical Literature (begun in 1949), and the
MLA bibliography (begun in 1921). Helpful in locating articles from
the point of view of the history of medicine was the Isis bibliography in the history of science.

James scholarship, like so much of the scholarship in American
philosophy, is somewhat unbalanced. There is a great deal of valuable
interpretative work, but there are fewer efforts to lay the scholarly
foundations, to provide reference tools.

None of the several published lists of James's writings is either
accurate or complete. While the missing items are unlikely to prove
of major importance, it is still true that we do not have a complete
picture of what James wrote. This gap should be filled by the critical edition of the writings of William James, published by the
Harvard University Press. The first volume, Pragmatism, appeared in
1975. The edition will provide standard, authoritative texts with
notes and supplementary material. The edition is to consist of about
16 volumes and should be completed in the early 1980's.

Many of James's manuscripts and books are preserved at the
Houghton Library of Harvard University. Perry, in Thought and Character (1935), published fragments of the manuscripts. James's marginalia on Christoph Sigwart, Emerson, and Lotze have been used in
various contexts. But much of this material remains unstudied. The
critical edition will be concluded with several volumes of unpublished
material, although major editorial decisions still have to be made
about the scope of these volumes. A few manuscripts are scattered in
other libraries.

James's letters, in spite of his often stated dislike for writing
them, survive in large numbers. His son, Henry James, collected many
letters while working on The Letters of William James (1920). He
wrote to friends, placed ads. Somewhat later, in connection with
Thought and Character (1935), Perry sought out William James letters.
Several thousand were collected in this way and deposited in the
Houghton Library. Since many of the holders asked that originals be
returned to them, in many cases Houghton has only typed copies. While
Houghton is the major depository, numerous letters are scattered in
other libraries or are still in private hands. It should be noted
that occasionally letters by some other William James, the combina-
tion was by no means rare, are added to these collections. F. J. D.
Scott, of California State University, San Jose, is trying to locate
James letters. Houghton has about 1200 letters to James.

Introduction

Several comments about the treatment of material should be made. Entries favor the first major form of publication. Articles which first appeared in newspapers and were later reprinted in journals or books are listed under the journal or book date. Articles which first appeared in journals and were then reprinted in books usually are listed under the journal date. An exception is made in cases where the article is incorporated into a book rather than simply reprinted. In such cases, items are listed under both dates.

Names of periodicals are given as they appear on the title pages of the issues in which the articles appeared. The entries, thus, reflect changes in the names of periodicals, but without any special notation. The Journal of Philosophy in its early years was titled the Journal of Philosophy, Psychology, and Scientific Methods. It is always mentioned by the shorter title. The French Revue Philosophique de la France et de l'Étranger is always called simply the Revue Philosophique.

Book reviews in the Nation and elsewhere often appeared unsigned. Where authorship has been established, the name is given without special notation.

Writings by James are referred to by title. A full citation is given in a special list.

Books translated into English out of languages other than French or German are listed under the English translation with a reference to the original publication. On several occasions, items translated into French were treated similarly.

Compound surnames were alphabetized in accordance with the Library of Congress practice. In the few cases where transliteration was required, Library of Congress rules were followed.

Many persons assisted with this project. Librarians too numerous to mention checked references and made xerox copies. I would like especially to thank Virginia Ashley and Claudia Drum, of McKissick Library, University of South Carolina, for help with the more difficult detective work and for arranging inter-library loans. Professor Viktoria Skrupskelis, of Oberlin College, and Dr. Elona Vaisnys were of great help in obtaining materials. Professors Wolfgang Elfe and John Basil, of the University of South Carolina, assisted with translations and transliteration. Professors Eugene Thomas Long and James Willard Oliver, of the Department of Philosophy, University of South Carolina, provided much good advice, encouragement, and assistance. Mrs. Annemarie Canova helped with the translations and did the bulk of the typing. My wife, Audrone Skrupskelis, helped with the preparation of the manuscript, especially the index.

Writings by James Referred to in Text

A - BOOKS

1   Collected Essays and Reviews. Edited by Ralph Barton Perry.
New York: Longmans, Green, 1920.

2   Essays in Radical Empiricism. Edited by Ralph Barton Perry.
New York: Longmans, Green, 1912.

3   Human Immortality: Two Supposed Objections to the Doctrine.
Boston: Houghton, Mifflin, 1898. New edition with replies
to criticism, 1899.

4   The Meaning of Truth: A Sequel to 'Pragmatism'. New York:
Longmans, Green, 1909.

5   Memories and Studies. Edited by Henry James, Jr. New York:
Longmans, Green, 1911.

6   A Pluralistic Universe. New York: Longmans, Green, 1909.

7   Pragmatism: A New Name for Some Old Ways of Thinking. New
York: Longmans, Green, 1907.

8   The Principles of Psychology. 2 vols. New York: Henry Holt,
1890.

9   Psychology. New York: Henry Holt, 1892.

10   Some Problems of Philosophy: A Beginning of an Introduction
to Philosophy. Edited by Henry James, Jr. New York:
Longmans, Green, 1911.

11   Talks to Teachers on Psychology: And to Students on Some of
Life's Ideals. New York: Henry Holt, 1899.

12   The Varieties of Religious Experience: A Study in Human
Nature. New York: Longmans, Green, 1902.

Writings by James

13 The Will to Believe and Other Essays in Popular Philosophy.
    New York: Longmans, Green, 1897.

B - SHORTER WRITINGS

1 "Address of the President before the Society for Psychical
   Research," Proceedings of the Society for Psychical
   Research (English), XII (1896), 2-10.

2 "Bradley or Bergson?", The Journal of Philosophy, VII (1910),
   29-33. Reprinted in Collected Essays.

3 "Controversy about Truth," The Journal of Philosophy, IV
   (1907), 289-296. With John E. Russell. Reprinted in
   Collected Essays.

4 "A Correction," The Journal of Philosophy, VII (1910), 183-184.
   Reply to W. P. Montague, "'A Pluralistic Universe' and the
   Logic of Irrationalism" (1910).

5 "The Doctrine of the Earth-Soul and of Beings Intermediate
   Between Man and God. An Account of the Philosophy of
   G. T. Fechner," The Hibbert Journal, VII (1909), 278-294.
   Reprinted with changes in A Pluralistic Universe.

6 "Does 'Consciousness' Exist?", The Journal of Philosophy, I
   (1904), 477-491. Reprinted in Essays in Radical
   Empiricism.

7 "The Energies of Men," The Philosophical Review, XVI (1907),
   1-20.

8 "Experimental Psychology in America," Science, NS II (1895),
   626.
      Reply to G. Stanley Hall, "Editorial" (1895).

9 "The Feeling of Effort," Anniversary Memoirs of the Boston
   Society of Natural History. Boston, 1880. Reprinted in
   Collected Essays.
      A pamphlet.

10 "Humanism and Truth," Mind, NS XIII (1904), 457-475. Reprinted
   with additions in The Meaning of Truth.

11 "Immediate Resemblance," Mind, NS II (1893), 509-510.
   Reprinted in Collected Essays.

WRITINGS BY JAMES REFERRED TO IN TEXT

12 "Is Life Worth Living?", The International Journal of Ethics, VI
    (1895), 1-24. Reprinted in The Will to Believe and elsewhere.

13 "The Knowing of Things Together," The Psychological Review, II
    (1895), 105-124. A portion titled "The Tigers in India"
    reprinted in The Meaning of Truth.

14 "The Laws of Habit," Popular Science Monthly, XXX (1887),
    433-451. Reprinted as Chapter IV of The Principles of
    Psychology.

15 "The Meaning of the Word Truth," Privately printed, 1908.
    Reprinted in The Meaning of Truth.

16 "Mr. Bradley on Immediate Resemblance," Mind, NS II (1893),
    208-210. Reprinted in Collected Essays.

17 "Mr. Pitkin's Refutation of 'Radical Empiricism'," The Journal
    of Philosophy, III (1906), 712. Reprinted in Essays in
    Radical Empiricism.

18 "The Moral Equivalent of War," International Conciliation
    (February 1910), no. 27. Reprinted in Memories and Stud-
    ies and elsewhere.

19 "On Some Hegelisms," Mind, VII (1882), 186-208. Reprinted in
    The Will to Believe.

20 "On the Function of Cognition," Mind, X (1885), 27-44.
    Reprinted in The Meaning of Truth.

21 "Philosophical Conceptions and Practical Results," The Univer-
    sity Chronicle (University of California), vol. I, no. 4
    (1898), 287-310. Reprinted in Collected Essays.

22 "The Physical Basis of Emotion," The Psychological Review, I
    (1894), 516-529. Reprinted in Collected Essays.

23 "A Pluralistic Mystic," The Hibbert Journal, VIII (1910),
    739-759. Reprinted in Memories and Studies.

24 Preface to Principii di psicologia, translated by G. C. Ferrari
    and A. Tamburini. Milan: Societa Editrice Libraria, 1901.
    Written in English, but published in Italian.

25 "Professor von Gizycki and Determinism," The Open Court, II
    (1888), 889.

Writings by James

26   "Quelques considérations sur la méthode subjective," <u>Critique</u>
        <u>Philosophique</u>, VI (1878), 407-413. Reprinted in <u>Collected</u>
        <u>Essays</u>.

27   "Rationality, Activity and Faith," <u>Princeton Review</u>, II (1882),
        58-86. Combined with other essays and reprinted as "The
        Sentiment of Rationality" in <u>The Will to Believe</u>.

28   "Reflex Action and Theism," <u>The Unitarian Review</u>, XVI (1881),
        389-416. Reprinted in <u>The Will to Believe</u>.

29   "Remarks on Spencer's Definition of Mind as Correspondence,"
        <u>The Journal of Speculative Philosophy</u>, XII (1878), 1-18.
        Reprinted in <u>Collected Essays</u>.

30   Review of Marcel Hébert, <u>Le Pragmatisme</u> (1909), <u>The Journal of</u>
        <u>Philosophy</u>, V (1908), 689-694. Reprinted in <u>The Meaning</u>
        <u>of Truth</u>.

31   Review of George Trumbull Ladd, <u>Psychology: Descriptive and</u>
        <u>Explanatory</u> (New York: Charles Scribner's Sons, 1894),
        <u>The Psychological Review</u>, I (1894), 286-293. Reprinted
        in <u>Collected Essays</u>.

32   "The True Harvard," <u>Harvard Graduates' Magazine</u>, XII (1903),
        5-8. Reprinted in <u>Memories and Studies</u>.

33   "What is an Emotion?" <u>Mind</u>, IX (1884), 188-205.
        Reprinted in <u>Collected Essays</u>.

34   "What is an Instinct?" <u>Scribner's Magazine</u>, I (1887), 355-365.
        Reprinted as part of Chapter XXIV of <u>The Principles of</u>
        <u>Psychology</u>.

35   "The Will to Believe," <u>The New World</u>, V (1896), 327-347.
        Reprinted in <u>The Will to Believe</u>.

36   "A World of Pure Experience," <u>The Journal of Philosophy</u>, I
        (1904), 533-543, 561-570. Reprinted in part as "The
        Relation between Knower and Known" in <u>The Meaning of</u>
        <u>Truth</u>; the whole reprinted in <u>Essays in Radical Empiricism</u>.

Writings about William James
1868 - 1974

1868 A BOOKS - NONE

1868 B SHORTER WRITINGS

1 AGASSIZ, LOUIS and AGASSIZ, ELIZABETH CARY. A Journey in
       Brazil. Boston: Ticknor and Fields.
          Records the expedition to Brazil headed by Louis
       Agassiz and financed by Nathaniel Thayer, March 1865 to
       July 1866. James was an unpaid assistant for part of it.
       The infrequent references to James provide a record of his
       travels in the Amazon basin.

1881 A BOOKS - NONE

1881 B SHORTER WRITINGS

1 SALTER, WILLIAM MACKINTIRE. "Dr. James on the Feeling of
       Effort," The Unitarian Review, XVI (December), 544-551.
          Summarizes contents. James has an "eye for the whole of
       man."

1882 A BOOKS - NONE

1882 B SHORTER WRITINGS

1 SALTER, WILLIAM MACKINTIRE. "Dr. James' Defence of Faith,"
       The Index, NS III (August 24), 88-89.
          Criticizes "Rationality, Activity, and Faith" (1882).
       Even our choices require justification. Duty is not what
       we wish, but what ought to be. There must be a mean be-
       tween full evidence and licence.

1884 A BOOKS - NONE

1884

1884 B SHORTER WRITINGS

1   GURNEY, EDMUND. "'What is an Emotion?'" Mind, IX (July),
        421-426.
            "What is an Emotion?" (1884) seems like an "extremely
        good joke." The theory might apply to fear and rage, but
        not to states where no close connection with the environ-
        ment exists.

2   MARSHALL, HENRY RUTGERS. "'What is an Emotion?'" Mind, IX
        (October), 615-617.
            Marshall claims to have reached a theory of emotion like
        James's independently.

1887 A BOOKS - NONE

1887 B SHORTER WRITINGS

1   ANON. Notice of "The Laws of Habit" (1887), Science, IX
        (February 4), 104.
            James's treatment is "scientific and philosophical," far
        removed from the old-fashioned literary treatment. James
        stresses the "plasticity" of organic materials and draws
        "ethical and pedagogical" conclusions.

2   ANON. Notice of "What is an Instinct?" (1887), Science, IX
        (March 18), 254.
            James is one of the "pleasantest and clearest" writers
        on psychology. He concludes with a "pedagogical rule of
        practice."

1888 A BOOKS - NONE

1888 B SHORTER WRITINGS

1   CARUS, PAUL. "Determinism and Free Will," The Open Court,
        II (April 12), 887-888.
            Comments on "Professor von Gizycki and Determinism"
        (1888). Free will and determinism are not exclusive but
        complimentary. Free actions are subject to law, in that
        a man's character determines what he will do.

2   GIZYCKI, GEORG VON. "Determinism Versus Indeterminism. An
        Answer to Prof. William James," The Open Court, I
        (February 2), 729-734; (February 16), 758-762.
            Science supposes that all events are subject to law and
        this applies to human acts. Before an act has taken place,

2

several possibilities are open. However this does not
mean that the act is an accident, but only that we do not
know what will be done. If indeterminism were true, the
actions of a person would be entirely unrelated to his
character.

1890 A BOOKS - NONE

1890 B SHORTER WRITINGS

1   ANON. Review of The Principles of Psychology, The Popular
     Science Monthly, XXXVIII (December), 272-275.
         Summarizes the contents. James declares that he will
     treat psychology as a natural science, but retains a
     "faith in metaphysics." As his personality directs, James
     is both a scientist and a metaphysician, an evolutionist
     and an anti-evolutionist.

2   ANON. Review of The Principles of Psychology, Science, XVI
     (October 10), 207-208.
         This work will influence the progress of psychology,
     but is not really suited as a text-book because it is too
     long, too advanced, and reflects too much the likes and
     dislikes of its author. James approaches psychology as a
     science, but does not identify scientific psychology with
     experimental psychology. He leaves room for introspection.
     Perry, in Thought and Character (1935), II, 104, attrib-
     utes this review to J. M. Baldwin.

1891 A BOOKS - NONE

1891 B SHORTER WRITINGS

1   ANON. Review of The Principles of Psychology, Harper's New
     Monthly Magazine, LXXXIII (July), 314-316.
         Reviewed in the "Editor's Study." James comes near to
     writing a popular book. While it is not "summer reading,"
     chapters on habit, consciousness of self, memory, imagina-
     tion, instinct, will, and hypnotism should appeal to per-
     sons of "average culture." James treats his facts as a
     moralist and as an "artist."

2   BALDWIN, JAMES MARK. "James' Principles of Psychology,"
     Educational Review, I, 357-371. Reprinted in Fragments in
     Philosophy and Science (New York: Charles Scribner's
     Sons, 1902).

1891

(BALDWIN, JAMES MARK)
It is a long awaited and very important book. James's
style is marked by "inverse perspective." James begins
by stating his views in their most radical form and then
gradually modifies them so that they approach current
views. James's positivistic interpretation of psychology
is not novel, but his interpretations of the psychological
facts are. Baldwin is primarily interested in drawing out
the philosophical implications of James's work and com-
paring them with his own views.

3 COUPLAND, W. C. Review of The Principles of Psychology, The
Academy, XXXIX (April 25), 396-397.
It is a very important book, but one which suffers from
poor organization and lengthy quotations. James's treatment of space is emphasized.

4 HALL, G. STANLEY. Review of The Principles of Psychology, The
American Journal of Psychology, III (February), 578-591.
The chapter on the stream of thought is the key-chapter
and James is at his best. The chapter on hypnotism is
hastily written and "meager." James is an "impressionist"
in psychology, giving us many sketches, old and new, good
and bad. The bad could be removed in a radically revised
edition. James is primarily interested in "states of
consciousness" and loves to dissect them. They are closely
related to brain states. James cannot dispense with the
soul, although he "nowhere stalwartly" asserts his
"pneumatology."

5 MYERS, FREDERIC W. H. Review of The Principles of Psychology,
Proceedings of the Society for Psychical Research (English),
vol. VII, part XVIII (April), 111-133.
James reveals to us an experimental science in its
infancy. Every page suggests needed psychological experiments. Myers considers James's psychology as it bears on
psychical research. While praising James's neutrality,
his refusal to engage in metaphysics, Myers holds that .
experimentation can go much further than is normally
supposed in dealing with the reality of the spiritual
principle in man.

6 PEIRCE, CHARLES SANDERS. Review of The Principles of Psychology, The Nation, LIII (July 2), 15; (July 29), 32-33.
It is one of the major products of American thought.
Unfortunately, James is constantly indulging in "tricks of
language." In its method, the work is materialistic.
James's setting aside certain questions as "metaphysics"
is only a "mode of objurgation" and expression of personal

distaste. James's discussion of the theory that perception is unconscious inference is logically very weak.

7   ROYCE, JOSIAH. "A New Study of Psychology," The International
    Journal of Ethics, I (January), 143-169.
        Review of The Principles of Psychology. James's stand-
    point is neither that of metaphysical psychology, nor of
    associationism, nor of the "neurological school." He is a
    naturalist who adopts moments of consciousness as the fun-
    damental units of psychological description. From the
    point of view of ethics, most important is James's analy-
    sis of volition as an act of attention.

8   SANTAYANA, GEORGE. Review of The Principles of Psychology,
    The Atlantic Monthly, LXVII (April), 552-556.
        There is no body of doctrine that can be called psychol-
    ogy and James has not produced a "system of the human
    mind." His work is a collection of monographs on subjects
    which happened to interest him. It is too big to serve as
    a text, but is certainly a book to be read and referred to.
    James's style is "homely and direct," while his "simplicity
    and genuineness" keeps him from ignoring his own ignorance.
    Instead of mental explanations, James offers us physio-
    logical ones. This is especially noteworthy in connection
    with the theory of the association of ideas and the theory
    of emotion.

9   SULLY, JAMES. Review of The Principles of Psychology, Mind,
    XVI (July), 393-404.
        Surveys the major topics treated in the book, with
    critical comments in most cases. In general, the work
    lacks structure, there are too many quotations, too much
    "padding," too many "vivid epithets" which tend to blur
    the exactness of a scientific terminology. The work is
    given some unity by a strong original personality. James's
    approach is empirical, but James cannot suppress a strong
    streak of mysticism.

1892 A BOOKS - NONE

1892 B SHORTER WRITINGS

1   ANON. Review of The Principles of Psychology, The Athenæum,
    no. 3382 (August 20), 246-248.
        The work is gigantic, but too full of controversy.
    James does "yeoman's work in the cause of unity of mind."
    But is James serious in his claim that the business of
    psychology is to correlate mental states with brain states?

1892

2 CARUS, PAUL. "The Nature of Mind and the Meaning of Reality,"
   The Monist, II (April), 434-437.
       James's image of a "blank mind" seeing a "hallucinatory
   candle" is self-contradictory. A blank mind would be no
   mind at all and could have no hallucinations.

3 GORDY, J. P. "Professor Ladd's Criticism of James's Psychology," The Philosophical Review, I (May), 299-305.
       Two aspects of The Principles of Psychology are "epoch-
   making": the treatment of psychology as a natural science
   and the claim that our ideas at a given time "form one
   undivided mental state." Gordy tries to defend James on
   both counts against criticism by Ladd (1892).

4 LADD, GEORGE TRUMBULL. "Psychology as So-called 'Natural
   Science,'" The Philosophical Review, I (January) 24-53.
       The Principles of Psychology is a personal book. Readers
   too will react personally, depending on the treatment their
   favorite figures receive. For James, psychology as science
   is to be both descriptive and explanatory. But James insists primarily on explanation, and to our great astonish-
   ment, restricts psychology to explanations of only one
   kind and these, the most "obscure and unattainable."
   James insists that psychology avoid metaphysics, but he
   himself weaves into his work "a vast amount of conjectural
   metaphysics of physics."

5 MARILLIER, LÉON. "La Psychologie de William James," Revue
   Philosophique, XXXIV, 449-470; 603-627; XXXV, 1-32;
   145-183.
       It is a glorious work, destined to take its place among
   the great psychologies. The notion of the continuity of
   thought clearly takes first place in James's mind. But
   the idea which unifies all of the separate discussions and
   is novel is the idea of selection. Discrimination, association, reasoning, perception, memory, are all matters of
   choice. All the acts of an individual are guided by
   interest.

6 STANLEY, HIRAM M. "Some Remarks Upon Professor James's Discussion of Attention," The Monist, III (October), 122-124.
       Denies James's contention that all acts of attention are
   preceded by "ideational preparation."

7 WARD, JAMES. Review of Psychology, Mind, NS I (October),
   531-539.
       James's abridgment will not be useful as a text, but will
   attract advanced students who want to learn the views of a
   new master of the science without the bulk of the larger

work. James's strength is his ability to look at the facts, and not at some writer's account of them. Ward analyzes at length the structure of the work and finds that the over-all organization is still poor. James's liking for Americanisms and colloquialisms sometimes gets the better of him. It is a truism that an emotion is accompanied by a feeling of a bodily state, but James becomes "perplexing" when he tries to explain how these bodily states arise.

8 WORCESTER, W. L. "Observations on Some Points in James's Psychology," The Monist, II (April), 417-434; III (January 1893), 285-298; IV (October 1893), 129-143.
   The first segment criticizes James's notion of belief. James's definition is poor, because some beliefs are not knowledge and some knowledge is not belief. James does not analyze adequately the relations between beliefs and other mental states such as emotions. His method of settling doubt is as likely to lead to error as to truth. The second segment deals with emotion. In adults few emotions follow directly the perception of the exciting object and we react quite differently to the same object depending on our expectations. It is not true that the awareness of bodily change is all there is to emotion. The third segment deals with the will. James holds that will follows attention, but the reverse is actually the case.

1893 A BOOKS - NONE

1893 B SHORTER WRITINGS

1 BRADLEY, F. H. "On Professor James' Doctrine of Simple Resemblance," Mind, NS II (January), 83-88. Reprinted in Collected Essays (1935).
   A criticism of The Principles of Psychology (1890), I, 532. In response to James's replies (1893), Bradley published two short notes, Mind, NS II (July), 366-369 and (October), 510; both were reprinted in Collected Essays (1935).

2 FORD, E. "The Original Datum of Space-Consciousness," Mind, NS II (April), 217-218.
   Criticizes the view of J. Ward and James that "'massiveness'" is the "only original element" in our space perceptions and that "distance" and "position" are later elaborations.

1894

1894 A BOOKS - NONE

1894 B SHORTER WRITINGS

1   BALDWIN, JAMES M. "The Origin of Emotional Expression," The
       Psychological Review, I (November), 610-623.
           Concludes with a "postscript" on James's "The Physical
       Basis of Emotion" (1894). Either James was so careless in
       his original statement of the view that everyone misunder-
       stood him or he has come to agree with critics. This paper
       ends the controversy and should be read instead of the
       chapter on emotion in The Principles of Psychology.

2   DEWEY, JOHN. "The Theory of Emotion," The Psychological
       Review, I (November), 553-569; II (January 1895), 13-32.
           An attempt to state a theory of emotion which would
       bring into "organic connection" Darwin's principles and
       the James-Lange theory, here called the "discharge theory."

3   GARDINER, HARRY NORMAN. Review of literature on emotion, The
       Psychological Review, I (September) 544-551.
           D. Irons (1894) at least proves that James's theory
       requires a careful restatement if misunderstandings are
       to be avoided.

4   IRONS, DAVID. "Prof. James' Theory of Emotion," Mind, NS III
       (January), 77-97.
           James makes two independent claims about emotion: that
       emotion follows bodily change and that it is only the con-
       sciousness of such change. There are no cases which sup-
       port both positions. The theory breaks down both for
       strong and for subtle emotions. In the end, psychology
       requires a self who takes certain attitudes towards ob-
       jects and this feeling is the "essential element" in an
       emotion.

5   LADD, GEORGE TRUMBULL. "Is Psychology a Science?" The
       Psychological Review, I (July), 392-395.
           Comments on James's review (1894) of Ladd's Psychology:
       Descriptive and Explanatory (New York: Charles Scribner's
       Sons, 1894). It is unfortunate that James should voice
       such "debilitating sentiments" at a time when young Amer-
       icans are turning to patient laboratory work in psychology.
       His longing for a psychological Galileo who will explain
       everything in terms of "brain-states" ignores genuine
       psychological work, careful observation and cautious
       generalization.

6 SOLLIER, PAUL. "Recherches sur les rapports de la sensibilité
     et de l'émotion," Revue Philosophique, XXXVII, 241-266.
        Discusses several experiments, which bear upon the
     James-Lange theory, without drawing any conclusions.

1895 A BOOKS - NONE

1895 B SHORTER WRITINGS

1 CATTELL, J. McKEEN.. "Princeton Meeting of the American Psy-
     chological Association," Science, NS I (January 11), 42-47.
        Meeting held on December 27-28, 1894. Pp. 44-45 contain
     a report of James's presidential address, "The Knowing of
     Things Together" (1895).

2 HALL, G. STANLEY. "Editorial," The American Journal of Psy-
     chology, VII (October), 3-8.
        While James is not mentioned, this editorial touched off
     a controversy involving James. Hall claimed that his The
     American Journal of Psychology and his department of psy-
     chology at Clark University were the initiators of experi-
     mental psychology in America. George Trumbull Ladd,
     J. Mark Baldwin, J. McKeen Cattell, and James wrote letters
     (Science, NS II [November 8, 1895], 626-628) protesting
     these claims.

3 _____. Letter to the editor, Science, NS II (November 29),
     734-735.
        Reply to letters mentioned in connection with Hall's
     editorial (1895). Hall has been misunderstood and has
     never made the claims attributed to him.

4 IRONS, DAVID. "The Physical Basis of Emotion. A Reply,"
     Mind, NS IV, 92-99.
        In his "The Physical Basis of Emotion" (1894), James
     modifies his view of the emotions considerably.

1896 A BOOKS - NONE

1896 B SHORTER WRITINGS

1 ANON. Notice of "Is Life Worth Living?" (1895), The Dial,
     XX (June 16), 366.
        James's defense of optimism avoids "shallow platitudes"
     and his refutation of pessimism is found in "the very
     heart of philosophical thought."

1896

2   BRYANT, SOPHIE. "Professor James on the Emotions," Proceed-
        ings of the Aristotelian Society, vol. III, no. 2, 52-64.
        The physical symptoms which accompany emotions do not
        appear in consciousness as parts of the emotions and often
        not even as their consequences. Bryant draws up a table
        of emotions and claims that James's theory is more adequate
        in some cases than in others.

3   CATTELL, J. McKEEN. Notice of "Address of the President before
        the Society for Psychical Research" (1896), The Psycholog-
        ical Review, III (September), 582-583.
        James reviews the work of the Society with "skill and
        moderation," but James's argument can be turned against
        him. James claims that "collectively" the evidence for
        psychical phenomena may carry great weight, although each
        item may seem doubtful when considered individually. How-
        ever, if after examining many instances we find none that
        is conclusive, we may suspect that no good evidence will
        ever be found.

4   DAVIDSON, THOMAS. "'Is Life Worth Living?'" The International
        Journal of Ethics, VI (January), 231-235.
        James tries to save us from suicide by the hope that the
        unknown world is better than the known. This may cure the
        sick but the well man requires an answer which will show
        him the value of life. This is to be sought in the spir-
        itual realm which is inaccessible to James since he iden-
        tifies nature with the scientifically knowable.

5   GARDINER, HARRY NORMAN. "Recent Discussion of Emotion," The
        Philosophical Review, V (January), 102-112.
        A survey of the controversy over emotion attempting to
        weigh the arguments for and against James's theory.

6   RIBOT, THÉODULE. La Psychologie des sentiments. Paris: Félix
        Alcan. English translation, The Psychology of the Emotions
        (London: Walter Scott, 1897).
        Includes chapter on emotion in which Ribot accepts a
        modification of the James-Lange theory. Ribot holds that
        the cause and effect relation in James's theory should be
        eliminated.

7   THOMSON, J. ARTHUR. "Professor James on 'Nature,'" The Inter-
        national Journal of Ethics, VI (January), 235-238.
        Comments on remarks about nature in "Is Life Worth
        Living?" (1895). For James nature is an indifferent
        "harlot," but it should be described as a progressive,
        orderly cosmos, a mother.

1897 A BOOKS – NONE

1897 B SHORTER WRITINGS

1   ANON. Notice of The Will to Believe, Dial, XXIII
       (September 16), 149–150.   °
       That faith is often needed before its object can exist,
     while undeniable as a "general proposition," is a dangerous
     guide for "untrained seekers." James himself in his com-
     ments on psychical research carries too far his principle
     of believing what one wants to believe. But it is a well-
     written book, the product of a "rich and acute mind."

2   ARMSTRONG, A. C., JR. Review of The Will to Believe, The
       Psychological Review, IV (September), 527–529.
       For the psychologist, the chief interest of the book lies
     in the emphasis placed on "emotional and volitional ele-
     ments in consciousness," the recognition of the "interplay
     of the several phases of consciousness." In spite of its
     originality, it can be compared with many contemporary
     works. One looks forward to the promised treatise on
     empiricism.

3   HODDER, ALFRED. Review of The Will to Believe, The Nation,
       LXV (July 8), 33–35.
       James's views, in spite of appearances, must be distin-
     guished from the sophistry of subordinating "intelligence
     to desire" in the name of God and morality. If James
     invokes the will as a last resort, it is within narrow
     limits and only in the practical sphere. James's thought
     is a celebration of the "strenuous mood."

4   SCHILLER, F. C. S. Review of The Will to Believe, Mind, NS
       VI (October), 547–554.
       While a collection of essays, the work reveals a remark-
     able degree of unity. It is held together by a "strong
     and picturesque personality." The essays are popular for
     they appeal to the many without ceasing to stimulate the
     few. James's work is a protest against "reckless ration-
     alism." It is thus far only a raid upon philosophy, but
     one which promises "solid conquests."

1898 A BOOKS – NONE

1898 B SHORTER WRITINGS

1   MILLER, DICKINSON S. Review of The Will to Believe, The Inter-
       national Journal of Ethics, VIII (January), 254–255.

1898

(MILLER, DICKINSON S.)
   A "most striking and powerful product," with numerous
temptations for the critic.

2   SCHILLER, F. C. S. Review of Human Immortality, The Nation,
   LXVII (December 1), 416-417.
      James answers the materialistic objection to immortality
   by accepting all the facts while insisting that the conclusion does not follow.

3   SETH, JAMES. Review of The Will to Believe, The American
   Journal of Theology, II (April), 393-396.
      James expands the notion of empiricism to include the
   moral and the aesthetic. He reaches a "moral and
   aesthetic idealism."

1899 A BOOKS - NONE

1899 B SHORTER WRITINGS

1   ANON. Notice of Talks to Teachers, The Dial, XXVII
   (October 16), 276.
      One of the best new works on the subject, full of good
   sense, which takes away the "terrors" of psychology for
   teachers.

2   CALDWELL, WILLIAM. "'The Will to Believe and the Duty to
   Doubt,'" The International Journal of Ethics, IX (April),
   373-378.
      Discusses the controversy between James and D. S. Miller
   (1899). James's apparent irrationalism, if properly understood, is a protest against limiting experience to the
   level of the understanding with its "antitheses and its
   enumeration of abstract possibilities." James's position
   can be compared with Hegel's and that of many religions.

3   CHAPMAN, JOHN JAY. "On Prof. James's Will to Believe," The
   Political Nursery (July), 2-3.
      Any plumber knows more psychology than James. James
   gives no picture of life because he has not studied people
   who have faith. James simply does not know what these
   words mean.

4   DAVIDSON, THOMAS. Review of Human Immortality, The International Journal of Ethics, IX (January), 256-259.
      James's position is unclear. Davidson lists almost
   two pages of questions which James's notion of "transmis-
   sive function" raises.

5   DeGARMO, CHARLES. Review of Talks to Teachers, Science, NS
     IX (June 30), 909-910.
         It is well that books on education are being written by
     "real leaders of thought." This is an important contribu-
     tion to education. But why did James copy a chapter from
     his earlier book? Nobody wants to buy the same book twice.
     James holds that from a science one cannot directly derive
     an art. A "mediator" is required, a "mind full of tact
     and invention."

6   GRIFFIN, EDWARD H. Review of Talks to Teachers, The Psycho-
     logical Review, VI (September), 536-539.
         It is dangerous in psychology to have partial points of
     view obtained by abstracting from the whole. James views
     men biologically, as organisms which adapt to their envi-
     ronment, and this obscures "the free activity of mind."
     But it is the work of a "master," never dull, and full of
     "wholesome and timely" instruction.

7   HODDER, ALFRED. Review of Talks to Teachers, The Nation,
     LXVIII (June 22), 481-482.
         James explains the value of psychology for teachers in a
     "popular" work marked by "sincerity and conviction."

8   HODGE, C. W. Review of Human Immortality, The Psychological
     Review, VI (July), 424-426.
         For James thought is a function of the brain, but the
     function is transmissive and not productive. However,
     if the brain only transmits a pre-existing consciousness,
     the term 'function' loses its meaning.

9   LEE, VERNON (VIOLET PAGET). "The Need to Believe: An Agnos-
     tic's Notes on Professor Wm. James," The Fortnightly
     Review, LXXII (November 1), 827-842. Reprinted with
     changes as "Professor James and the 'Will to Believe',"
     Gospels of Anarchy (London: T. Fisher Unwin, 1908).
         James's essays are "brilliant, delicate, violent." To
     James's need to believe one should oppose a "need not to
     believe," in fact, a will not to believe. Lee attempts to
     depict a mind which does not need to believe.

10   MARSHALL, HENRY RUTGERS. "Belief and Will," The International
     Journal of Ethics, IX (April), 359-373.
         Sides with James in the controversy between James and
     D. S. Miller (1899).

11   MILLER, DICKINSON S. "'The Will to Believe' and the Duty to
     Doubt," The International Journal of Ethics, IX (January),
     169-195.

1899

(MILLER, DICKINSON S.)
Kant, Fichte, Arthur Balfour appeal to the will to overcome religious skepticism. James goes further by refusing
to sanction faith by reason. The will to believe is the
"will to deceive." James's method is to take as certain
what is not, to "hypnotize" the mind.

12 PAULSEN, FRIEDRICH. Introduction to Der Wille zum Glauben,
translated by Th. Lorenz. Stuttgart: Fr. Frommann.
James builds idealism upon a positivistic basis.

1900 A BOOKS - NONE

1900 B SHORTER WRITINGS

1 ADICKES, ERICH. Review of Der Wille zum Glauben, translated
by Th. Lorenz (Stuttgart: Fr. Frommann, 1899), Deutsche
Literaturzeitung, vol. XXI, no. 32 (August 4),
cols. 2074-2077.
James is more prudent than others who hold similar views.
He holds that decisions are based on inner need.

2 CALDWELL, WILLIAM. "Pragmatism," Mind, NS IX (October),
433-456.
An exposition of "Philosophical Conceptions and Practical
Results" (1898). Pragmatism is part of a tendency to
replace ontology with teleology. Most of the things it
stands for are good and should form a part of true
philosophy.

3 KAFTAN, [?]. Review of Der Wille zum Glauben, translated by
Th. Lorenz (Stuttgart: Fr. Frommann, 1899), Theologische
Literaturzeitung, XXV (June 9), 375-377.
Deserves serious attention and is appropriate for the
modern spiritual situation. However, there are many
doubts and questions which could be raised.

4 PAYOT, JULES. Preface to Causeries pédagogiques, translated
by L. S. Pidoux. Lausanne and Paris: Payot.
Consists primarily of quotations illustrating the great
merits of James's work. For James, psychology is a science,
while teaching is an art. Inventive individuals are needed
to apply the principles of science to the complex field of
education.

5 PRATT, CORNELIA ATWOOD. "Teachers, Students, and Professor
James," The Critic, XXXVI (Fall), 119-121.

14

A review of <u>Talks to Teachers</u>. James correctly recognizes that teaching is an art, the practice of which
depends upon the personalities of students and teachers,
and which is thus not derivable from the science of psychology. James also correctly holds up character as the
goal of education.

6   SHERRINGTON, C. S. "Experimentation on Emotion," <u>Nature</u>, LXII
(August 2), 328-331.
      The James-Lange theory can be refuted experimentally.
Dogs with severed spinal cords continue to display emotion
even though their capacity for receiving sense stimuli is
severely restricted.

7   _____. "Experiments on the Value of Vascular and Visceral
Factors for the Genesis of Emotion," <u>Proceedings of the
Royal Society of London</u>, LXVI, 390-403.
      The experiments yield no support for the James-Lange
theory of emotion and to an extent refute it.

1901 A BOOKS - NONE

1901 B SHORTER WRITINGS

1   BRÖMSE, H. Review of <u>Der Wille zum Glauben</u>, translated by
Th. Lorenz (Stuttgart: Fr. Frommann, 1899), <u>Zeitschrift
für Philosophie und philosophische Kritik</u>, CXVIII,
247-254.
      Summarizes the contents, with special emphasis on
James's preface. While James is eager to defend the having
of faith, he gives no details as to its contents.

2   HOWISON, GEORGE HOLMES. "Human Immortality: Its Positive
Argument" in <u>The Limits of Evolution and Other Essays
Illustrating the Metaphysical Theory of Personal Idealism</u>.
New York: Macmillan.
      <u>Human Immortality</u> barely leaves room for faith. Howison
attempts to raise this "ideal hypothesis" to the level of
demonstrated fact. Only once does James approach the
"idealistic doctrine of an eternal pluralism." On the
whole, for James, our personalities are only fragments,
transmitted by the brain, of the vast "mind-ocean" beyond
our consciousness. And once the transmitter dies, our
personalities will die with it and "vanish into nameless
nothing."

1901

3   J. C. Review of Human Immortality, Revue Néo-Scolastique, VIII
       (November) 430-431.
          James's willingness to let every leaf that has ever
       existed become immortal is too paradoxical to be advanced
       without proof.

4   MYERS, CHARLES S. "Experimentation on Emotion," Mind, NS X,
       114-115.
          Sherrington's "Experimentation on Emotion" (1900) pro-
       vides no evidence against the James-Lange Theory. He does
       not consider the possibility that the experimental dog may
       feel no emotion even though there are some outward signs.

5   SERGI, GIUSEPPE. Les Émotions, translated by R. Petrucci.
       Paris: Octave Doin.
          French translation of Dolore e piacere (1894), with an
       added chapter defending the James-Lange theory of emotion
       on philosophical grounds. Sergi believes that his version
       of the theory is an advance on James's.

1902 A BOOKS - NONE

1902 B SHORTER WRITINGS

1   ANON. Review of Varieties, The Outlook, LXXII (December 27),
       991-995.
          James subjects religion to scientific scrutiny, something
       which is almost never done. James is devoted to "men in
       their highest life" and writes dramatically. He can put
       himself in the place of his subjects. The effects James
       describes can only be explained by spirit and they neces-
       sitate belief in a "personal God," although James himself
       does not draw this conclusion.

2   ANON. "Varieties of Religious Experience," The Independent,
       LIV (September 18), 2251-2253.
          James presents an extraordinary "collection of intimate
       spiritual confessions" and an essay on the "truth of reli-
       gion," containing the grounds of James's "own belief in
       the fundamental tenets of religion." There is much to
       dissent from, but more valuable than specific doctrines is
       the author's spirit.

3   BISHOP, W. S. Review of Varieties, The Sewanee Review, X
       (October), 493-497.
          James has collected a "mass of testimony" to the power
       of religious belief. As a psychological study, it cannot
       contribute to the "objective content" of religion. In

Lecture 18, James makes "short work" of positive doctrines concerning God.

4   COCKERELL, T. D. A. Review of Varieties, The Dial, XXXIII (November 16), 322-323.
      "One of the great books of our time" which finds the origin of religion in the "feelings and impulses of individuals." The fact that a religious experience may originate in a psychopathological condition does not rule out the "influx of some external spiritual force."

5   CROZIER, J. B. "The Problem of Religious Conversion," The Fortnightly Review, LXXVIII (December 1), 1004-1018.
      James's contention that conversions are due to the presence of God is contradicted by the fact that adherents of different religions in their mystical states experience only what they expect and that similar states can be induced by other means. Conversions are better explained by the fact that some centers of the brain become detached from others and cease being subject to their control.

6   DUMAS, GEORGES. Introduction to La Théorie de l'émotion, translated by G. Dumas. Paris: Félix Alcan.
      Dumas contrasts the views of James and Lange and prefers James's. For James emotions are not simply physiological, they are also peripheral.

7   FLOURNOY, THÉODORE. Review of Varieties, Revue Philosophique LIV (November), 516-527. Reprinted in La Philosophie de William James (1911).
      James's philosophy of religion is empirical and practical. He wishes to embrace all the detail of the world and considers vain all mere speculation. This last view is called pragmatism. Flournoy emphasizes James's refutation of "medical materialism" and his efforts to justify religion.

8   GARDNER, P. Review of Varieties, The Hibbert Journal, I (October), 182-187.
      James works on a higher level than others who have dealt with the psychology of religion. Of special interest is his attempt to justify religious beliefs.

9   PILLON, F. Review of La Théorie de l'émotion, translated by G. Dumas (Paris: Félix Alcan, 1902), L'Année Philosophique, XIII, 156-158.
      Primarily a quotation from the Introduction by Dumas.

1902

10   SAGE, M. Mme Piper et la société anglo-américaine pour les recherches psychiques. Paris: Leymarie. An abridged translation, Mrs. Piper & The Society for Psychical Research translated by Noralie Robertson (New York: Scott-Thaw, 1904).
     Many references to James's work with Mrs. L. Piper, a medium.

11   SCHILLER, F. C. S. Review of Varieties, The Nation, LXXV (August 21), 155.
     Scientific methods are introduced into a field which hitherto contained nothing but "dogmatizing." James gives us only glimpses of the new philosophy. It is hoped that James's health will allow him to produce the promised work on pragmatism.

1903 A BOOKS

1   STETTHEIMER, ETTIE. Die Urteilsfreiheit als Grundlage der Rechtfertigung des religiösen Glaubens, mit besonderer Berücksichtigung der Lehre von James. Wittenberg: Herrose & Ziemsen. Translated into English, The Will to Believe as a Basis for the Defense of Religious Faith (New York: Science Press, 1907).
     A criticism of The Will to Believe primarily on the grounds that it results in subjectivism.

1903 B SHORTER WRITINGS

1   BERLE, A. A. "The Psychology of Christian Experience," The Bibliotheca Sacra, LX (January), 1-27.
     Varieties is to be judged by considering whether or not it will make a person's religious life deeper and stronger. Here, James fails. He is guilty of many blunders obvious to anyone practiced in the "cure of souls." It is, however, good to see a Harvard professor taking such experiences seriously.

2   COE, GEORGE ALBERT. Review of Varieties, The Philosophical Review, XII (January), 62-67.
     James takes us for a walk through a great forest. We enjoy the variety and detail and the sense of not always knowing where we are going. It is hoped that the promised second volume will consider the "criterion" of the truth of the religious consciousness.

3   DELACROIX, H. "Les Variétés de l'expérience religieuse par William James," Revue de Métaphysique et de Morale XI (September), 642-669.

James and others working along similar lines have placed the study of religion within the study of human nature. After an extended account of the contents, Delacroix finds that James exaggerates the importance of individual experience and ignores the social aspects of religion.

4   HIBBEN, JOHN GRIER. Review of Varieties, The Psychological Review, X (March), 180-186.
    Makes a permanent contribution to our understanding of "religious experience and of human nature." Emphasis on the exceptional pushes aside "common experiences" expressed in "institutional religion," which, however, are the final court of appeal. James's view that the divine operates through the subconscious is suspect, since the subconscious may be the "region of chimeras." James's suggestion that every man may have his own God does away with the unity of religion.

5   KING, IRVING. "Pragmatism as a Philosophic Method," The Philosophical Review, XII (September), 511-524.
    James and Peirce emphasize the practical. The test of concrete experience is attractive to those impatient with the "vagaries" of methaphysics. But pragmatism has not analyzed adequately the relations between thought and action. The ambiguities of pragmatism would disappear if pragmatists realized that thought arises out of definite crises in activity.

6   MUIRHEAD, JOHN HENRY. Review of Varieties, The International Journal of Ethics, XIII (January), 236-246.
    A major contribution to psychology, but defective philosophically. James totally misrepresents idealists, for no serious writer attempts to construct religious objects by means of logic. James himself appeals to the "full fact," but this leads to idealism, like Royce's. James's proposed substitute for idealistic philosophy is the science of religion. This can give us the "subliminal," but never the "sublime."

7   OSTWALD, WILHELM. Review of Varieties, Annalen der Naturphilosophie, II, 142-143.
    An unusually interesting work, filled with a wealth of observations.

8   RASHDALL, HASTINGS. Review of Varieties, Mind, NS XII, 245-250.
    James undertakes a worth-while task and does it well. He makes prominent kinds of human experience undreamed of by philosophers and theologians. But he overemphasizes

1903

(RASHDALL, HASTINGS)
exceptional cases and does not realize that their social
uselessness may be due to their abnormality. By exagger-
ating the mystical side, he misses the true significance
of some religious figures. In his philosophical conclusions, James revives "Pyrrhonism," abandons the search
for truth, and hands religion and morality over to the
"sway of wilful caprice."

9   SEWALL, FRANK. "Professor James on Religious Experience,"
     The New-Church Review, X (April), 243-264.
         A review of Varieties. At times, James seems to view
     religion as a disease. He overemphasizes the morbid. In
     a book full of surprises, a major surprise is the absence
     of references to Swedenborg. James's style is "engaging,"
     marked by a "catholicity of spirit."

10   STEVENS, GEORGE B. Review of Varieties, The American Journal
     of Theology, VII (January), 114-117.
         James proposes utility as a test of religion and promises
     to develop his views at greater length in a second volume.
     The book is a "rather succinct volume of dogma" yielded
     by empirical philosophy.

1904 A BOOKS - NONE

1904 B SHORTER WRITINGS

1   ANON. "The Human Sympathy of William James," The Critic,
     XLIV (March), 244.
         A poem written after reading "The Diversities of
     Religious Belief."

2   BAWDEN, H. H. "What Is Pragmatism?" The Journal of Philosophy,
     I (August 4), 421-427.
         'Pragmatism', although less attractive, is a more dis-
     tinctive term than Schiller's 'humanism' and is to be
     preferred. As opposed to Schiller and Dewey, the pragma-
     tists offer a method for estimating the "practical value
     and results of philosophical conceptions."

3   BRADLEY, FRANCIS HERBERT. "On Truth and Practice," Mind, NS
     XIII (July), 309-335. Reprinted with an introductory note
     and many changes in Essays on Truth and Reality (1914).
         Aimed primarily at Schiller, but contains critical re-
     marks about James. Bradley argues that the pragmatic iden-
     tification of truth with the "practical working of an idea"
     is mistaken.

4   BROWN, FRANCIS THEODORE. "William James and the Philosophy of
        Emerson," Methodist Review, LXXVI (September), 747-756.
        James has avoided the half-truths of Emersonian monism
        by his emphasis on activity and the human personality.
        While James does overlook the uniqueness of Christianity,
        his The Will to Believe can easily be placed in an "admi-
        rable modern library of Methodist apologetics."

5   FUNK, ISAAC K. The Widow's Mite and Other Psychic Phenomena.
        New York: Funk & Wagnalls.
        Contains some accounts of James's experiments with
        Mrs. L. Piper, a noted medium, and a letter from James on
        the "widow's mite" incident.

6   LEUBA, JAMES H. "Professor William James' Interpretation of
        Religious Experience," The International Journal of Ethics,
        XIV (April), 322-339.
        What James concludes about the universal element in reli-
        gion is already well known. The work is better viewed as
        preparation for a startling pluralism, akin to polytheism.
        The way to the other world is through the subliminal con-
        sciousness. This is why James emphasizes mystical states.
        But why substitute spirits who "crawl in through the sub-
        liminal door" for an omnipotent God?

7   ROYCE, JOSIAH. "The Eternal and the Practical," The Philo-
        sophical Review, XIII (March), 113-142.
        Royce isolates "pure pragmatism," a doctrine not held by
        anyone, to reveal the basis of actual pragmatism. For
        pure pragmatism, experience consists of objects character-
        ized "through and in your thoughtful deeds." This leads
        to absolute idealism.

8   RUNZE, GEORG. Review of Varieties, Zeitschrift für Psychologie
        und Physiologie der Sinnesorgane, XXXVII, 129-143.
        James's work is interesting, but disappointing to the
        exact thinker. Runze discusses the treatment of James in
        Julius Baumann, Deutsche und ausserdeutsche Philosophie der
        letzen Jahrzehnte (Gotha: F. A. Perthes, 1903).

9   STARBUCK, EDWIN D. Review of Varieties, The Biblical World,
        NS XXIV, 100-111.
        James turns the psychology of religion into a science.
        He finds the sources of religion in feeling, but this is
        not what we expect on the basis of his theory of emotion.
        The feelings themselves are manifestations of "life-
        movements" in the organism and these "life-movements" are
        the sources of religion.

1904

10   STRONG, CHARLES AUGUSTUS. "A Naturalistic Theory of the Refer-
        ence of Thought to Reality," The Journal of Philosophy, I
        (May 12), 253-260.
            The James-Miller theory of cognition, stated by James in
        "The Function of Cognition" (1885) and D. S. Miller in
        "The Meaning of Truth and Error" (The Philosophical Review,
        II [1893], 408-425) has been ignored. With the rise of
        pragmatism it is time for that theory to be revived and
        supplemented. James interprets knowledge as involving the
        relations of resemblance and operation.

11   TAYLOR, ALFRED EDWARD. "Some Side Lights on Pragmatism,"
        University Magazine (McGill), III (April), 44-66.
            James infers the truth of a belief from its existence,
        but this is illegitimate, even though the belief enjoys
        universal consent. James ignores the fact that we can
        have evidence without complete proof and that to adopt
        something as a working hypothesis is far from holding that
        to be true. James admits that some truths can be proved
        and this is a fatal admission. The existence of a truth
        independent of my will shows that to be true means some-
        thing different from being willed.

1905 A BOOKS - NONE

1905 B SHORTER WRITINGS

1   BERGSON, HENRI. Letter to the editor, Revue Philosophique,
        LX (August), 229-230.
            G. Rageot ("Ve Congrès international de psychologie,"
        Revue Philosophique, LX [July 1905], 68-87) is mis-
        taken in attributing similarities between James and
        Bergson to accidental influences. They are due to general
        and profound causes. James's "stream of thought" and
        Bergson's "durée réelle" have different meanings. Rageot
        comments on the letter, pp. 230-231.

2   BODE, BOYD HENRY. "'Pure Experience' and the External World,"
        The Journal of Philosophy, II (March 2), 128-133.
            "Thoroughgoing" empiricists find unacceptable that thought
        refers to a reality external to itself. James's is the
        latest attempt to do away with "objective reference" and
        to reduce everything to pure experience. But such efforts
        are "futile" since they lead to solipsism.

3   DESSOULAVY, C. "Le Pragmatisme," Revue de Philosophie, VII,
        89-94.

Surveys the pragmatism controversy. Pragmatism arises from three modern movements: Kantianism and the practical reason, evolutionism, and utilitarianism. Perhaps it resembles medieval scholasticism which identified the true and the good.

4 HOERNLÉ, R. F. ALFRED. "Pragmatism v. Absolutism," Mind, NS XIV, 297-334, 441-478.
   Includes a brief discussion of The Will to Believe. For James, beliefs must be proved in action and cannot remain mere "intellectual ballast." James's vision is prospective since the past is fixed and unalterable. James upholds indeterminism and this brings him into conflict with the scientific view.

5 JOSEPH, H. W. B. "Prof. James on 'Humanism and Truth,'" Mind, NS XIV (January), 28-41.
   Truths may have practical consequences, but we want to settle questions of truth or falsity apart from them. Do pragmatists identify truth with the consequences of an assertion's truth, or the consequences of believing it true, or with a beneficial reaction to an idea? If our categories evolve, how can the conception of man as adapting to his environment be taken as true "anteriorly" to them?

6 JUDD, CHARLES H. "Radical Empiricism and Wundt's Philosophy," The Journal of Philosophy, II (March 30), 169-176.
   Wundt's views are like James's. Both have similar definitions of reality and favor abandoning the notion of consciousness. Wundt's thought is superior because it recognizes the "possibility of transcending original experience."

7 McTAGGART, JOHN McTAGGART ELLIS. "The Inadequacy of Certain Common Grounds of Belief," The Hibbert Journal, IV, 116-140. Incorporated in Some Dogmas of Religion (London: Edward Arnold 1906).
   While James is not mentioned, this is in part a criticism of The Will to Believe. We have no right to assume that the universe is not "intolerably bad." The rejection of any dogma need not make action either absurd or impossible.

8 MELLONE, S. H. "Is Humanism a Philosophical Advance?" Mind, NS XIV (October), 507-529.
   A criticism of Schiller and James, focusing on the problem of the independence of the object. It is true that our efforts mold the world, but one should specify the extent of this. James gives us no answer for he both

1905

(MELLONE, S. H.)
recognizes a resisting real and says that reality is an
"accumulation of our intellectual inventions."

9 PILLON, F. Review of L'Expérience religieuse, translated by
F. Abauzit (Paris: Félix Alcan, 1906), L'Année
Philosophique, XVI, 214-219.
Primarily extended quotations. The translation is good.

10 SABINE, GEORGE H. "Radical Empiricism as a Logical Method,"
The Philosophical Review, XIV (November), 696-705.
Radical empiricism is an empirical method for solving
metaphysical problems with emphasis on "introspection" and
observation of individual experiences. But this can only
yield psychological facts and not principles of unity and
explanation. The method is inappropriate for metaphysics.

11 SCHILLER, F. C. S. "The Definition of 'Pragmatism' and
'Humanism,'" Mind, NS XIV (April), 235-240. Incorporated
in Studies in Humanism (London: Macmillan 1907).
The narrow pragmatism of Peirce can be expanded into a
wider one, a "general view of the mind," by the realization
that only practical consequences are needed to "account"
for current truths. The wider pragmatism is an epistemological method which, however, does not force the acceptance
of the general philosophical principle called humanism.
Thus, Schiller would like to dissent in part from the
limits proposed by James in "Humanism and Truth" (1904).

12 SOLLIER, PAUL. Le Mécanisme des émotions. Paris: Félix Alcan.
Critizes the James-Lange theory. Emotions disappear in
cases of extended anaesthesia, but this is due to a general
mental inhibition typical of that state. It is the brain
which is the center of the emotions.

13 TAYLOR, ALFRED EDWARD. "Truth and Practice," The Philosophical
Review, XIV (May), 265-289.
In the discussion of truth, three issues arise: what is
the meaning of 'true' and 'false'; to which propositions
are they to be ascribed; how in a given case we consider a
proposition true. The last is a psychological question and
must be distinguished from the first two. 'True' cannot
mean the same thing as 'useful' and it is false that utility is always a sign of truth. Taylor hopes his analysis
will lead the contending sides to greater understanding.

14 TOWER, C. V. "A Neglected 'Context' in 'Radical Empiricism',"
The Journal of Philosophy, II (July 20), 400-408.

In "Does 'Consciousness' Exist?" (1904), James correctly discards consciousness as an entity and keeps it as a function. We can accept its definition of consciousness as "a context of experiences." However, radical empiricism ignores one context, the "total context," which includes an indefinite fringe of objects.

15   WEIGLE, L. A. Review of "Does 'Consciousness' Exist?" (1904) and "A World of Pure Experience" (1904), The Psychological Bulletin, II (March 15), 99-102.
      James is a radical empiricist for whom the terms and the relations are given in experience. His view of relations saves him from the atomism which afflicts ordinary empiricism.

1906 A BOOKS - NONE

1906 B SHORTER WRITINGS

1   ABAUZIT, FRANK. Preface to L'Expérience religieuse, translated by F. Abauzit. Paris: Félix Alcan, 1906.
     Cites a letter from James authorizing the translation.

2   BOUTROUX, ÉMILE. Introduction to L'Expérience religieuse, translated by F. Abauzit. Paris: Félix Alcan, 1906. Also published as L'Expérience religieuse selon William James, (Nimes: La Laborieuse, 1907).
     James seeks the wealth of the immediately given. His method for deciding the truth of religious beliefs is empirical. Religion is to be judged by its fruits. The function of thought is to produce habits of action.

3   COLVIN, STEPHEN S. "Pragmatism, Old and New," The Monist, XVI (October), 547-561.
     Pragmatism is not novel. Its subjectivism, pluralism, empiricism, and utilitarianism only restate old doctrines more carefully. A consistent pragmatist must offer an absolute, while the absolutist, has only a pragmatic warrant for his absolute.

4   LALANDE, ANDRÉ. "Pragmatisme et pragmaticisme," Revue Philosophique, LXI (February), 121-146. A summary by George H. Sabine, The Philosophical Review, XV (November 1906), 673-674.
     The pragmatism of James and Peirce is a revolt against dilettantism, a demand that metaphysics be subjected to a new standard of truth. Both are empiricists, reject the

1906

(LALANDE, ANDRÉ)
Kantian notion of a priori forms, and find the universal in experience. James holds that both the thing and its relations are elements of experience.

5   LEIGHTON, J. A.   "Cognitive Thought and 'Immediate' Experience," The Journal of Philosophy, III (March 29), 174-180.
James's doctrine of pure experience confuses logical and psychological treatments of thought. What holds only of "possible" experience is asserted of "actual" and "personal" experience, and vice versa.

6   MICHAUD, E.   Review of L'Expérience religieuse, translated by F. Abauzit (Paris: Félix Alcan, 1906), Revue Internationale de Théologie, XIV, 351-354.
It is not reasonable to emphasize abnormal cases and ignore metaphysics and theology. In spite of many points subject to criticism, it is a valuable book, expecially in its refutation of medical materialism.

7   NICHOLS, HERBERT.   "Professor James's 'Hole,'" The Journal of Philosophy, III (February 1), 64-70.
Having rejected the soul and association, James uses the notion of continuous transition to preserve the unity of the self. Past states no longer exist when new ones have replaced them. However, when James talks of two minds knowing one thing, he returns to the reality of past states. Nichols tries to explain what leads to this error.

8   PILLON, F.   "Sur la mémoire et l'imagination affectives," L'Année Philosophique, XVII, 45-123.
Pp. 90-96 contain critical comments on James's theory of emotion.

9   PITKIN, WALTER B.   "A Problem of Evidence in Radical Empiricism," The Journal of Philosophy, III (November 22), 645-650.
While James is not mentioned, his writings are quoted. For the radical empiricist, experience is autonomous. The physical and the psychical both fall within it, but experience itself rests on nothing. Arguments in support of radical empiricism fail since description is confused with evidence.

10   ROGERS, A. K.   "Professor James's Theory of Knowledge," The Philosophical Review, XV (November), 577-596.
Discussions of pragmatism leave many questions unanswered. While pragmatism as a method is acceptable, its metaphysics

is questionable. How are we to interpret the view that "reality is actually in every sense created" in the process of knowledge?

11   RUSSELL, JOHN E. "Solipsism: The Logical Issue of Radical Empiricism," The Philosophical Review, XV (November), 606-613.
      For radical empiricism, experience alone is real and reality is known only by experience. But experience must be mine and no provision is made for reaching the experience of others.

12   _____. "Some Difficulties with the Epistemology of Pragmatism and Radical Empiricism," The Philosophical Review, XV (July), 406-413.
      Pragmatism confuses psychology with logic, the situation in which knowledge arises with knowledge, the consequences of truth with truth. It eliminates all relations, except that of "nextness." Its interpretation of truth leads to a dilemma. An idea is not true unless it has been verified, but once verified, it no longer exists, since the transition from the idea to the terminus has taken place. Finally, radical empiricism involves solipsism.

1907 A BOOKS

1   PAETZ, W. Die erkenntnis-theoretischen Grundlagen von William James "The varieties of religious experience." Eilenburg: Ewald Lesske.
      Consists primarily of quotations from Varieties organized around the problem of knowledge and examines James's claim that the science of religion can be given an exact basis.

2   PORRET, J. ALFRED. Au sujet de la conversion: remarques sur la théorie émise par M. William James, dans son livre "L'Expérience religieuse." Geneva: H. Robert. Reprinted from Revue de Théologie et de Philosophie.
      Discusses conversion as described in Varieties. James thinks it only possible that conversion involves divine intervention, but certain facts cannot be explained without God and intervention is necessary.

1907 B SHORTER WRITINGS

1   ALDEN, HENRY M. Discussion of Pragmatism in "Editor's Study," Harper's Monthly Magazine, CXV (September), 645-646.
      Philosophy has been more tolerant of generalities than science, but now science has forced its hand. James brings philosophy from "her aerial heights to the ground."

1907

2   ANON. Comments on Pragmatism. The Expository Times, XIX,
        (October), 1-3.
           After James's classification of temperaments, we expect
        a treatise on philosophical predestination. Instead,
        James insists that in philosophy we are free to come and
        go as we please.

3   ANON. "The Fascinations of the Pragmatic Method," Current
        Literature, XLIII (August), 183-186.
           Pragmatism is "in the air" and can be found in many
        writers who themselves may be unaware of it. James is
        "perhaps" its "ablest" exponent.

4   ANON. "A New Philosophy," Harper's Weekly, LI (August 31),
        1264.
           James is the "high priest" of a new philosophy and pro-
        vides "racy reading for the common man." Pragmatism is
        "witty summer reading."

5   ANON. "The Philosophy of a Renunciation," Harper's Weekly,
        LI (September 21), 1370.
           James's "The Energies of Men" (1907) is used to recom-
        mend that Theodore Roosevelt renounce his ambitions for a
        third term.

6   ANON. "Pragmatism," The Independent, LXIII (September 12),
        630-631.
           Pragmatism is a "unifying point" for different fields.
        Many find that they have been pragmatists all along.
        James left his Harvard chair to appeal to wider audiences
        and this shows his "faith in pragmatism as a philosophy
        for the people."

7   ANON. "Pragmatism," The Spectator, XCIX (July 6), 9-11.
           With a reputation as a psychologist and defender of
        religious belief, James "in what many think was an evil
        day" turned his attention to metaphysics. Pragmatism con-
        tains a bold creed. James's style, often brilliant, at
        times is obscure. James insists upon the practical value
        of truth. But how many theories lead to no direct applica-
        tions and yet help us to understand experience?

8   ANON. "Pragmatism, the Newest Philosophy," Current Literature,
        XLII (June), 652-653.
           James is "prophet-in-chief" of pragmatism in America and
        gave up his professorship to devote himself to its propa-
        ganda. Body of article consists of quotations from
        Edwin E. Slosson (1907).

9   ANON. "The Pragmatist Microbe," Current Literature, XLIII
     (October), 418-420.
         Surveys comments on Pragmatism with extensive quotations
     and emphasis on criticism.

10   ANON. "Professor James's 'Pragmatism,'" Harvard Graduates'
     Magazine, XVI (September), 20-25.
         Everyone should read the book, bound to arouse much con-
     troversy. At present, philosophers say it is not philoso-
     phy, psychologists, not psychology, and theologians, not
     theology.

11   BAKEWELL, CHARLES M. Review of Pragmatism, The Philosophical
     Review, XVI (November), 624-634.
         In depicting the "intellectualists," James caricatures
     their views. Philosophical problems are ignored and not
     solved. James gives us unobjectionable advice to be cau-
     tious and patient, and not a method. Like positivists,
     James seeks to turn philosophy into a science, but one with
     more scope than other sciences.

12   BJÖRKMAN, EDWIN. Interview with James, The New York Times,
     November 3, 1907, p. 8.
         James's books are "selling by the thousands," "business
     men are caught disputing over their lunches," while
     "matrons and maids display equal eagerness."

13   BLANCHE, F. A. "Pragmatisme et humanisme," Revue des Sciences
     Philosophiques et Théologiques, VI (January), 105-129.
         Surveys the pragmatism controversy. The Will to Believe
     receives most of the attention in James's case, especially
     "The Sentiment of Rationality." James calls himself a
     radical empiricist, because even our most certain beliefs
     are subject to correction and because he accepts the plu-
     ralism we find in our experience. James follows Peirce in
     holding pragmatism to be a method. Schiller proposes to
     enlarge it into a philosophy.

14   BODE, BOYD HENRY. Review of A. K. Rogers, "Professor James's
     Theory of Knowledge" (1906), The Journal of Philosophy,
     IV (March 28), 192-194.
         Rogers is "clear and forcible," but does not handle well
     James's thesis that knowledge can be reduced to a resem-
     blance leading to a "beneficial reaction towards an
     object."

15   BORRELL, PHILIPPE. "La Notion de pragmatisme," Revue de
     Philosophie, XI (December), 587-590.

1907

(BORRELL, PHILIPPE)
Criticism of F. Mentré (1907). To show the value of
rationalism, Mentré has to resort to a pragmatic approach.
For pragmatists, the practical is not restricted to what
is useful in industry.

16 BROWN, WILLIAM ADAMS. "The Pragmatic Value of the Absolute,"
The Journal of Philosophy, IV (August 15), 459–464.
In Pragmatism, the 'absolute' is shown to be the giver
of "moral holidays." It is a source of action as well.

17 HODGES, GEORGE. "William James: Leader in Philosophical
Thought," The Outlook, LXXXV (February 23), 448–451.
Surveys James's thought emphasizing his empiricism and
open-mindedness. James is one of the most religious of
philosophers.

18 JANSSENS, EDGAR. Review of L'Expérience religieuse, translated
by F. Abauzit (Paris: Félix Alcan, 1906), Revue Néo-
Scolastique, XIV (February), 136–140.
James's method of valuing religion by its moral results
contains much truth, but is not as harmless as it appears.
It leads James into certain contradictions and to concen-
trate on the affective side of religion, excluding the
intellectual and voluntary.

19 KALTENBORN, HANS VON. "William James at Harvard," The Harvard
Illustrated Magazine, VIII (February), 93–95.
Contains anecdotes about James's last class and his
examination for the degree of M. D., written to mark
James's retirement.

20 McGILVARY, EVANDER BRADLEY. "The Stream of Consciousness,"
The Journal of Philosophy, IV (April 25), 225–235.
Consciousness is a continuous stream and not a succession
of pulses of thought, little egos. James makes the mistake
in The Principles of Psychology because he attributes to
the ego the discreteness found in the objects of thought.
"Feelings of transition" and the "quality of warmth and
intimacy" are made to serve as glue to restore unity, but
they work as badly as Hume's association.

21 MENTRÉ, FRANCOIS. "Complément à la note sur la valeur pragmatique du pragmatisme," Revue de Philosophie, XI (December),
591–594.
Reply to Borrell (1907). Mentré refers to a letter by
James in which James tried to convert Mentré to pragmatism.

22 _____. "Note sur la valeur pragmatique du pragmatisme," Revue de Philosophie, XI (July), 5-22. Abstract in The Philosophical Review, XVI (November 1907), 666-667.
Pure science requires disinterested effort. If science is to bear practical fruit, initial investigations must be conducted without thought of utility. Thus pragmatism is not a useful approach to pure science and fails by its own favorite criterion.

23 MÜNSTERBERG, HUGO. "Professor James as a Psychologist," The Harvard Illustrated Magazine, VII (February), 97-98.
James's basic method is "self-observation." He is more of a descriptive than an explanatory psychologist. Written to mark James's retirement.

24 NEILSON, WILLIAM ALLAN. "William James as Lecturer and Writer," The Harvard Illustrated Magazine, VII (February), 98-99.
Occasioned by James's retirement. James is concerned with thought, not form. Harvard English professors were envious of the writing ability of the philosophers.

25 NICHOLS, HERBERT. "Pragmatism Versus Science," The Journal of Philosophy, IV (February 28), 122-131.
Pragmatists distinguish a man from a percept of him, but not a percept from a thing. Identifying the two, they conclude that "science has broken down," that its laws are only human devices. We can accept the physical world without dualism and thereby avoid skepticism.

26 NOËL, L. "Bulletin d'epistemologie. Le pragmatisme," Revue Néo-Scolastique, XIV, 220-243.
Surveys pragmatic writings and literature on pragmatism.

27 PERRY, RALPH BARTON. "Professor James as a Philosopher," The Harvard Illustrated Magazine, VII (February), 96-97.
Occasioned by James's retirement. James dislikes sharp distinctions and finds "food" for both psychology and philosophy in an event. He is in the tradition of British empiricism. Even his "nearest disciples" would not claim that his right hand always knows what his left is doing.

28 PITKIN, WALTER B. "In Reply to Professor James," The Journal of Philosophy, IV (January 17), 44-45.
Reply to "Mr. Pitkin's Refutation of 'Radical Empiricism'" (1906). The "common sense realism" of some passages in the radical empiricism essays cannot be reconciled with the idealism of others.

1907

29   PRATT, JAMES BISSETT. "Truth and Its Verification," The
       Journal of Philosophy, IV (June 6), 320–324.
          It is "non-pragmatic" to define truth in terms of veri-
       fiability since verifiability is not something found in
       an individual's experience, but is a "general condition"
       which "transcends every single finite experience."

30   SCHILLER, F. C. S. Review of Pragmatism, Mind, NS XVI
       (October), 598–604.
          Novel are James's recognition that "correspondence"
       within experience is acceptable to pragmatism and his
       discussion of potential truth. We also receive new hints
       about James's metaphysics. James's description of pragma-
       tism as anarchic is misleading. That each man ought to
       interpret his own experience is only a long overdue recog-
       nition of "human freedom and responsibility."

31   SLOSSON, EDWIN E. "Pragmatism," The Independent, LXII
       (February 21), 422–425.
          Pragmatism is not yet a school but a "focus" of converg-
       ing lines of thought. This new humanism does not originate
       in the humanities but is the "gift of modern science."
       The fact that both James and Schiller engage in psychical
       research is giving rise to the fear that pragmatism will
       bring with it "Mrs. Piper" and "the whole host of devils."

32   STUDENT. "Pragmatism," Century Path, vol. X, no. 36 (July 14),
       p. 4.
          Pragmatism is a "new darkness." It begins by ruling
       out the soul and ends with "eat, drink, and be merry; for
       tomorrow we die." "A Pragmatist" rules out as of no con-
       sequence controversies over materialism and idealism. But
       if you take two men, in all respects alike, but one is a
       spiritualist and the other a materialist, in a few years,
       one will be "fine" and the other "gross."

33   _____. "Pragmatism and Chaos," Century Path, vol. X, no. 52
       (November 3), p. 4.
          Materialism has receded, but it has left a "lot of sea-
       weed" which assumes the "well-sounding name of Pragmatism."
       For the pragmatists there is no universe with its laws,
       "except what I think there is."

34   THOMAS, WM. I. Review of "The Energies of Men" (1907), The
       Journal of Philosophy, IV (May 9), 268–271.
          James suggests that we can remain in equilibrium while
       living at a much faster pace. He discloses the technique
       of Yoga and "its patent bearing on educational theory."

35 WATSON, JOHN. The Philosophical Basis of Religion. Glasgow:
        James Maclehose and Sons.
            Pp. 141-164 deals with James. After an extensive summary
        of "The Will to Believe," Watson claims that James is mis-
        taken in holding that nothing can be verified except what
        belongs to "external nature" and that there is an "absolute
        opposition between faith and knowledge." James's philosophy
        of religion is an "abstraction" which ignores the "higher
        elements." Watson adds a highly critical "Note on the
        Pragmatic Conception of Truth."

36 WENLEY, R. M. Review of Pragmatism, Science, NS XXVI
        (October 11), 464-468.
            Pragmatism is only the "raw material" for a philosophy
        and one hopes that James and his allies will actually
        state one. It represents a "protestant attitude" towards
        orthodox university philosophy. But the work "fails to
        rise to the level of its author's reputation" and contains
        "cheap stuff."

37 WOBBERMIN, GEORG. Introduction to Die religiöse Erfahrung,
        translated by G. Wobbermin. Leipzig: J. C. Hinrichs.
            Primarily an exposition of the views of Friedrich Daniel
        Ernst Schleiermacher, in view of Wobbermin's thesis that
        James is much like Schleiermacher.

38 WOODBRIDGE, FREDERICK J. E. "Pragmatism and Education," Edu-
        cational Review, XXXIV (October), 227-240.
            The pragmatic method remains obscure, much of the obscu-
        rity revolving around the term "practical." Pragmatism
        abolishes the separation between ideas and facts and claims
        that experience knows no distinct "orders of existence."
        This is unobjectionable if kept within proper limits, but
        it is sometimes extended to mean that ideas produce the
        whole realm of facts. In education, pragmatism urges us
        to make ideas clear by showing where they lead to and
        emphasizes the principle of continuity.

1908 A BOOKS - NONE

1908 B SHORTER WRITINGS

1   ANGELL, JAMES ROWLAND. Review of Pragmatism, The International
        Journal of Ethics, XVIII (January), 226-235.
            Pragmatism has aroused much controversy. With age, it
        promises to become one of the "real progressive factors"
        in the history of thought. James does not pay enough
        attention to the stubbornness of reality, to that to which

1908

(ANGELL, JAMES ROWLAND)
our truths must conform. James also tends to slur over the
social aspects of establishing truth.

2   ANON. "Proceedings of the American Philosophical Association:
The Seventh Annual Meeting, Cornell University, December
26-28, 1907," The Philosophical Review, XVII (March),
167-190.
Includes abstracts, pp. 180-186, of a discussion on "The
Meaning and Criterion of Truth." The discussion was begun
with James's "The Meaning of the Word Truth" (1908). J. E.
Creighton, Charles M. Bakewell, John Grier Hibben, and
Charles A. Strong took part.

3   ANON. "La Signification du pragmatisme," Bulletin de la
Société Francaise de Philosophie, VIII, 249-296.
A discussion of pragmatism at a meeting of the society
on May 7, 1908. Leon Brunschvicg, André Lalande, X. Léon,
Lucien Laberthonnière, Édouard Le Roy, Lucien Lévy-Brühl,
Dominique Parodi, Georges Sorel, were among those present.
A letter from Max Leclerc is added as an appendix.

4   ARMSTRONG, A. C. "The Evolution of Pragmatism," The Journal of
Philosophy, V (November 19), 645-650.
The confused controversy over pragmatism has begun to
clear up. Pragmatists agree that pragmatism is primarily
a method, although it is not clear that this can be distinguished from the theory of truth. Pragmatism is not subjectivism. It is less open to metaphysics than Schiller's
humanism.

5   BJÖRKMAN, EDWIN. "William James, the Man and the Thinker,"
The American Review of Reviews, XXXVII (January), 45-48.
James, the leading exponent of pragmatism, has retired
from Harvard to devote himself to writing. James became
well known through his The Principles of Psychology which
states the James-Lange theory of emotion. He first
announced his pragmatism in The Will to Believe.

6   BOUTROUX, ÉMILE. Science et religion dans la philosophie
contemporaine. Paris: Flammarion. English translation,
Science and Religion in Contemporary Philosophy, translated
by Jonathan Nield (London: Duckworth, 1909).
Recent philosophers are either naturalists or spiritualists. James is a spiritualist. Both religion and science
arise from experience. Religious experience originates
in the subconscious self, while scientific, in the conscious self. Both kinds of experience lead to a belief in
the reality of something outside the self.

7 _____. "William James et l'expérience religieuse," Revue de
Métaphysique et de Morale, XVI, 1-27. Reprinted in Science
et religion (1908).
James's method is radical empiricism. For him, consciousness is a field containing multiplicity, fluid and
continuous. He deals with the truth of religion pragmatically, by considering its fruits. For understanding the
religious object, James uses the theory of the subliminal
consciousness of F. W. H. Myers. Boutroux asks whether
this treatment of religion is scientific and how it compares with other sciences. James's emphasis on the inner
life gives us the soul of religion, but we also need the
body of religion, the system of beliefs and institutions.

8 BRADLEY, FRANCIS HERBERT. "On the Ambiguity of Pragmatism,"
Mind, NS XVII (April), 226-237. Reprinted in Essays on
Truth and Reality (1914).
It is difficult to say whether Bradley himself has
always been a pragmatist, because its exponents are so
unclear as to what pragmatism is. 'Practice' and 'practical' can be given narrow or broad interpretations. If
understood in the latter way, pragmatism would hardly
exclude anyone.

9 CARUS, PAUL. "Pragmatism," The Monist, XVIII (July), 321-362.
Reprinted in Truth on Trial (1911).
It would be a misfortune if James's thought was to become
influential because pragmatism advocates the useful lie.

10 DEWEY, JOHN. "What Does Pragmatism Mean by Practical?" The
Journal of Philosophy, V (February 13), 85-99. Reprinted
in Essays in Experimental Logic (Chicago: The University
of Chicago Press, 1916).
Comments on Pragmatism. 'Practical' is triply ambiguous.
It may mean "attitudes exacted of us by objects," the
capacity of an idea to effect changes in existences, or
the "desirable or undesirable quality of certain ends."
James has achieved a synthesis of various pragmatic
strains, what is now needed is analysis. Perhaps it would
be best if pragmatism as a "holding company" for allied
but different interests be dissolved.

11 GUTBERLET, C. "Der Pragmatismus," Philosophisches Jahrbuch
der Görres-Gesellschaft, XXI, 437-458.
Pragmatism is a new fashion from the land of the dollar.
It is a religion, but one built on sand.

12 HAWTREY, RALPH GEORGE. "Pragmatism," The New Quarterly, I
(March), 197-210.

1908

(HAWTREY, RALPH GEORGE)
James can define words as he pleases and the word 'true' means what James says it does. But then, we will use 'correctness' to mean what we ordinarily mean by truth. 'Correctness' would not mean what the pragmatists mean by 'truth'.

13 HÉBERT, MARCEL. Le Pragmatisme: étude de ses diverses formes anglo-américaines, francaises, italiennes et de sa valeur religieuse. Paris: E. Nourry. A French translation of James's review (1908) of the book was added in the second edition (1910).
Pragmatism is subjectivism. Its emphasis on the practical leaves no room for knowledge in the proper sense.

14 HIBBEN, JOHN GRIER. "The Test of Pragmatism," The Philosophical Review, XVII (July), 365-382.
The test of "working" should be applied to pragmatism. It works in some cases, but fails in others.

15 JACOBY, GÜNTHER. Review of Pragmatism, Kant-Studien, XIII, 478-480.
This long awaited work is a disappointment because it does not make clear the basis of James's thought. James's conclusions are not based upon scientific investigation, but upon his preferences.

16 JOHNSON, WM. HALLOCK. "Pragmatism, Humanism, and Religion," The Princeton Theological Review, VI, 544-564.
Pragmatism is friendly to religion and has helped it by revitalizing philosophy. Pragmatism emphasizes personality and insists on the right to believe. But it appeals only to the strong and offers nothing to sick souls. It fails to support the view that man is dependent upon God.

17 JUDD, CHARLES H. Review of Pragmatism, The Psychological Bulletin, V (May 15), 157-162.
A psychologist can review this book since pragmatists approach their problems from a psychological point of view. The distinction between tough-minded and tender-minded is psychological and shows that philosophical disputes are a clash of temperaments. Pragmatism risks subjectivism. In spite of James's claims, it is hard to distinguish pragmatism from his other philosophy.

18 LALANDE, ANDRÉ. "Pragmatisme, humanisme, et vérité," Revue Philosophique, LXV (January), 1-26. Summary by C. West, The Philosophical Review, XVII (September 1908), 567.

Pragmatists are correct that truth satisfies needs. But we should insist upon the unity of truth, the need to reach agreement.

19 LOVEJOY, ARTHUR ONCKEN. "Pragmatism and Theology," The American Journal of Theology, XII, 116-143. Reprinted in The Thirteen Pragmatisms (1963).

James proposes as a criterion of meaning that propositions refer to concrete future experience. But some propositions are meaningful which have no such reference and pragmatism must be restated as a test of verifiability. When this fails, we realize that James is proposing a test of the importance of a belief. Connected with pragmatism is belief in a genuine future, and here we find the contribution of pragmatism to theology.

20 _____. "The Thirteen Pragmatisms," The Journal of Philosophy, V (January 2), 5-12; (January 16) 29-39. Reprinted in The Thirteen Pragmatisms (1963).

There are at least thirteen doctrines, different and sometimes incompatible, which are often confounded and discussed as pragmatism.

21 McTAGGART, JOHN McTAGGART ELLIS. Review of Pragmatism, Mind, NS XVII (January), 104-109.

Pragmatism is said to look away from "principles" and "necessities" and turn towards "consequences." But all philosophers consider consequences, while James himself uses principles and asserts necessities. James's exposition of a theory of truth while "picturesque" is not "lucid."

22 MEYER, MAX. Review of Pragmatism, Zeitschrift für Psychologie und Physiologie der Sinnesorgane. I. Abteilung. Zeitschrift für Psychologie, XLVIII, 279-280.

The term pragmatism is not known in Germany, but the idea is. It can be found in Avenarius, Mach, and G. Heymans.

23 MOORE, GEORGE EDWARD. "Professor James' 'Pragmatism,'" Proceedings of the Aristotelian Society, NS VIII (1907-1908) 33-77. Reprinted in Philosophical Studies (London: Routledge & Kegan Paul, 1922)..

James finds a connection between truth and verification and usefulness. However, not all true ideas can be verified, not all true ideas are useful, not all useful ideas are true. For James, truth is mutable and truths are man-made. However, it is reality that is mutable. When James talks about man-made truths, he seems to be talking about the process of coming to believe.

1908

24   OESTERREICH, K.   Review of Die religiöse Erfahrung, translated
       by G. Wobbermin (Leipzig: Hinrich, 1907), Kant-Studien,
       XIII, 474-478.
          Kant would have found it interesting, but would have
       insisted on a critique of religious experience.

25   OSTWALD, WILHELM.   Review of Pragmatism, Annalen der Natur-
       philosophie, VII, 510-512.
          James's lecturers are popular and filled with humor.
       Ernst Mach has recently presented similar views.

26   PARODI, DOMINIQUE.   "Le Pragmatisme d'après Mm. W. James et
       Schiller," Revue de Métaphysique et de Morale, XVI
       (January), 93-112.
          Reviews Schiller's Studies in Humanism (1907) and
       James's Pragmatism. Utility has been held to be a sign of
       truth, the originality of pragmatism lies in claiming that
       utility constitutes truth. Pragmatism is ambiguous and
       cannot be maintained on pragmatic grounds.

27   PRATT, JAMES BISSETT.   "Truth and Ideas," The Journal of Phi-
       losophy, V (February 27), 122-131.
          Criticizes the pragmatic conception of truth. In his
       most recent attempts, James fails to clarify his position
       which cannot always be distinguished from that of the
       intellectualist.

28   ROYCE, JOSIAH.   The Philosophy of Loyalty. New York:
       Macmillan.
          Royce agrees that consciousness is purposive and beliefs
       lead to action. However, truth cannot rest on momentary
       successes, but must lead to the whole of life.

29   RUSSELL, BERTRAND.   "Transatlantic 'Truth,'" The Albany Review,
       II (January), 393-410. Reprinted as "William James's Con-
       ception of Truth," Philosophical Essays (London: Longmans,
       Green, 1910; revised edition, London: George Allen & Unwin,
       1966).
          A review of Pragmatism. Many of James's views are shared
       by all empiricists. James states them in a manner "insin-
       uating, gradual, imperceptible." They seep in like "hot
       water running in so slowly that you don't know when to
       scream." If the pragmatic definition of truth is to be
       useful, we must be able to know that a belief pays without
       knowing that it is true. It is often easier to know·
       whether a belief agrees with the facts than to know its
       consequences. To the preface of Philosophical Essays,
       Russell added a tribute to James written shortly after
       James's death.

38

30   SALTER, WILLIAM MACINTIRE. "Pragmatism: A New Philosophy,"
     The Atlantic Monthly, CI (May 1908), 657-663.
        A survey of the pragmatism controversy. James fails to
     show that belief is reasonable. He confuses two senses of
     working: fitting in with other experience and pleasing us.

31   SCHOTT, [?]. Review of Die religiöse Erfahrung, translated by
     G. Wobbermin (Leipzig: J. C. Hinrichs, 1907), Zeitschrift
     für Religionspsychologie, II, 220-229.
        A chapter by chapter summary of the contents.

32   STEIN, LUDWIG. "Der Pragmatismus," Archiv für systematische
     Philosophie, XIV (February), 1-9; (May), 143-188.
        The first segment surveys the pragmatism controversy and
     praises James for maintaining a high level. The second,
     traces the history of pragmatism. It is the outcome of
     certain English tendencies, nominalism, voluntarism, and
     utilitarianism. The controversy between pragmatists and
     idealists parallels the controversy between psychologists
     and logicians in Germany.

33   STRONG, CHARLES AUGUSTUS. "Pragmatism and Its Definition of
     Truth," The Journal of Philosophy, V (May 7), 256-264.
        Pragmatism has a sound core of empirical truth. But its
     one-sided practicalism and its psychologism must be cor-
     rected. Strong's paper consists of two parts, one written
     before and the other after James's "The Meaning of the
     Word Truth" (1908).

34   WITMER, LIGHTNER. "Mental Healing and the Emmanuel Movement,"
     The Psychological Clinic, II (December 15), 212-223;
     (January 15, 1909), 239-250; (February 15, 1909), 282-300.
        A critical review of the mental healing movement asso-
     ciated with the work of Richard C. Cabot and Elwood
     Worcester. In the third part, James is singled out. His
     support of psychical research and his opposition to medical
     licensing are parts of his campaign against science. The
     Principles of Psychology is a work for beginners and its
     popularity is evidence for the low level of science. In
     the last edition of his Grundzüge der physiologischen
     Psychologie, Wundt refers to James three times and not a
     fact or theory is introduced on James's authority. James
     is the "spoiled child" of American psychology, "exempt from
     all serious criticism."

1909

1909 A BOOKS

1   SANBORN, HERBERT C. Über die Identität der Person bei William
James. Leipzig: Böhme & Lehmann.
On personal identity, James tries to take the middle
ground between the views of Hume and those of Leibniz and
Kant. His theories do not agree with empirical data.
Sanborn devotes much attention to problems of terminology.

2   SHARGHA, IKBAL KISHEN. Examination of Prof. William James's
Psychology. Allahabad, India: Ram Narain Lal.
Beginning students should not "take everything on
trust," when studying James's shorter Psychology. On the
mind-body relation James wanders between materialism,
dualism, idealism, and skepticism, but favors materialism.
It is hoped that in the future James will "steer clear of
the rocks and shallows of materialism."

1909 B SHORTER WRITINGS

1   ANON. "Comments on James's Pluralistic Philosophy," Current
Literature, XLVII (August), 182-185.
Quotes reviews of A Pluralistic Universe by Horace M.
Kallen in the Boston Evening Transcript and Paul Elmer
More in the New York Evening Post, and others.

2   ANON. "Is the Psychology Taught at Harvard a National Peril?"
Current Literature, XLVI (April), 437-438.
Summary of the article by Lightner Witmer (1908) and a
long quotation from an article by Raymond St. James Perrin,
published in The Bang, in which James, Royce, Santayana,
and Münsterberg are accused of spreading "fake philosophy."

3   ANON. "Professor James's New 'Pluralistic' Philosophy,"
Current Literature, XLVI (June), 647-650.
Tired of academic life, James gave up his professorship
to engage in "free-lance propaganda." Pragmatism was the
first result; this second, is bound to be less popular
since it lacks immediate applications. Many will discover
that they have been pluralists without knowing it.

4   ANON. Review of A Pluralistic Universe, The Athenæum,
no. 4255 (May 15), 577-578.
James insists on intimacy with the divine, but co-
consciousness surely does not offer intimacy. James's
approach to religion is experiential and sometimes seems
no more than "analogy tinged with emotion."

5   ANON. Review of <u>The Meaning of Truth</u>, <u>The Athenaeum</u>, no. 4280 (November 6), 549-550.

> Compromise is now in the air. James acts as if he had never left the fold. There are almost no traces of the pragmatic appeal to the individual conscience. James "abjures subjectivism."

6   BAUDIN, E. "La Méthode psychologique de W. James," preface to <u>Précis de psychologie</u>, translated by E. Baudin and G. Bertier. Paris: Marcel Rivière.

> James's psychology studies the living individual. James accepts physiological research as a preliminary, but for psychology itself he uses introspection. James attempts to find the immediately given which for him is the stream of consciousness.

7   BLANCHE, F. "La Notion de vérité dans le pragmatisme," <u>Revue de Philosophie</u>, XV (July), 5-25.

> The conceptions of truth of James, Dewey, and Schiller stress its dynamic character. They fail to see that truth as the conformity of thoughts to things is prior to action. Rightly they emphasize psychological circumstances, but this becomes an exclusive interest.

8   BOURDEAU, JEAN. <u>Pragmatisme et modernisme</u>. Paris: Félix Alcan.

> A collection of articles from the <u>Journal des Débats</u>, 1907-1908. Articles from this newspaper were reprinted in the <u>Revue Hebdomadaire du Journal des Débats</u> and are more readily available in this form. References are to the <u>Revue Hebdomadaire</u>: "Agnosticisme et pragmatisme," vol. XIV, part II (August 30, 1907), 401-403; (September 27, 1907), 592-594; "Une Sophistique du pragmatisme," (November 8, 1907), 880-882; (November 22, 1907), 975-977; "Le Pragmatisme contre le rationalisme," vol. XV, part I (January 24, 1908), 161-163; "L'Illusion pragmatiste," (February 28, 1908), 400-402. Pragmatism is the reaction of the American mind against "le rationalisme latins." It is a philosophy of gestures, without words.

9   CARUS, PAUL. "The Philosophy of Personal Equation," <u>The Monist</u>, XIX (January), 78-84. Reprinted in <u>Truth on Trial</u> (1911).

> Pragmatism insists upon the "personal equation" in matters of belief, but the personal factor is not equally important in all cases.

10   _____. "A Postscript on Pragmatism," <u>The Monist</u>, XIX (January), 85-94.

1909

(CARUS, PAUL)
Comments on James's review of Hébert (1908). It is strange that all of James's critics misunderstand him.

11 ESHLEMAN, CYRUS H. "Professor James on Fechner's Philosophy," The Hibbert Journal, VII (April), 671-673.
A reader of "The Doctrine of the Earth-Soul" (1909) regrets that James did not give a fuller account of soul-life.

12 LADD, GEORGE TRUMBULL. "The Confusion of Pragmatism," The Hibbert Journal, VII, 784-801.
Pragmatism makes assumptions regarding the "method and aim of philosophy," the "nature and guarantee of truth," and the scope of the ideas of value. In all three cases, what is actually taken for granted differs from what is said to be so taken. While it is good that pragmatism seeks to satisfy the "deeper needs of humanity," its disregard of intellectual obligations will defeat its good intentions.

13 LANGE, HERMANN. Review of Pragmatismus, translated by W. Jerusalem (Leipzig: W. Klinkhardt, 1908), Zeitschrift für Philosophie und Pädagogik, XVI, 155-158. The same review also appeared in Zeitschrift für lateinlose höhere Schulen, XX, 169-171.
It is desirable that James's work have an influence in Germany like it has had elsewhere. His method needs elaboration.

14 LORENZ-IGHTHAM, THEODOR. "Das Verhältnis des Pragmatismus zu Kant," Kant-Studien, XIV, 8-44.
Kant's practical reason and James's will to believe coincide. Both postulate a supersensible world as a basis for moral actions. Kant's conception of the regulative function of the ideas, his views on teleology and the ideas of reason, his distinction between appearances and things in themselves, are important for pragmatism.

15 MARGRETH, JACOB. "Amerikanische Religionspsychologie, in ihrer Grundlage geprüft," Katholik, series 4, vol. 4, 223-229.
A very critical review of Varieties. James's work is marked by a poor selection of cases. His treatment is light. His basic mistake is a completely false epistemology which denies the power of reason to know truth.

16 MOORE, THOMAS VERNER. "The Pragmatism of William James," Catholic World, XC (December), 341-350.

James is like a lawyer skillfully defending a guilty criminal. At first pragmatism seems innocent, but when we understand it fully, it is guilty of all the charges which "so many philosophers have heaped upon it."

17 NEURATH, OTTO. Notice of Pragmatismus, translated by W. Jerusalem (Leipzig: W. Klinkhardt, 1908), Der Kunstwart, XXIII (October), 138-141.
    Treated with several philosophical, sociological books. The basis of pragmatism is the view that theories test themselves in practice. Jerusalem is the major representative of this view in Germany.

18 OFFNER, M. Review of Psychologie und Erziehung, translated by F. Kiesow, 2nd edition. (Leipzig: Engelmann, 1908), Zeitschrift für Psychologie und Physiologie der Sinnesorgane. I. Abteilung. Zeitschrift für Psychologie, LII, 319-320.
    James warns against the over-emphasizing of psychology in education. For him, man is an active being, the mind, an instrument of adaptation.

19 PILLON, F. Review of Précis de psychologie, translated by E. Baudin and G. Bertier (Paris: Marcel Rivière, 1909), L'Année Philosophique, XX, 195-196.
    Expresses reservations on several points.

20 PRATT, JAMES BISSETT. What is Pragmatism? New York: Macmillan.
    Pragmatism arises from two sources. Less influential is Kant's emphasis on the practical reason, more important, the "modern scientific view of the meaning of hypotheses." James's moderate pragmatism holds that the object of a true assertion actually exists, that the assertion can be true before it is verified, and that the workings only verify it. Dewey's radical pragmatism does not require an object and holds that verification makes the truth.

21 RILEY, ISAAC WOODBRIDGE. "Transcendentalism and Pragmatism: A Comparative Study," The Journal of Philosophy, IX (May 13) 263-266.
    Both James and Emerson reject tradition and intellectualism, both wish to revive individualism and "emotional responsiveness."

22 RUSSELL, BERTRAND. "Pragmatism," Edinburgh Review, CCIX, 363-388. Reprinted in Philosophical Essays (London: Longmans, Green, 1910; revised edition, London: George Allen & Unwin, 1966).

1909

(RUSSELL, BERTRAND)
Reviews several works by pragmatists, including The Will to Believe.

23   SCHINZ, ALBERT. Anti-pragmatisme: examen des droits respectifs de l'aristocratie intellectuelle et de la démocratie sociale. Paris: Félix Alcan. English edition with replies to critics, Anti-Pragmatism: An Examination of the Respective Rights of Intellectual Aristocracy and Social Democracy (Boston: Small, Maynard, ©1909).
Pragmatism, while a good attitude in life, is poor philosophy. It is important to preserve reason and not allow life to swallow up philosophy. Is James a pragmatist? There is a higher pragmatism in the name of which James opposes a lower pragmatism. In an appendix, Schinz complains that James has met the book with silence.

24   SCHNEIDER, KARL. "Die Philosophie des Pragmatismus," Die Grenzboten, LXVIII, 584-591.
Pragmatism is a philosophy which denies itself and wishes to serve the practical ends of life.

25   TAUSCH, EDWIN. "William James, The Pragmatist—A Psychological Analysis," The Monist, XIX (January), 1-26.
A philosophy is best understood in terms of genetic psychology. This is difficult in James's case, since he has published no autobiography. James is an "ethical voluntarist," a "dualistic pluralist," an "active optimist," and an anti-intellectualist.

26   TAYLOR, ALFRED EDWARD. Review of A Pluralistic Universe, Mind, NS XVIII (October), 576-588.
James does what he accuses others of doing. He defines monism and then attributes to every monist everything implied by his definition. Monism should not be identified with intellectualism. What James really hates is logic, the "habit of asking for reasons." James misunderstands Zeno's paradoxes. They were intended as a reductio ad absurdum of pluralism and prove only that our logic is crude. Surprising is James's adherence to Bergson. James does not dive into the stream of experience, he carries analysis up to a point, but never explains why it should not be carried further.

27   WODEHOUSE, HELEN. "Professor James on Conception," The Journal of Philosophy, VI (September 2), 490-495.
James holds that concepts cut up reality and distort it, but they do no such thing. There is more agreement between James and Bradley than James allows.

1910 A BOOKS

1   DRAHN, HERMANN. Prüfung des "Pragmatismus" von William James
    als Philosophie. Greifswald: Hans Adler.
        The effective principle of James's metaphysics is the
    will. Our decisions are conditions of a better universe.
    James's metaphysics is not entirely free of psychology.
    It would be better if pragmatism freed itself of a one-
    sided emphasis on practice and realized that science is an
    expression of the whole person.

2   MÉNARD, ALPHONSE. Analyse et critique des principes de la
    psychologie de W. James. Lyon: Imprimeries réunies.
        Cited as in the catalogue of the Bibliotheque Nationale,
    but edition consulted is dated Paris: Félix Alcan, 1911.
    James abandons atomism and gives a better interpretation of
    the psychical datum in terms of continuity and the stream
    of consciousness. As a result, psychology becomes primar-
    ily descriptive. Here, radical empiricism accepts the
    risk that psychology as a rigorous science may become
    impossible. James differs from Bergson on the question
    of memory, recognition, and attention because he explains
    mental phenomena in sensory-motor terms. James and Wundt
    together define the double task of psychology, empirical
    description and the analysis of conditions, and thus are
    not opposed to each other.

*3   _____. Le Phénomène religieux, essai de psychologisme
    pragmatique au suject des expériences religieuses d'après
    W. James. Lyon: A. Maloine.
        Not seen. Listed in the catalogue of the Bibliotheque
    Nationale. Doctoral thesis at the University of Lyon.

1910 B SHORTER WRITINGS

1   ABAUZIT, FRANK. "William James," La Semaine Littéraire
    (Geneva), no. 872 (September 17), 445-447; no. 873
    (September 24), 457-460.
        James was more a psychologist and less a metaphysician.
    In 1901, Abauzit asked James about James's intent to de-
    velop a philosophical system. Abauzit reconstructs
    James's reply.

2   ANON. "Death of Professor James," Journal of the American
    Society for Psychical Research, IV (September-October),
    526-528.
        James died before he was able to decide scientifically
    about the truth of "spiritistic theories."

1910

3   ANON. "Dr. James on the Moral Equivalent of War," The Socio-
     logical Review, III, 315-316.
        James's paper displays a side of his work little known
     in England. James's "practical suggestion" is quoted at
     length.

4   ANON. "Münsterberg Replies to Criticism," The Psychological
     Clinic, III (January 15), 248.
        According to "rumor," Hugo Münsterberg asked the American
     Psychological Association to expel Lightner Witner for his
     article (1908), threatening not to invite the Association
     to meet at Harvard unless it did so.

5   ANON. "Our Foremost Philosopher," Current Literature, XLIX
     (October), 415-418.
        Surveys opinions occasioned by James's death. James was
     "one of the freshest, most vital, most fascinating minds
     of our time."

6   ANON. "William James," Nature, LXXXIV (September 1), 268-269.
        James's lack of philosophic training enabled him to look
     at problems directly, without a "thick fog of historic
     errors." He found psychology entangled in metaphysics
     and insisted that it describe its facts anew and become a
     natural science.

7   ANON. "William James," Science, NS XXXII (November 11),
     659-660. Also appeared in Harvard University Gazette, VI,
     29-30.
        Minute on the life and services of James adopted by the
     Faculty of Arts and Sciences of Harvard University,
     October 18, 1910. G. H. Palmer (1920) states that he
     wrote it.

8   ARCHIBALD, WARREN S. Letter to the editor, The Nation, XCI
     (October 6), 312.
        In "A Pluralistic Mystic" (1910), James's closing words,
     among the last he wrote, ring with the "lure of enchanted
     cities."

9   BARON, E. Review of The Meaning of Truth, Revue de Philosophie,
     XVI, 426-428.
        James is an ardent propagandist of the new gospel and
     gives us a collection of essays on its most controversial
     point. Pragmatism, it becomes clear, is not a matter of
     believing what one wants to believe, but recognizes an
     object with which we come to agree through the working of
     our ideas. Pragmatism should not be confounded with the
     metaphysics--Schiller's humanism, James's pluralism--which
     it makes possible.

10   BERGSON, HENRI. "À Propos d'un article de Mr. Walter B. Pitkin
     intitulé: 'James and Bergson,'" The Journal of Philosophy,
     VII (July 7), 385-388. Reprinted in Mélanges (1972).
     Defends James against Pitkin (1910). James's exposition
     of Bergson's theory of concepts and of the place of the
     intellect in reality is correct.

11   BJÖRKMAN, EDWIN. "William James: Builder of American Ideals,"
     The American Review of Reviews, XLII (October), 463-467.
     James was unusually "charming" with the "power to move
     and inspire." His life was marked by "watchful calm and
     quiet application." He tried to bring philosophy back to
     the "service of life."

12   BORNHAUSEN, KARL. "William James als Philosoph," Die
     Christliche Welt, nr. 34 (August 25), cols. 794-801.
     A popular survey of James's psychology and pragmatism.
     Pragmatism is an American philosophy which emphasizes
     practice. It is a pure utilitarianism.

13   BOUTROUX, ÉMILE. Décès de M. William James. Paris: Alphonse
     Picard et Fils.
     Extract from the transactions of the Académie des
     Sciences Morales et Politiques (Institut de France),
     October-December, 1910. Memorial address by the president.

14   _____. "William James," Revue de Métaphysique et de Morale,
     XVIII (November), 711-743.
     Serves as basis for William James (1911).

15   BOVET, PIERRE. Review of The Meaning of Truth, Archives de
     Psychologie, IX, 149-150.
     James's humanism seems to be nothing else than his
     radical empiricism.

16   _____. William James psychologue: l'intérêt de son œuvre
     pour des éducateurs. Neuchâtel: Rossier & Grisel.
     A pamphlet, perhaps also published in the Bulletin
     Mensuel du Département de L'Instruction Publique (Neuchâtel),
     1910, pp. 117-132; text of a lecture given on September 24,
     1910 to the Société Pédagogique Neuchâteloise. Bovet is
     not summarizing James's views on education, but rather
     drawing out the implications of James's psychology for
     education. For James, psychology must become a natural
     science while man himself is primarily an active being.

17   BRADLEY, FRANCIS HERBERT. "A Disclaimer," The Journal of
     Philosophy, VII (March 31), 183. Reprinted in Collected
     Essays, (1935), vol. II.

1910

(BRADLEY, FRANCIS HERBERT)
   Bradley cannot claim the originality attributed to him
   in "Bradley or Bergson?" (1910). Hegel already saw that
   immediate feeling is not "all disconnectedness."

18   BRUCE, H. ADDINGTON. "William James," The Outlook, XCVI
   (September 10), 68-70.
   A general survey of James's career with some emphasis
   on psychical research. James was the "most influential of
   present-day American philosophers."

19   CALDECOTT, A. "The Work of William James. I. As Pragmatist,"
   The Sociological Review, III, 310-314.
   James was a leader of thought, but after his death, his
   work appears impermanent. It is too literary. He emphasized the subject of knowledge and had a supreme trust in
   the emotional side of human nature.

20   CARUS, PAUL. "The Pragmatist View of Truth," The Monist, XX
   (January), 139-153.
   Review of The Meaning of Truth. Some misunderstandings
   of pragmatism are due to James's style.

21   CHAPMAN, JOHN JAY. "William James: A Portrait," Harvard
   Graduates' Magazine, XIX (December), 233-238. Reprinted
   in Memories and Milestones (New York: Moffat, Yard, 1915);
   The Selected Writings of John Jay Chapman, edited by
   J. Barzun (New York: Farrar, Straus and Cudahy, 1957).
   In spite of his playfulness, James was deeply sad. Perhaps, he hated philosophy and pursued it only as a dis-
   tasteful but necessary task. James did not have the gift
   of expression, but rather the "gift.of suggestion" and his
   audiences never grasped what James actually meant.

22   CHAUMEIX, ANDRÉ. "William James," Revue des Deux Mondes, LIX,
   836-864.
   Surveys James's character and thought, written after
   James's death. James is the heir of British empiricism and
   fought against intellectualism.

23   CHESTERTON, G. K. "Our Notebook," The Illustrated London News,
   XLVII, (September 17), 432.
   A "childishly unworldly" man who marks a turning point in
   the history of our time in his manner of teaching philosophy. James forced metaphysics to "join the undignified
   dance of commonsense." "Pragmatism is bosh" because in
   the ordinary way of thinking we always separate utility
   from truth.

24 DEWEY, JOHN. "William James," The Independent, LXIX
    (September 8), 533-536. Reprinted in Characters and Events,
    edited by Joseph Ratner, (New York: Henry Holt, 1929),
    vol. I.
        James wrote for "semi-popular" audiences because for him
    philosophy was a "human affair." He did not need to write
    a treatise on ethics, because he was everywhere a moralist.
    He is one of the few philosophers whose death marks a pub-
    lic event. In psychology, his great achievement was the
    "union of the physiological and laboratory attitude with
    the introspective method."

25 _____. "William James," The Journal of Philosophy, VII
    (September 15), 505-508. Reprinted in Characters and
    Events, edited by Joseph Ratner (New York: Henry Holt,
    1929), vol. I.
        An appreciative notice. James's most marked trait was
    his sense of reality, his refusal to ignore or reject
    experience for the sake of theory.

26 GOLDSTEIN, JULIUS. "William James," Deutsche Rundschau,
    CXLV (December), 455-461.
        James is the first original American thinker, an empiri-
    cist with religious interests. James wrote to Goldstein
    that Some Problems was to be his last work and would bring
    peace and completion.

27 GROBE-WUTISCHKY, ARTHUR. Review of Psychologie, translated by
    M. Dürr (Leipzig: Quelle und Meyer, 1909), Psychische
    Studien, XXXVII (February), 110-113.
        A favorable review with emphasis on James's efforts to
    establish psychology as a science and his treatment of the
    self.

28 GROOS, KARL. "Was ist Wahrheit? Betrachtungen über die
    Erkenntnistheorie von William James," Internationale
    Wochenschrift für Wissenschaft, IV, cols. 1351-1364.
        For James, truth is what has proven itself in practice.
    Experience contradicts James's contention that all truths
    are plastic.

29 GRUENBERG, BENJAMIN. "William James," Scientific American,
    CIII (September 10), 198-199.
        James developed a "functional" psychology and held a
    dynamic view of life and conduct.

30 HUBBACK, F. W. Review of A Pluralistic Universe, The Inter-
    national Journal of Ethics, XX (April), 366-369.

1910

(HUBBACK, F. W.)
James does not separate what ought to be from what is as
does G. E. Moore. James shows that if we believe strongly
enough, what ought to be will influence what is.

31 JEANNIÈRE, RENÉ. "La Théorie des concepts chez M. Bergson et
M. James," Revue de Philosophie, XVII (December), 578-598.
Summary by Christian A. Ruckmich in The Philosophical
Review, XX (September 1911), 577-578.
A review of the controversy aroused by "Bradley or
Bergson?" (1910).

32 JERUSALEM, WILHELM. "William James," Die Zukunft, LXXIII,
186-190.
An obituary notice, emphasizing James's conception of
mental life. James is through and through an American.

33 KALLEN, HORACE M. "James, Bergson and Mr. Pitkin," The Journal
of Philosophy, VII (June 23), 353-357.
Criticism of Pitkin (1910).

34 _____. "William James," The Nation, XLI (September 8), 210-211.
James is the only American philosopher whose work is
studied in China and in Finland, everywhere where there is
concern about "human destiny." James had a strong capacity for "immediate intuition" of reality. He insisted that
ideals are not irrelevant.

35 KALTENBACH, JACQUES. "William James: souvenirs personnels,"
Foi et Vie, 13th year, 582-584.
James was one of the least abstract of philosophers. He
valued French thought highly and affirmed the usefulness
of religion.

36 KELLER, H. Review of Psychologie, translated by M. Dürr
(Leipzig: Quelle & Meyer, 1909), Zeitschrift für
mathematischen und naturwissenschaftlichen Unterricht, XL,
501-503.
In this rich work, James holds that our mental life is
teleological in origin.

37 L. L. Review of A Pluralistic Universe, Revue de Philosophie,
XVI, 194-199.
A chapter by chapter summary. Why does James try to
persuade us with syllogisms if philosophy is simply the
expression of character?

38 LADD, GEORGE TRUMBULL. Review of The Meaning of Truth, The
Philosophical Review, XIX (January), 63-69.

James shifts from question to question and alters the
meaning of terms. Pragmatists claim that truth is agreement with reality, thus making reality authoritative over
our ideas. But in trying to explain how we recognize
truth, James claims that truth is agreement of portions
of experience with other portions and thus approaches
solipsism.

39 LALANDE, ANDRÉ. Review of A Pluralistic Universe, Revue
Philosophique, LXIX, 70-78.
A summary of the major aspects. It is an ingenious
book. However, James at times uses poor arguments.

40 LEE, VERNON (VIOLET PAGET). "The Two Pragmatisms," The North
American Review, CXCII (October), 449-463. Included in
Vital Lies (1912).
There are two very different pragmatisms, that invented
by C. S. Peirce and the "Will to Believe" pragmatism of
James.

41 LÉO, ALBERT. "William James chez lui," Foi et Vie, 13th year
(November 20), 664-666.
Reminiscences by a student at Harvard in the fall of
1904.

42 LIPPMANN, WALTER. "An Open Mind: William James," Everybody's
Magazine, XXIII (December), 800-801.
James was tolerant, willing to evaluate any idea no matter what its source. His interest in psychical research
shows this. James had agreed that after his death he would
try to communicate with the living.

43 McDOUGALL, WILLIAM. "The Work of William James. II. As
Psychologist," The Sociological Review, III, 314-315.
James has done more than anyone since Aristotle to make
psychology the "basis of all the humanities."

44 MacEACHRAN, JOHN M. Pragmatismus: Eine neue Richtung der
Philosophie. Leipzig: Dieterich.
Little can be said in favor of pragmatism. Philosophy
is a matter of intellect and it is not its business to
create moral standards. The term humanism is not appropriate here. Pragmatism is a reaction against the idealism
which has dominated Oxford. While pragmatists accuse ideal-
ists of writing in a technical way, their own popular,
rhetorical style is not an improvement.

1910

45   McGILVARY, EVANDER BRADLEY.   Review of The Meaning of Truth,
         The International Journal of Ethics, XX (January), 244-250.
            To one who has suspected that James was capable only of
         "random excursions," the work proves that behind them
         stands a "thoroughly systematic plan." James shows that
         he is not a subjectivist. However, James's attribution of
         truth to ideas which never intended to be true or false
         confuses the issue. Schiller's account which begins with
         claims to truth is preferable even if unsatisfactory.

46   MARSHALL, HENRY RUTGERS. "William James," Science, NS XXXII
         (October 14), 489-492.
            James's most "striking traits" were those that "men of
         science hold as their ideals"; he could have spent his
         life in "pure science." Had he lived longer, he would have
         developed the ethical implications of pragmatism.

47   MILLER, DICKINSON S. "Some of the Tendencies of Professor
         James's Work," The Journal of Philosophy, VII (November 24),
         645-664.
            For James, psychology is the study of human nature. All
         of his work is either a contribution to psychology or from
         its point of view, for he did not allow philosophy to
         "ignore the way life feels." He approached psychology as
         a doctor, artist, and a sympathetic human being.

48   MITCHELL, A. W. Review of A Pluralistic Universe, Review of
         Theology and Philosophy, VI, 179-187.
            An exposition with little criticism. Pluralism seems to
         have room for both the human and the divine and is supe-
         rior to the absolute unity of the Hegelians.

49   MONTAGUE, WILLIAM PEPPERELL. "An Explanation," The Journal of
         Philosophy, VII (March 31), 184-185.
            A reply to James's criticism, Journal of Philosophy,
         pp. 183-184, of Montague's review (1910) of A Pluralistic
         Universe.

50   _____. "'A Pluralistic Universe' and the Logic of Iration-
         alism," The Journal of Philosophy, VII (March 16), 141-155.
            Review of A Pluralistic Universe. James gives us a con-
         vincing critique of absolutism, but a very unconvincing
         defense of Bergson's critique of intellectualism. Montague
         gives a general criticism of Bergson.

51   MORE, PAUL ELMER. "The Pragmatism of William James" in
         Shelburne Essays, 7th series. New York: G. P. Putnam's
         Sons.

A philosopher of flux when attacked just flows into
another form. It is amusing to watch a rational defense
of an attack on "rationalism." In A Pluralistic Universe
James's main purpose is to discard metaphysics.

52 MÜLLER-FREIENFELS, RICHARD. Review of The Meaning of Truth,
    Zeitschrift für Psychologie und Physiologie der
    Sinnesorgane. I. Abteilung. Zeitschrift für Psychologie,
    LVII, 195-196.
        James answers accusations that pragmatism leaves no room
    for an external world. He wants a radical empiricism.
    Pragmatism does not clarify the difference between estab-
    lished truth and personal belief, even where this differ-
    ence would be useful.

53 _____. Review of A Pluralistic Universe, Zeitschrift für
    Psychologie und Physiologie der Sinnesorgane.
    I. Abteilung. Zeitschrift für Psychologie, LV, 215-217.
        Having in other works made usefulness the criterion of
    truth, James turns to a different problem, the controversy
    between monists and pluralists.

54 NOËL, L. Review of Précis de psychologie, translated by E.
    Baudin and G. Bertier (Paris: Marcel Rivière, 1909),
    Revue Néo-Scolastique de Philosophie, XVII (February),
    142-143.
        It was a happy thought to translate James's Psychology
    for a public which knows him as the adoptive father of
    pragmatism and for work on religious experience. Some of
    the chapters are classics. The translation is excellent.

55 PERRY, RALPH BARTON. "William James," Harvard Graduates' Maga-
    zine, XIX (December), 212-225.
        Surveys James's professional career.

56 PILLON, F. Review of Philosophie de l'expérience, translated
    by E. Le Brun and M. Paris (Paris: Flammarion, 1910),
    L'Année Philosophique, XXI, 211-213.
        French translation of A Pluralistic Universe. The
    English title indicates the object studied, while the
    French, the method used, radical empiricism.

57 PITKIN, WALTER B. "James and Bergson: Or, Who is Against the
    Intellect," The Journal of Philosophy, VII (April 28),
    225-231.
        In A Pluralistic Universe, James mistakenly represents
    his position to be like Bergson's. In spite of some simi-
    larities, the two are sharply opposed, particularly concern-
    ing conceptual knowledge. James is an anti-intellectualist,

1910

(PITKIN, WALTER B.)
Bergson is not. For Bergson, concepts make things more
intelligible.

58   PUTNAM, JAMES JACKSON. "William James," The Atlantic Monthly,
      CVI (December), 835-848.
          Reminiscences by James's fellow student at the Harvard
      Medical School, hiking companion, and life-long friend.
      Excerpts from letters from James to Putnam are quoted.

59   ROYCE, JOSIAH. "A Word of Greeting to William James," Harvard
      Graduates' Magazine, XVIII, 630-633.
          Speech at a dinner, January 18, 1910, celebrating the
      completion of James's portrait for Harvard University.
      Royce recalls his relations with James.

60   RUSSELL, BERTRAND. "The Philosophy of William James," The
      Nation (London), VII (September 3), 793-794. Reprinted
      in The Living Age, CCLXVII (October 1), 52-55.
          James is at his best when dealing with facts, but in the
      rarified atmosphere of metaphysics his mind fails to find
      its full scope. His pragmatism is a philosophy for those
      who love battle more than victory. He urges us to accept
      any faith we find congenial.

61   RUSSELL, JOHN E. Review of The Meaning of Truth, The Journal
      of Philosophy, VII (January 6), 22-24.
          In his anti-pragmatist days (see "Controversy about
      Truth" [1907]), Russell would have viewed the volume dif-
      ferently. Now he finds it a challenge to the rejectors of
      pragmatism. James opposes a concrete conception of truth
      to the empty abstraction of the anti-pragmatists. He
      answers critics who claim that radical empiricism leads
      to solipsism.

62   RUTTMANN, W. J. "Die Hauptpunkte der James'schen Psychologie,"
      Die deutsche Schule, XIV, 751-757.
          James is not a psychologist in a narrow sense. The whole
      of his work is marked by a strong literary flavor. Rutt-
      man surveys the main aspects of James's psychology with
      emphasis on James's conception of the self.

63   SCHILLER, F. C. S. Review of The Meaning of Truth, Mind, XIX
      (April), 258-263.
          Shows how the "pragmatic conceptions actually grew up in
      a first-class" mind. James upholds the "solidarity" of the
      leading pragmatists, although somewhat hesitant about
      Dewey. This is due to a realistic strain in James, his
      views on "real objects." Here, James is not pragmatic

WILLIAM JAMES: A REFERENCE GUIDE

enough, for he does not ask what is meant by real objects.
Schiller cannot agree that Schiller's contributions to
humanism are primarily psychological.

64 SWITALSKI, W. Der Wahrheitsbegriff des Pragmatismus nach
    William James. Braunsberg: Heynes Buchdruckerei.
        For the question "What is truth?" pragmatists substitute
    "What are the grounds of the validity of my judgment?"
    But answers are to be sought in Christian philosophy, in
    the Aristotelian tradition. Aristotle gives an objective
    interpretation of our knowledge of truth.

65 THORNDIKE, EDWARD L. "William James," The Journal of Educa-
    tional Psychology, I (September), 473-474.
        A note marking James's death.

66 TITCHENER, EDWARD BRADFORD. A Text-book of Psychology. New
    York: Macmillan.
        Discusses the James-Lange theory of emotion.

67 WALKER, LESLIE J. Theories of Knowledge: Absolutism, Pragma-
    tism, Realism. London: Longmans, Green.
        Criticizes pragmatism and radical empiricism from the
    scholastic point of view. Pragmatism, while not a Kantian
    philosophy, can be traced to Kant's practical reason. Its
    major difficulty is to explain the origin of knowledge.

1911 A BOOKS

1 BÖCKER, THEODOR. Die James-Lange'sche Gefühlstheorie in ihrer
   historischen Entwicklung. Leipzig: Breitkopf & Härtel.
       James for the first time formulated a peripheral theory
   of the emotions in terms of physiological and pathological
   evidence. Much attention is devoted to the work of psychologists who proposed modifications of the theory.

2 BOUTROUX, ÉMILE. William James. Paris: Armand Colin.
   English translation, Archibald Henderson and Barbara
   Henderson, (New York: Longmans, Green, 1912).
       Surveys James's psychology, religious psychology, prag-
   matism, metaphysics, and philosophy of education. James's
   philosophy is anti-academic and is guided only by experience. James establishes a novel relation between science
   and philosophy. He begins with science as if it were the
   whole of knowledge and excluded metaphysics. However, the
   development of science itself leads him into metaphysics.
   James's metaphysics identifies reality with the deepest
   life of consciousness.

1911

3   BUSCH, KARL AUGUST. William James als Religionsphilosoph.
    Göttingen: Vanderhoeck & Ruprecht.
        Discusses the psychological religious philosophy of
    Varieties, the relation between pragmatism and religion,
    and James's pluralism in connection with God and meliorism.
    This exposition is followed by a brief evaluation.

4   FLOURNOY, THÉODORE. La Philosophie de William James. Saint-
    Blaise: Foyer Solidariste. English translation, The
    Philosophy of William James, translated by Edwin B. Holt
    and William James, Jr. (New York: Holt, 1917).
        Surveys the major aspects of James's thought. The intro-
    duction includes two letters from James to a group of stu-
    dents who had invited him to lecture. Flournoy gives some
    personal reminiscences.

1911 B SHORTER WRITINGS

1   ANGELL, JAMES ROWLAND. "William James," The Psychological
    Review, XVIII (January), 78-82.
        The Principles of Psychology appeared at the right time
    and completely changed psychology. James introduced
    "habit as the basic principle of mental organization,"
    revolutionized views of emotion, gave instinct a place in
    the forefront of human psychology, demanded recognition of
    the vague and fugitive in consciousness, more so than other
    English writers, used materials from the pathological side
    of human life. His account of space perception still
    remains valuable. His support of psychical research in
    the face of severe criticism should teach us "honest inde-
    pendence." His greatest contribution lies not in his doc-
    trines but in his spirit.

2   ANON. "A List of the Published Writings of William James,"
    The Psychological Review, XVIII (March), 157-165.
        A preliminary list, now outdated. Perry, Annotated Bib-
    liography (1920) attributes this to Henry James, Jr. and
    Edwin B. Holt and gives The Journal of Philosophy as
    publisher.

3   ANON. Review of Memories and Studies, The Athenaeum, no. 4389
    (December 9), pp. 726-727.
        A "garden of rare flowers, fragrant with the personality
    of a great philosopher."

4   ANON. Review of Some Problems, The Athenaeum, no. 4365
    (June 24), pp. 709-710.
        Summarizes the contents. "To face facts, and be brave
    and loyal," that is James's philosophy.

5   ANON. Review of <u>The Meaning of Truth,</u> <u>The North American</u>
    <u>Review</u>, CXCIII (February), 298-300.
        With James, for the first time, ideas originating in the
    United States have influenced thinkers in Europe.

6   BALDWIN, BIRD T. "William James's Contributions to Education,"
    <u>The Journal of Educational Psychology</u>, II (September),
    369-382.
        James is primarily responsible for the present-day
    "empirical and experimental" treatment of education.

7   BERGSON, HENRI. Introduction to <u>Le Pragmatisme</u>, translated by
    E. Le Brun. Paris: Flammarion. Reprinted as "Sur le
    pragmatisme de William James," in <u>La Pensée et le mouvant</u>
    (Paris: Félix Alcan, 1934). English translation, <u>The</u>
    <u>Creative Mind</u>, translated by M. L. Andison, (New York:
    Philosophical Library, 1946).
        If we understand James, we will change our conception of
    the universe. The world will no longer seem like a play.
    In the world, scenes do not follow each other in order,
    things do not fit, there are no finally decisive events.
    The world is fluid. James's conception of truth is suited
    to his conception of the world.

8   BERTHELOT, RENÉ. <u>Un Romantisme utilitaire: étude sur le</u>
    <u>mouvement pragmatiste</u>. Vol. I, <u>Le Pragmatisme chez</u>
    <u>Nietzsche et chez Poincaré</u>. Paris: Félix Alcan.
        Part of the Introduction is titled "La Vulgarisation
    de l'idée et de l'équivoque pragmatistes: William James
    et M. Schiller (1898-1909)." James's main interests are
    religious. He denies that there is a single truth and
    holds that there are particular truths. In all truths,
    there is an indemonstrable element where we have to rely
    on postulates.

9   BOODIN, JOHN E. "From Protagoras to William James," <u>The</u>
    <u>Monist</u>, XXI (January), 73-91.
        James has been compared with Protagoras. This is apt
    because Protagoras was not a subjectivist but a "genuine
    empiricist." Pragmatism has not always been clearly
    stated. It must make clear that conduct refers to our
    "entire human nature in realizing its tendencies" and
    clarify its relations to nominalism.

10 BRADLEY, FRANCIS HERBERT. "On Some Aspects of Truth," <u>Mind</u>,
    NS XX (July), 305-341. A part, titled "On Prof. James's
    'Meaning of Truth,'" reprinted with changes in <u>Essays on</u>
    <u>Truth and Reality</u> (1914).

1911

(BRADLEY, FRANCIS HERBERT)
It is not clear in what sense James is a relativist, since it is not clear what James means by humanity. James's view that where there is truth there is a "temporal process" connecting idea and object is also criticized.

11 BUSCH, KARL AUGUST. "William James," Zeitschrift für Religionspsychologie, IV, 300-303.
An obituary notice. For the Kantian, James was an "enfant terrible." He was an individualist and a poet. Busch had visited James in Cambridge late in James's life.

12 CARUS, PAUL. Truth on Trial: An Exposition of the Nature of Truth Preceded by a Critique of Pragmatism and an Apprecia- tion of its Leader. Chicago: Open Court.
A collection of articles from The Monist, two of which are listed separately (1908) (1909). Contains writings on truth and pragmatism.

13 COOK, HELEN D. "The James-Lange Theory of the Emotions and the Sensationalistic Analysis of Thinking," The Psycholog- ical Bulletin, VIII (March 15), 101-106.
Some of the arguments used by Titchener against the James-Lange theory can be used against Titchener. Dis- cusses Titchener rather than James.

14 ENRIQUES, F. Review of Philosophie de l'expérience, translated by E. Le Brun (Paris: Flammarion, 1910), Scientia (Série physico-mathématique), IX, 226-228.
In spite of James's declared opposition to science and rationalism, his position is closer to science and reason than that of the pseudo-rationalists he opposes. James simply claims that we also need an artistic understanding of reality, and what scientist could object?

15 JACKS, L. P. "William James and His Message," The Contemporary Review, XCIX, 20-33.
James's philosophy would be a stimulating influence because it is a call to undertake a "daring and risky expe- dition into the unknown." For James, words were "pointers" into a "concrete whole of experience," for his critics, words were to be taken at face value.

16 JACOBY, GÜNTHER. Review of Psychologie, translated by M. Dürr (Leipzig: Quelle & Meyer, 1909), Zeitschrift für Philoso- phie und philosophische Kritik, CXLIV, 66-67.
James's text-book cannot be compared with others. Beginning students will come to take much pleasure in psychology.

17 JASTROW, JOSEPH. "An American Academician," Educational
    Review, XLI (January), 27-33.
       Contains some reminiscences.

18 KALLEN, HORACE M. "Pragmatism and its 'Principles'," The
    Journal of Philosophy, VIII (November 9), 617-636.
       The principles of pragmatism are found not in H. Heath
    Bawden, The Principles of Pragmatism (Boston: Houghton
    Mifflin, 1910), but in James. Pragmatism holds that the
    core of reality is duration. From this can be derived an
    empirical method and the view that "mind is value." For
    James, mind and nature have equal standing. Other pragma-
    tists upset this delicate balance and schools of pragmatism
    arise.

19 LALANDE, ANDRÉ. "L'Idée de vérité d'après William James et ses
    adversaires," Revue Philosophique, LXXI (January), 1-26.
    Summary by Corrinne Stephenson, The Philosophical Review,
    XX (July 1911), 465.
       For pragmatism, ideas and objects are parts of the one
    whole of experience and thus are in harmony. True is
    what is expedient. If this seems to emphasize the lower
    aspects, James replies that human nature has two sides and
    both are to be considered. To avoid relativism, James
    emphasizes consequences.

20 LINDSAY, JAMES. Review of The Meaning of Truth, Archiv für
    systematische Philosophie, XVII, 133-134.
       James is too polemical and the result is not very satis-
    fying. Some rationalists are absurd, but this is no
    reason to "proscribe the legitimate place" of the intellect.

21 _____. Review of A Pluralistic Universe, Archiv für
    systematische Philosophie, XVII, 134-135.
       James is too polemical and extreme. James confuses
    theism with deism and gives a "discreditable travesty" of
    theism.

22 LOVEJOY, ARTHUR O. "William James as Philosopher," The Inter-
    national Journal of Ethics, XXI (January) 125-153.
    Reprinted in The Thirteen Pragmatisms (1963).
       Contrary to common belief, James had more logical
    scrupulosity than most and followed his analyses wherever
    they led. James was devoted to individuality and had a
    sense for the flow of time. We should not from the sim-
    plicity of his style infer the simplicity of his thought.
    It is complex and delicately balanced.

1911

23 McDOUGALL, WILLIAM. "In Memory of William James," Proceedings
    of the Society for Psychical Research (English), vol. XXV,
    part LXII (March), 11-29.
        James was a leader of the society, but had the society
    never existed, he still would have done much for psychical
    research. His aim was to reconcile science and religion
    on empirical grounds and this is identical with the aim of
    the society. James's psychical research provided data for
    the attack on mechanical materialism.

24 McGILVARY, EVANDER BRADLEY. "The 'Fringe' of William James's
    Psychology the Basis of Logic," The Philosophical Review,
    XX (March), 137-164.
        The doctrine of the 'fringe' can serve as the basis of
    a wider logic than James himself developed. This wider
    logic centers around the "non-pragmatistic correspondence
    between ideas and realities."

25 MILLER, DICKINSON S. Review of Some Problems, The Nation,
    XCIII (September 14), 240-241.
        The work centers around three problems: the relation
    of thought to things; the problem of the one and the many;
    the problem of novelty. James rebels against control and
    his treatment of the three can be reduced to this
    rebellion.

26 MUIRHEAD, JOHN HENRY. "William James as Philosopher," Pro-
    ceedings of the Society for Psychical Research (English),
    vol. XXV, part LXII (March), 30-37.
        James wanted to see everything in human terms and was
    part of a general humanistic movement. James's attack on
    impersonal idealism kept him from developing his thought
    in its natural direction. On the subjects of truth, rela-
    tion of concepts to reality, and pluralism, he should have
    moved towards idealism.

27 NOËL, L. "William James," Revue Néo-Scolastique de Philoso-
    phie, XVIII (February), 28-57.
        In every line we find "la rondeur du boy américain."
    James's work is national, expressing the practical con-
    cerns of his race, with the rigid honesty of the puritans
    and religious fervor. He is a major representative of
    pragmatism. Metaphysics is his weakest point.

28 OGDEN, R. M. Review of É. Boutroux, William James (1911) and
    A. Ménard, Analyse et critique (1911), The Philosophical
    Review, XX (November), 658-662.
        James roused the American mind from the "lethargy of its
    German rationalism." Boutroux "convincingly" outlines

James's thought and shows how it bridges the gap between mind and matter. Ménard views James through Bergsonian glasses. His work lacks criticism.

29 PALANTE, GEORGES. "Le Débat sur l'intelligence," Mercure de France, XCII (August), 823-829.
    Pragmatism is reviewed together with other books on the value of reason. Pragmatism finds intellectual truth too threatening and leaves the comfort and security of moral truth in its place. It seeks social utility. James tries to preserve intellectual truth, but ends up by confounding everything with everything else.

30 PERRY, RALPH BARTON. "The Philosophy of William James," The Philosophical Review, XX (January), 1-29. Reprinted in Present Philosophical Tendencies (1912).
    A "rude sketch" of James's philosophy. James's thought is a system, it is "one philosophy" although James died before he could make explicit its structure. His thought was "a study of man."

31 PILLON, F. Review of Le Pragmatisme, translated by E. Le Brun (Paris: Flammarion, 1911), L'Année Philosophique, XXII, 213-214.
    The traditional conception considers truth after a truth has been established, while pragmatism deals with it before verification. It is difficult to see how James deals adequately with all kinds of truth.

32 PRATT, JAMES BISSETT. "The Religious Philosophy of William James," The Hibbert Journal, X (October), 225-234.
    James was hospitable to all beliefs sincerely held. He is accused of believing what he wanted to, but he rejected monism, in spite of its attractiveness, because it was inconsistent with the actual universe which is pluralistic. James was a "believer" rather than a "skeptic," although he never worked out a theology. Included is a long quotation from James's letter to James H. Leuba on religion.

33 RILEY, ISAAC WOODBRIDGE. "Continental Critics of Pragmatism," The Journal of Philosophy, VIII (April 27), 225-232; (May 25) 289-294.
    Surveys how French and Italian critics have cut up pragmatism, especially the "land of James."

34 RITTER, EUGÈNE. Charles Ritter: ses amis et ses maîtres. Lausanne: Payot & Cie.
    Contains several letters from James to Charles Ritter.

1911

35 ROYCE, JOSIAH. "William James and the Philosophy of Life" in
William James and Other Essays On the Philosophy of Life.
New York: Macmillan. Also appeared in Science, XXXIV
(July 14), 33-45; Harvard Graduates' Magazine, XX (1911-
1912), 1-18; The Boston Evening Transcript, June 29, 1911,
p. 13.
The Phi Beta Kappa oration before the Harvard Chapter,
June 29, 1911. When James died, many asked Royce to write
about him, but this is his only public statement. With
Edwards and Emerson, James is a representative American
philosopher. His work is related to three major movements:
evolution, the new psychology, and the social transformation of America.

36 RUSSELL, BERTRAND. Review of Memories and Studies, The Cambridge Review, XXXIII (November 16), 118.
James's maxim that a worthy pursuit will make a man's
face shine does little for chimney-sweeps. The essay on
Spencer is amusing, those on war, delightful.

37 SANTAYANA, GEORGE. "The Genteel Tradition in American Philosophy," The University of California Chronicle, XIII
(October), 357-380. Reprinted in Winds of Doctrine:
Studies in Contemporary Opinion (New York: Charles
Scribner's Sons, 1913).
Raised in the genteel tradition, James cast off most of
it. A romanticist, James viewed the spirit of the world
as a "romantic adventurer." The world is a "gradual
improvisation."

38 SCHILLER, F. C. S. Review of Some Problems, Mind, NS XX
(October), 571-573.
James has been writing introductions to philosophy since
The Principles of Psychology. Had it been completed, it
would still have given us only a fragment of James's vision. It teaches philosophy to be "profound without ped-
antry." The treatment of the problem of being is novel
and so are the chapters on percept and concept.

39 SCHINZ, ALBERT. "La Portée philosophique de l'œuvre de
William James," Bibliothèque Universelle et Revue Suisse,
Series IV, vol. LXII, 519-539.
For James, truth is important, but life is more impor-
tant. He began with the study of nature, then turned to
psychology, then, to philosophy. Against spiritualists,
James held that body acts on mind, but against material-
ists, that men have spontaneity.

40 SLATTERY, CHARLES LEWIS. "The Debt of the Church to William James," The Outlook, XCVIII (July 22), 643-646.
James had the spirit of Christ. While outside the church, he still rendered it great services. None who has read James on habit can approve of "wild oats," since laws are needed to build character. His studies in religion revealed the influence of the "Unseen God," while his pragmatism required that the church be judged not by dogmas but by fruits. James's thought has been reproduced in thousands of sermons.

41 SMITH, H. ARTHUR. "Commemorative Address: William James and Frank Podmore," Proceedings of the Society for Psychical Research (English), vol. XXV, part LXII (March), 1-4.
Memorial remarks.

42 WUNDT, WILHELM. Probleme der Völkerpsychologie. Leipzig: Ernst Wiegandt, 1911.
Surveys the impact of pragmatism upon the German theologians Ernst Troeltsch and Georg Wobbermin. Wundt is critical of the resulting individualistic tendencies in the study of religion. Much better are the methods of social psychology.

1912 A BOOKS

1 OLTRAMARE, HUGO. Essai sur la prière d'après la pensée philosophique de William James. Geneva: H. Robert.
Faithful to James's spirit and method, rather than to specific doctrines, the author discusses the problem of evil in relation to James's radical empiricism, pragmatism, and his "théorie anatomo-physiologique." Presented as a thesis for the degree of Bachelor of Theology at the University of Geneva. Copy at Columbia University.

1912 B SHORTER WRITINGS

1 ANON. Review of Essays in Radical Empiricism, The North American Review, CXCVI (November), 716-717.
James proposes a revolutionary method for philosophy, that of looking at the primary facts.

2 ANON. "William James and Empiricism," The Athenæum, no. 4421 (July 20), 57.
Review of Essays in Radical Empiricism. No momentous contributions to philosophy are to be found in it.

1912

3   BERKELEY, HASTINGS. "The Kernel of Pragmatism," Mind, NS XXI,
    84-88.
        It is futile to argue with pragmatists. They simply do
    not see a certain quality their opponents claim is essen-
    tial. James could admit in theory a difference between
    the truth of a belief and its working, but claim that this
    difference has never been discerned. Anti-pragmatists,
    like B. Russell, fail to understand pragmatism.

4   BODE, BOYD HENRY. Review of Essays in Radical Empiricism, The
    Philosophical Review, XXI (November), 704-705.
        This book should help to distinguish James's pragmatism
    from that of others.

5   BOURDEAU, JEAN. La Philosophie affective. Paris: Félix
    Alcan.
        James is an anti-intellectualist. Discusses Albert
    Schinz (1909) and James's pluralism.

6   FERRIÈRE, AD. "Deux philosophes de l'expérience: William
    James et Théodore Flournoy," Coenobium, V (May), 1-13.
        Based upon Flournoy's La Philosophie de William James
    (1911). Both James and Flournoy fought against the cancer
    of materialistic monism. It is appropriate that Flournoy
    should be the author of this tribute to James.

7   HENRY, J. "Pragmatisme anglo-américain et philosophie
    nouvelle," Revue Néo-Scolastique de Philosophie, XIX (May),
    264-272.
        The pragmatism of James and Schiller is quite different
    from Bergsonism and what Le Roy calls the new philosophy.
    Pragmatism begins with epistemological problems and is
    compatible with various kinds of metaphysics, the new
    philosophy begins with a metaphysical view, radical
    evolutionism.

8   JACOBY, GÜNTHER. "Der amerikanische Pragmatismus und die
    Philosophie des Als Ob," Zeitschrift für Philosophie und
    philosophische Kritik, CXLVII, 172-184.
        Pragmatism is often presented as an American philosophy
    of dollars. It is American, but a philosophy of life and
    creativity. Jacoby concludes that the philosophy of Hans
    Vaihinger is more deeply grounded than pragmatism. The
    pragmatic conception of truth is obtained from general
    considerations, Vaihinger's from a detailed investigation
    of science.

9   JASTROW, JOSEPH. "The Legacy of William James," The Dial, LII
    (January 1), 12-14.

A review of J. Royce, William James and Other Essays (1911), Some Problems, and Memories and Studies. James could be fair even to those he disliked. "The humanist persists in the philosopher."

10   _____. Notes in Psychology On Lectures Supplementary to James' Psychology. Madison, Wisc.: Privately printed for the use of classes in the University of Wisconsin. No direct references to James.

11   KELLER, ADOLF. "William James," Wissen und Leben, V (June 15), 370-391.
       James exemplifies the empirical method in its purest form. His thought is like a pyramid, with concrete fact forming the base and the point reaching towards the heights of metaphysics. He is a representative of a country which is not tied down by tradition.

12   KNOX, HOWARD V. Review of Memories and Studies, Mind, NS XXI (July), 453-455.
       Indicates a number of important points. As always, James is delightful reading.

13   LEE, VERNON (VIOLET PAGET). Vital Lies: Studies of Some Varieties of Recent Obscurantism, 2 vols. London: John Lane; New York: John Lane.
       There are two pragmatisms: the valuable pragmatism intended to "make our ideas clear," introduced by Peirce and taken over by James and Schiller, and the worthless pragmatism of the "will to believe." James is a "delightful thinker," marked by "a certain lack of grip and continuity," a victim of a "virus" in the air. The will to believe would have "made havoc in latter day thought" even if James had not espoused it.

14   _____. "What is truth? (A Criticism of Pragmatism)," Yale Review, NS I (July), 600-619. Included in Vital Lies (1912).
       A dialogue. The anti-pragmatist at last realizes that it is in religious experience that the "cash-value" of truth must be sought.

15   LEUBA, JAMES H. A Psychological Study of Religion: Its Origin, Function, and Future. New York: Macmillan.
       In Varieties, James examined mystical states to find evidence for the "transcendent hypothesis." James held that the presence of "reconciliation" and union pointed to the superhuman but he had no warrant for such a claim. His efforts are a "fiasco."

1912

16   LINDSAY, A. D. Review of Some Problems of Philosophy, The
      Hibbert Journal, X (January), 489-492.
          Perhaps the most interesting of James's works. James
      sometimes describes philosophy as the residue of questions
      not yet capable of scientific treatment, but he holds that
      philosophy co-ordinates the sciences and that it treats
      the general and leaves the particulars to science.

17   M. S. Review of Le Pragmatisme, translated by E. Le Brun
      (Paris: Flammarion, 1911) and É. Boutroux, William James
      (1911), Revue de Philosophie, XX, 94-97.
          A sense for the concrete may suffice for experimental
      psychology, but does not go far in philosophy. James's
      radical empiricism is sterile.

18   MILLER, DICKINSON S. Review of Memories and Studies, É.
      Boutroux, William James (1911), J. Royce, William James
      and Other Essays (1911), The Nation, XCIV (April 11),
      362-363.
          The essays mark James as among the best American essay-
      ists. Boutroux's treatment is too light, and one would do
      better to read James. Royce interprets James as a repre-
      sentative American, but it is easy to exaggerate James's
      Americanism.

19   MONTAGUE, WILLIAM PEPPERELL. Review of Some Problems, The
      Journal of Philosophy, IX (January 4), 22-25.
          It is disappointing that the book breaks off just at the
      beginning of the treatment of certain metaphysical
      problems.

20   MOORE, EDWARD CALDWELL. An Outline of the History of Christian
      Thought Since Kant. London: Duckworth.
          Pp. 238-241 deal with James. Modern religious thought
      begins with Kant's view that "religion is a fact of the
      inner life" and James's religious psychology continues
      this. It suggests that lower religions are to be under-
      stood in terms of higher, and not the reverse.

21   MURRAY, DAVID LESLIE. Pragmatism. London: Constable.
          Pragmatism is the product of several lines of thought,
      the "most fertile" of which is James's "new psychology."
      James destroyed the empiricist view that knowledge begins
      with discrete elements. We are initially given a whole
      which is later broken up by analysis.

22   O'KEEFFE, D. "Pragmatism," The Irish Ecclesiastical Record,
      4th series, vol. XXXI (June), 561-569; XXXII, 31-40;
      268-277; 354-361.

Pragmatism is an extreme form of skepticism which has shaken philosophers out of their dogmatic slumber, especially where a naive copy-theory of truth is concerned. The pragmatic claim to free our beliefs is illusory. We get another form of control. O'Keeffe shows that James is usually mistaken in his comments about scholasticism.

23 PARKER, CHARLES B. "Plato and Pragmatism" in Harvard Essays on Classical Subjects, edited by Herbert Weir Smith. Boston: Houghton, Mifflin.
For "ultimate instruction," James refers us to the flux of sensations while Plato, to the world of essence. But perhaps both reach the same "mystical region" where "rational thinking" fails.

24 PERRY, RALPH BARTON. Present Philosophical Tendencies: A Critical Survey of Naturalism, Idealism, Pragmatism, and Realism Together with a Synopsis of the Philosophy of William James. New York: Longmans, Green.
Most of the appendix is a reprint of "The Philosophy of William James" (1911). Perry discusses the pragmatic theory of knowledge, "immediatism versus intellectualism," pluralism, indeterminism, and religious faith, with frequent references to James.

25 PETERSON, HARVEY A. "Note on a Retrial of Professor James' Experiment on Memory Training," The Psychological Review, XIX (November), 491-492.
Attempts to duplicate experiments in memory training described in The Principles of Psychology (1890), I, 666-667.

26 RUSSELL, BERTRAND. Review of Essays in Radical Empiricism, Mind, NS XXI (October), 571-575.
Radical empiricism is by now "indubitable," except for the term 'experience' which James uses without adequate analysis. James's attempt to identify the mental with the physical through the notion of pure experience is "profoundly original." However, James should have just shown that there is no "mental," no act which is distinct from its object.

27 SABINE, GEORGE H. Review of Some Problems, The International Journal of Ethics, XXII (January), 217-221.
The theory of conception is the root of James's thought. A great philosopher can teach even by errors. James is mistaken in opposing conception to perception as sharply as he does. He resembles Kant and his solution of the difficulty is as artificial as Kant's.

1912

28　SCHILLER, F. C. S.　Preface to D. L. Murray, Pragmatism.
London:　Constable.
　　Pragmatism while a work of genius is too untechnical for
professional philosophers and no longer "covers the whole
ground."

29　SÉROL, M.　"La Fin de l'homme selon William James," Revue de
Philosophie, XXI, 564-574.
　　The study of James shows that empiricism is too limited
to provide answers about the ultimate destiny of man.
James cannot find redemptive truths and ends by contradict-
ing experience.

30　TROELTSCH, ERNST.　"Empiricism and Platonism in the Philosophy
of Religion:　To the Memory of William James," Harvard
Theological Review, V (October), 401-422. ·
　　James's is the first "thorough-going" American contribution to the philosophy of religion.　James presents his
views as a working hypothesis, while European thinkers see
in theirs a demand of reason.　The European tradition is
Platonic, while James turns religious philosophy into
psychology.　James draws our attention to the concrete but
we should not forget that the abstract is the sphere of
philosophy.

31　WATERLOW, SIDNEY.　"The Philosophy of Henri Bergson," The
Quarterly Review, CCXVI (January), 152-176.
　　A review of works by and about Bergson, but includes A
Pluralistic Universe and Some Problems.　Waterlow tries
to discuss the ties between James and Bergson beyond the
fact that both have a "strongly emotional cast of mind"
and both are in revolt against their predecessors.

1913 A BOOKS

1　BLOCH, WERNER.　Der Pragmatismus von James und Schiller nebst
einem Exkurs über die Hypothese.　Leipzig:　Johann
Ambrosius Barth.　A different version was published as
Der Pragmatismus von James und Schiller nebst Exkursen über
Weltanschauung und über die Hypothese. (Leipzig:　Johann
Ambrosius Barth, 1913).　Also appeared in the Zeitschrift
für Philosophie und philosophische Kritik, CLII (1913),
1-41, 145-214.
　　Pragmatism is not a philosophy but a world-view and is
not well-grounded.　In addition, one can prove its falsity.
Bloch concentrates on the pragmatic theories of meaning
and of truth.

2   HARBERTS, W. William James' Religionsphilosophie, begründet
    auf persönlicher Erfahrung. Erlangen: E. Th. Jacob.
        For James, religious experience is supersensible,
    personal, and mystical. Harberts discusses James's concep-
    tion of God, the sick-soul, faith, conversion, saintliness,
    and prayer.

3   REVERDIN, HENRI. La Notion d'expérience d'après William
    James. Geneva: Georg et Co.
        The concept of experience is central in the philosophy
    of James. James approached experience as a spokesman for
    empiricism, a psychologist dealing with the stream of con-
    sciousness, an epistemologist, a radical empiricist, and
    a student of religious experience. These approaches can-
    not all be reconciled.

4   SCHULTZE, MARTIN. Das Problem der Wahrheitserkenntnis bei
    William James und Henri Bergson. Erlangen: Junge & Sohn.
        The emphasis is on Bergson. Some ten pages are given
    to an exposition of James's views and another ten to a
    criticism of the pragmatic and positivistic conception of
    truth.

1913 B SHORTER WRITINGS

1   BOISSE, LOUIS. "Le Pragmatisme pédagogique," Revue
    Pédagogique, NS LXII (May 15), 401–428.
        An exposition and criticism of James's philosophy of
    education as stated in Talks. Boisse disagrees with
    James's view that knowledge of psychology is neither nec-
    essary nor sufficient for good education and ₒwith his ten-
    dency to ignore the theoretical power. Boisse does agree
    with James's emphasis on activity in education.

2   BORNHAUSEN, KARL. "James der Philosoph des heutigen Amerika,"
    Die Christliche Welt, no. 6 (February 6), cols. 122–130.
        Bornhausen contributes a brief introduction to the trans-
    lation of Royce's "William James and the Philosophy of
    Life" (1911).

3   BUSH, WENDELL T. "The Empiricism of James," The Journal of
    Philosophy, X (September 25), 533–541.
        Since James, philosophers have come to respect their
    power of observation. Yet, in the Essays in Radical
    Empiricism, James does not quite speak the "language of
    empiricism." Words such as 'flux', 'pure experience',
    and James's attachment to the "supernatural," tend to
    "compromise" it in empiricist eyes.

1913

4   CARR, H. WILDON. Review of Essays in Radical Empiricism, The
    Hibbert Journal, XI (January), 451–453.
        Was it necessary for the editors to present this as a
    treatise? It is actually a collection of polemical
    articles.

5   CROOKS, EZRA B. "Professor James and the Psychology of Reli-
    gion," The Monist, XXIII (January), 122–130.
        Varieties gave rise to the field of psychology of reli-
    gion. James's method was "sympathetic interpretation" and
    an "imaginative entering" into religious experience. We
    find illuminated the "oddities" of our consciousnesses.
    Fascinated by this, we tend to forget that these oddities
    are only a small part of our life.

6   DUGAS, L. "Un Paradoxe psychologique: la théorie de James-
    Lange," Revue Philosophique, LXXV, 289–296.
        The theory in its dualistic form must face the problem
    of mind-body interaction. Furthermore, it misunderstands
    the nature of consciousness by declaring it to be of no
    consequence.

7   E. D. Review of Essays in Radical Empiricism, Revue de
    Philosophie, XXII, 193–195.
        Summarizes the contents with emphasis on the claim that
    for radical empiricism relations too are part of
    experience.

8   FOERSTER, NORMAN. "Open Minds: A Text from William James,"
    The Dial, LIV (May 1), 364–367.
        This is the age of open-mindedness, which however is not
    always good. There is the democratic open-mind which
    espouses everything, the snobbish one, which emphasizes the
    novel, and the aristocratic one, which sifts things in
    accordance with standards. Probably, James meant the
    third kind, but pragmatism itself tended to be democratic.

9   GILLOUIN, RENÉ. "William James" in Essais de critique litté-
    raire et philosophique. Paris: Bernard Grasset.
        James does not excel at philosophical technique. His
    major aim is to encompass the whole of life and reconcile
    the sacred and the profane.

10 HOERNLÉ, R. F. ALFRED. Review of J. Royce, William James and
    Other Essays (1911); É. Boutroux, William James (1911);
    É. Boutroux, William James, translated by Archibald and
    Barbara Henderson, Mind, NS XXII (October), 563–566.
        Royce presents the less familiar side of James's teach-
    ing, the religious and ethical. Among American ideals are

"efficiency" and "playing the game." James expresses
these and purifies them by insisting upon "high ideals."
Boutroux presents James's philosophy faithfully and
vividly. The translation is only "average," with serious
mistranslations.

11 HUNEKER, JAMES GIBBONS. The Pathos of Distance. New York:
Charles Scribner's Sons.
      In "A Philosophy for Philistines," Huneker claims that
pragmatism has been influenced by Nietzsche, is "old-
fashioned utilitarianism with a dollar mark," "a thin
doctoral thesis." It revives the Jesuitical maxim that
the end justifies the means. "Jacobean Adventures"
reviews A Pluralistic Universe. James is trying to exor-
cise monism, his "haunting devil." He has written a
"large, lucid, friendly book," which attempts to "humanize
rationalism."

12 JACOBY, GÜNTHER. Review of Essays in Radical Empiricism,
Kant-Studien, XVIII, 508–510.
      James dislikes systems and enters more deeply into the
human spirit than most.

13 JAMES, HENRY. A Small Boy and Others. London: Macmillan.
      An account of James's childhood by his brother Henry
James. In places, it becomes an autobiography and a
general account of family life.

14 KNOX, HOWARD V. "William James and His Philosophy," Mind, NS
XXII (April), 231–242.
      In The Principles of Psychology James shows how for the
psychologist the abstract distinction between philosophy
and psychology breaks down. James's later work only ex-
pands and enforces the "underlying philosophy" of the
Principles.

15 LANGE, HERMANN. Review of Psychologie, translated by M. Dürr
(Leipzig: Quelle & Meyer, 1909), Zeitschrift für
Philosophie und Pädagogik, XX, 253–255.
      Cites instances where James explains mental processes
physiologically.

16 LEGRAND, GEORGES. "'L'Expérience religieuse' et la philosophie
de William James," Revue Néo-Scolastique de Philosophie,
XX (February), 69–87.
      Central in James's study of religion is the subconscious.
This leads him to the error of identifying the experiences
of a religious mystic and a drug user. He solves the
question of the worth of religion pragmatically and

1913

(LEGRAND, GEORGES)
ignores rational proofs. This is again an error. James's
work is valuable for clearing away materialistic prejudices,
but it must be viewed with reservations.

17 MIÉVILLE, HENRI L. "La Notion d'expérience d'après William
James," Revue de Théologie et de Philosophie, NS I,
378-384.
An exposition of Reverdin's La Notion d'expérience
d'après William James (1913), emphasizing the vagueness of
James's terms.

18 MOORE, JARED SPARKS. "The Religious Significance of the Philosophy of William James," The Sewanee Review, XXI
(January), 41-58.
James's thought passed from the problems of the body, to
the problems of the mind, to the "deeper problems of the
soul." James is favorable to religion, but the consequences of his pragmatism are not.

19 PILLON, F. Review of L'Idée de vérité, translated by L. Veil
and Maxime David (Paris: Félix Alcan, 1913), L'Année
Philosophique, XXIV, 202-203.
Summarizes the contents. James protests against the
view that pragmatism ignores theoretical interests and is
a philosophy of action.

20 SCHILLER, F. C. S. Review of R. B. Perry, Present Philosophical Tendencies (1912), Mind, NS XXII (April), 280-284.
This review touched off a controversy between Perry and
Schiller over the application of the terms 'idealism' and
'realism' and Perry's interpretation of pragmatism. Also
at issue was the importance of radical empiricism.
Schiller maintained that the radical empiricism essays
were "tentative," that James recognized difficulties and
would not have republished them as they stood, that the
term itself had wider and narrower meanings. Perry replied
in "Realism and Pragmatism," Mind, NS XXII (October 1913),
544-548; this was countered by Schiller, "Prof. Perry's
Realism," Mind, NS XXIII (July 1914), 386-395; followed by
Perry, "Dr. Schiller on William James and on Realism,"
Mind, NS XXIV (April 1915), 240-249; and Schiller, "Realism,
Pragmatism, and William James," Mind, NS XXIV (October
1915), 516-524.

21 SEILLIÈRE, ERNEST. "La Morale de W. James et les éléments de
l'activité mystique," Revue Germanique, IX (January-
February), 1-35.

In Varieties, James advocates salvation through faith alone. He holds that mystical experiences lead to peace and believes in mind-cure. He thus fails to understand the importance of works. Moral progress is the result not of mystical but of practical experience.

22 SÉROL, M. "La Valeur religieuse du pragmatisme de William James," Revue de Philosophie, XXIII (December), 507-540.
    If we apply the pragmatic test to James's own pragmatism, its value for religion is slight. It gives us a faith far short of certainty and this is too fragile a basis for an intense and vigorous religious life.

23 VORBRODT, G. "W. James' Philosophie," Zeitschrift für Philosophie und philosophische Kritik, CLI, 1-27.
    Surveys main points in James's thought with reference to the work of G. Jacoby (1912), Th. Flournoy (1911), and É. Boutroux (1911).

1914 A BOOKS

1 GEYER, DENTON LORING. The Pragmatic Theory of Truth as Developed by Peirce, James, and Dewey. [n.p.].
    Doctoral thesis at the University of Illinois. Up to 1904, James accepted the pragmatism of Peirce as a device for clarifying meanings, then began to write about the pragmatic theory of truth as a sympathetic onlooker, until with Pragmatism he made that theory his own. In James, truth has a double meaning of which James himself was not aware. Ideas are true if they work as one expects them to, truth in the sense of "fulfilled expectations"; as opposed to truth as "value of results," when ideas are true if they lead to desirable results.

2 KALLEN, HORACE M. William James and Henri Bergson: A Study in Contrasting Theories of Life. Chicago: University of Chicago Press.
    James breaks with the philosophic tradition while Bergson remains within it. James describes experience, while Bergson "interprets and transmutes." Kallen places special emphasis on the contrast between Bergsonian intuition and the pragmatic method. Metaphysical differences lead the two to different conceptions of God, freedom, and individuality.

3 KNOX, HOWARD V. The Philosophy of William James. London: Constable.
    Summarizes in James's own words, the central portions of James's thought. James broke down the barriers between

1914

(KNOX, HOWARD V.)
metaphysics and psychology and discovered a new territory.
James restored to us our world by showing that consciousness is a "means of action and adaptation." Theories
derive their meaning from their applicability to the world
and this leads to the "decisive step," the viewing of
truth as "successful application."

1914 B SHORTER WRITINGS

1   ALIOTTA, ANTONIO. The Idealistic Reaction Against Science,
translated by Agnes McCaskill. London: Macmillan, 1914.
Translation of La reazione idealistica contra la scienza
(Palermo: Casa Editrice "Optima," 1912).
    Pragmatism is only a form of English empiricism. James
is an anti-intellectualist who denies the subject-object
distinction.

2   BICKNELL, PERCY F. "Glimpses of a Gifted Family," The Dial,
LVI (April), 289-291.
    Review of Henry James, Notes of a Son and Brother (1914).

3   BOISSE, LOUIS. "Le Pragmatisme et la vie religieuse," La
Grande Revue, LXXXV (May 25), 302-322.
    Pragmatism is a vile spirit, invented to diminish the
value of philosophy, and now being applied to religion,
politics, aesthetics, and education.

4   BOUTROUX, ÉMILE. Preface to Aux étudiants, translated by
H. Marty. Paris: Payot.
    James's thought is a living force. This can be shown by
his doctrine of the subliminal consciousness and by his
tolerance.

5   BRADLEY, FRANCIS HERBERT. Essays on Truth and Reality. Oxford:
Clarendon.
    Papers published elsewhere are listed separately (1904)
(1908) (1911). In republishing "On Truth and Practice"
(1904), Bradley added an introductory note explaining why
some material was omitted and replying to criticisms. Also
not published elsewhere is a note "On Professor James's
'Radical Empiricism'." James identifies reality with
experience, but leaves unclear the status of past and
possible experience. James seems to hold both that experience is a continuous flux with no terms and relations and
that terms and relations are given in experience.

6   GALLOWAY, GEORGE. The Philosophy of Religion. Edinburgh:
T. & T. Clark.

References to James emphasize pragmatism and the tests of truth.

7   GOLDSTEIN, JULIUS. Introduction to Das pluralistische Universum, translated by J. Goldstein. Leipzig: Alfred Kröner.
    Will introduce James's metaphysics into Germany which thus far has known only his psychology and theory of knowledge. James is a radical empiricist who, however, appreciates man's higher spiritual life. The central problem is the conflict between monism and pluralism.

8   HEDGES, M. H. "The Physician as a Hero: William James," The Forum, LII (December), 875-881.
    James is one of the "illustrious physicians" and most deserving of the title of hero. James sought "balm for the souls of men." James answered the questions of the day with a "materialistic mysticism" and a "scientific religion."

9   JAMES, HENRY. Notes of a Son and Brother. New York: Charles Scribner's Sons.
    Henry James's reminiscences of his youth. A number of family letters, including some from James, are published.

10 KALLEN, HORACE M. "James, Bergson, and Traditional Metaphysics," Mind, NS XXIII (April), 207-239.
    Traditional metaphysics builds systems, considers experience to reveal appearances only, and holds that ultimate reality conserves human values. Bergson sides with the tradition, while James's radical empiricism breaks off completely. However, there are aspects in which James could owe a debt to Bergson.

11 _____. Review of H. Reverdin, La Notion d'expérience d'après William James (1913), The Philosophical Review, XXIII (May), 357-359.
    Reverdin lists the several concepts of experience adopted by James at various times. However, he finds in this a contradiction whereas it should be viewed as a development.

12 KNOX, HOWARD V. Review of H. Reverdin, La Notion d'expérience d'après William James (1913), Mind, NS XXIII (October), 604-608.
    A carefully done book, but Reverdin fails, as he admits, to catch the central thread. It is pragmatism which unifies James's thought, the insistence on a "functional" rather than a "structural" approach to every problem.

1914

(KNOX, HOWARD V.)
Reverdin fails to see the radical transformation of empiricism which James effects.

13 M. S. Review of Introduction à la philosophie, translated by R. Picard (Paris: Marcel Rivière, 1914), Revue de Philosophie, XXIV, 431-435.
Radical evolutionism and a defiance of reason marks James's other works. The present one appears the beginning of a return to the "philosophia perennis" of Aristotle and St. Thomas.

14 M. T. M. "The Pragmatic Test," Harper's Weekly, LVIII (April 18), 10-12.
Reminiscences by a woman who in her late thirties read The Principles of Psychology and decided to enter college so that she could teach the subject. Contains letters from James to her.

15 MASSIS, HENRI. "William James, ou le manager de l'idéal," L'Opinion, 7th year, no. 21 (May 23), 655-656.
Pragmatism turns philosophy away from its true purpose which is the contemplation of intelligible being. James gives us a rough version of what in Bergson we find in a more cultured form.

16 METZGER, WILHELM. Review of Das pluralistische Universum, translated by J. Goldstein (Leipzig: A. Kröner, 1914), Vierteljahrsschrift für wissenschaftliche Philosophie und Sociologie, XXXVIII, 259-261.
James does not give proofs, but attempts to persuade by describing the attractive features of his views.

17 STEBBING, L. SUSAN. Pragmatism and French Voluntarism. Cambridge, England: At the University Press.
A study of the notion of truth in French philosophy from Maine de Biran to Bergson. James exaggerates his agreement with Bergson, for while James wants a mixture of concepts and percepts, for Bergson, "a fuller knowledge" can be attained only by a "deeper kind of knowing faculty," by intuition which transcends both perception and conception. James converts the claim that truth is useful into the grotesque claim that what is useful is true.

18 SURYANARAYANAN, S. S. "William James and His Philosophy," East & West, XIII, 1094-1101.
James tried to overcome the divorce of philosophy from life. His work is valuable not for its results but for its pragmatic method, "a newer and clearer way of solving old problems."

19   TITCHENER, EDWARD BRADFORD. "An Historical Note on the James-Lange Theory of Emotion," The American Journal of Psychology, XXV (July), 427-447.
       It is surprising that in support of his theory James did not add an argument from the history of psychology. Titchener cites many works in which James's theory is anticipated.

20   VOGT, P. B. "From John Stuart Mill to William James," The Catholic University Bulletin, XX (February), 139-165.
       James moves in "Mill's orbit," for both subordinate logic to psychology, abandon absolute truth in favor of relative, and limit knowledge to sense experience. But whereas Mill interprets everything in terms of association, James has "teleological evolution." Both hold that "reality is intrinsically subjective," but for Mill this is a truth, while for James, only a hypothesis. Future experience could lead us to a realism. Pragmatic ideas were in the air and it is difficult to establish direct lines of influence.

21   WOBBERMIN, GEORG. Introduction to Die religiöse Erfahrung, translated by G. Wobbermin. 2nd edition. Leipzig: J. C. Hinrichs.
       In the additional introduction, Wobbermin replies to criticisms, especially Wundt's in Probleme der Völkerpsychologie (1911). Wundt criticized the whole of James's work in terms of pragmatism, but pragmatism is only a part of James's thought. It is necessary to combine Schleiermacher's critique with James's psychological approach to attain an adequate standpoint.

1915 A BOOKS - NONE

1915 B SHORTER WRITINGS

1   BERGSON, HENRI. Extracts from letter to Horace M. Kallen, The Journal of Philosophy, XII (October 28), 615-616. Reprinted in Écrits et paroles (Paris: Presses Universitaires de France, 1959) and Mélanges (1972).
       A favorable discussion of Kallen's William James and Henri Bergson (1914).

2   DRISCOLL, JOHN T. Pragmatism and the Problem of the Idea. New York: Longmans, Green.
       Pragmatism rests on a false conception of the idea. It is dangerous because it excludes the idea of God, in the Christian sense, from human thought and destroys morality. Royce, James, Dewey, Schiller, and Bergson are criticized.

1915

3   HEDGES, M. H. "Seeking the Shade of William James," The Forum,
     LIII (April), 441-448.
          After reading The Will to Believe, Hedges began a
     "romantic quest" for the spirit of James. He did not find
     it at Harvard and Harvard professors denied James three
     times. James's spirit lives in his books, which show him
     a "fellow-loving democrat" who believed in the "sovereignty
     of the mediocre man," and a "materialistic mystic" who
     saw "God in dirt."

4   HÖFFDING, HARALD. Modern Philosophers. Translated by
     Alfred C. Mason. London: Macmillan. Originally published
     in Danish.
          Lectures given in autumn of 1902. James approaches reli-
     gion from epistemological, ethical, and psychological
     points of view. The last is predominant. Since James
     recognizes the variety of religious consciousnesses, a
     major problem for him is their classification. James
     correctly distinguishes personal from institutional
     religion. He takes too lightly the problem of historical
     continuity.

5   LEUBA, JAMES H. "William James and Immortality," The Journal
     of Philosophy, XII (July 22), 409-416.
          In psychical research, James was critical and never
     committed himself to spiritism. He had no desire for
     personal survival, having early discarded the notion of a
     soul. He surmised that death does not end everything and
     we become parts of a "superhuman consciousness." Varieties
     sought evidence of this.

6   LOVEJOY, ARTHUR ONCKEN. Review of H. M. Kallen, William James
     and Henri Bergson (1914), The Nation, C (April 8) 388-390.
          Kallen identifies James's thought with radical empiri-
     cism, for which, he claims, all the data of experience are
     equals. But this would show that pragmatism is false,
     since, for Kallen, pragmatism is the view that all think-
     ing is biased by the desires of the thinker.

7   PORTERFIELD, ALLEN WILSON. "Lessing and Wackenroder as
     Anticipators of William James," Modern Language Notes,
     XXX (December), 263-264.
          The James-Lange theory is anticipated in Lessing's
     Hamburgische Dramaturgie and in Wilhelm Heinrich
     Wackenroder's Phantasien über die Kunst fur Frëunde der
     Kunst (1799).

8   RILEY, WOODBRIDGE. American Thought From Puritanism to Prag-
     matism. New York: Henry Holt.

James makes a new phase in pragmatism, a shift from the logical to the psychological. Knowledge is reduced to the satisfaction of "felt needs, to the emotional thrill." When faced with alternatives, James tries to adapt one to the other psychologically. In metaphysics, James is a complete phenomenalist.

1916 A BOOKS - NONE

1916 B SHORTER WRITINGS

1 ANGELL, JAMES R. "A Reconsideration of James's Theory of Emotion in the Light of Recent Criticisms," The Psychological Review, XXIII (July), 251-261.
    A survey of the literature on the James-Lange theory of emotion purporting to show that recent experiments, particularly those by C. S. Sherrington and W. B. Cannon, do not refute the core of James's theory.

2 HACKETT, F. "William James as Highbrow," The New Republic, VIII (September 23), 184-186.
    Quotations from The Principles of Psychology are used to show that highbrows are cold and unemotional. James himself was a "superior" man who still remained human.

3 SABIN, ETHEL E. "James's Later View of Consciousness and the Pragmatic View: A Contrast" (Abstract), The Journal of Philosophy, XIII (July 6), 382-383.
    A pragmatism which realizes that stability is relative to purpose would have saved James from errors in his conception of knowledge.

4 SCHROEDER, THEODORE. "Intellectual Evolution and Pragmatism," The Monist, XXVI (January), 86-112.
    A "psycho-analytical" study intended to show that James was blind to various aspects of his problem and to explain by reference to James's personality why he was blind.

1917 A BOOKS - NONE

1917 B SHORTER WRITINGS

1 BAKEWELL, CHARLES M. Introduction to William James, Selected Papers on Philosophy. New York: E. P. Dutton. Reprinted in Modern English Essays, edited by E. Rhys, vol. V (New York: E. P. Dutton, 1922).

1917

(BAKEWELL, CHARLES M.)
James wrote in a popular style because he interpreted
life. He disliked philosophical schools and became uneasy
once pragmatism became a school. His radical empiricism
teaches that mind is never a passive spectator.

2   KALLEN, HORACE M. "William James," The Dial, LXIII
(August 30), 141-143. Prepared for the Warner Library.
Unlike most American philosophy, James's is not deriva-
tive, but arises from a direct vision of man and his
destiny. He interpreted the life of pioneers who insisted
that men are not born good, "they make good." James
gives us a "metaphysical democracy" in which ideas too
must make good.

3   LOEWENBERG, JACOB. "The James-Lange Theory in Lessing," The
American Journal of Psychology, XXVIII (April), 301.
Cites a passage from Lessing's Hamburgische Dramaturgie
in which the James-Lange theory is anticipated.

4   SCHOLZ, HEINRICH. Review of Die religiöse Erfahrung, translated by G. Wobbermin, 2nd edition. (Leipzig: Hinrichs,
1914), Preussische Jahrbücher, CLXVII, 478-483.
An important book. James overemphasizes pathological
details which are of secondary interest in the study of
religion. Germans, influenced by different traditions,
will be dissatisfied with the treatment of truth.

5   SETH PRINGLE-PATTISON, ANDREW. The Idea of God in the Light
of Recent Philosophy, Oxford: Clarendon.
Numerous references to James, with emphasis on James's
notion of a finite God and pluralism.

1918 A BOOKS

1   SABIN, ETHEL ERNESTINE. William James and Pragmatism.
Lancaster, Pa.: The New Era Printing Co.
Chapter I, "Some Difficulties in James's Formulation of
Pragmatism" (1918) is listed separately. Compares James's
"old" with Dewey's "new" pragmatism. Thesis, University of
Illinois, 1916.

1918 B SHORTER WRITINGS

1   PERRY, RALPH BARTON. The Present Conflict of Ideals: A Study
of the Philosophical Background of the World War. New
York: Longmans, Green.
James is discussed in two chapters, "The Pragmatic Justification of Faith" and "Pluralism and the Finite God."

2 SABIN, ETHEL E. "Some Difficulties in James's Formulation of Pragmatism," The Journal of Philosophy, XV (June 6), 309-322. Reprinted in William James and Pragmatism (1918).
Pragmatism has advanced beyond James. James never did escape dualism. He confused truth and reality, and in the guise of radical empiricism, returned to sensationalism.

3 SINGER, EDGAR A. "The Empiricism of William James," University of Pennsylvania: University Lectures Delivered by Members of the Faculty in the Free Public Lectures Course, V, 325-345. Reprinted with a few omissions in Modern Thinkers and Present Problems (New York: Henry Holt, 1923).
An interpretation of "The Will to Believe," by one who heard it read while a student at Harvard and found it a shock to his "laboratory mind." Pragmatism tries to show that the "moral and religious aspects" of the world "are things to work and fight for" and not merely to find. But Singer himself would prefer in this struggle to rely upon science.

4 SLATTERY, CHARLES LEWIS. "William James" in Certain American Faces: Sketches from Life. New York: E. P. Dutton.
Anecdotes about James, current among James's students.

1919 A BOOKS

1 TURNER, J. E. An Examination of William James's Philosophy: A Critical Essay for the General Reader. Oxford: B. H. Blackwell.
James's philosophy tends to "lower the life of the spirit," although he was a noble person. James's wide sympathies led him to adopt each new movement and as a result his pragmatism, pluralism, empiricism, and philosophy of religion, cannot be reconciled with each other. James's genius was to stimulate thought and show that philosophy is not "aloof" from everyday concerns.

1919 B SHORTER WRITINGS

1 ANON. "William James: A Belated Acknowledgment," The Atlantic Monthly, CXXIII (April), 568-570.
A little girl's reminiscences of James while both were vacationing in the same hotel on Cape Ann, Mass. (perhaps summer of 1874). James is described as catching and dissecting a frog.

1919

2 COHEN, MORRIS RAPHAEL. "William James," The New Republic, XX
(October 1), 255-257. The substance of this article
appears in the Cambridge History of American Literature,
©1921.
    James's humanistic thought has little in common with the
supposed American practicality. He was dominated by a
"religious vision of life," which from the very beginning
was united with an empiricism. Sometimes James falls into
the intellectualistic trap of recognizing only extremes.
We must either believe or not believe and no room is left
for suspension of judgment, for acting without belief, and
the like.

3 GRONAU, GOTTHARD. Die Philosophie der Gegenwart. Langensalza:
Wendt & Klauwell.
    Contains a chapter titled "Der Pragmatismus von James
und Schiller." Germans are a nation of poets and thinkers,
Americans, a practical people for whom money is God.
James's philosophy is American. It will be quickly for-
gotten especially in Germany, a land in which idealism has
found a home.

4 SABIN, ETHEL E. "Pragmatic Teleology," The Journal of Philosophy, XVI (August 28), 488-493.
    A reply to Warbieke (1919). Many of the charges apply
to James's humanism, but to this humanism Dewey's instru-
mentalism must be opposed. James himself often went beyond humanism.

5 WARBIEKE, JOHN. "A Medieval Aspect of Pragmatism," The Journal
of Philosophy, XVI (April 10), 207-215.
    James's pragmatism by subordinating knowledge to an
ethical ideal is like medieval doctrine in which everything was subordinated to salvation.

1920 A BOOKS

1 JAMES, HENRY, ed. The Letters of William James. 2 vols.
Boston: The Atlantic Monthly Press. Also published in a
limited edition of 600 sets with illustrations (Boston:
The Atlantic Monthly Press, 1920); reprinted in a one-
volume edition (Boston: Little, Brown, 1926).
    Selected letters, with emphasis on personal correspon-
dence. Corrections were made in the 1926 edition and an
appendix with two previously unpublished letters added.

2 PERRY, RALPH BARTON. Annotated Bibliography of the Writings
of William James. New York: Longmans, Green. Reprinted,

Dubuque, Iowa: Wm. C. Brown (n.d.) and North Salem, N. H.: Christian F. Verbeke, 1968.

An incomplete list, superseded by McDermott (1967). It remains, however, the most complete list of translations into other languages. The 1968 reprinting lists additional translations and one item by James--Preface to the Italian translation of The Principles of Psychology--not listed elsewhere.

1920 B SHORTER WRITINGS

1 JORDAN, MARY AUGUSTA. "An Unpublished Letter of William James," Smith College Studies in Modern Languages, vol. II, no. 1 (October), pp. 5-7.

Text of letter from James to Miss Jordan, June 29, 1891, who had published an anonymous review of The Principles of Psychology in "Kate Fields' Washington."

2 LITTELL, P. "Books and Things," The New Republic, XXV (December 29), 145-146.

Notice of Letters (1920). The Letters reveal the many interests which James's growing absorption in philosophy pushed into the background. Contains reminiscences by a former student.

3 LUBBOCK, PERCY, ed. The Letters of Henry James. 2 vols. New York: Charles Scribner's Sons.

Many letters to James as well as many references.

4 MAURICE-DENIS, NOELE. "La Pensée francaise et l'empirisme américain," La Revue Universelle, III (November 1), 362-366.

American military and diplomatic intervention in Europe was preceded by an intellectual one. James's work was studied. American thinkers had an appeal because they offered moral sincerity in place of dilettantism. But sincerity is not enough and a simple and realistic philosophy is not necessarily true.

5 PALMER, GEORGE HERBERT. "William James," Harvard Graduates' Magazine, XXIX (September), 29-34.

Reminiscences by a faculty colleague. James always sided with the under-dog. His praise of Peirce sprang as much from "pity as from admiration." He rarely spoke at faculty meetings. He attended Palmer's seminar on Hegel and wrote "On Some Hegelisms" (1882) to wash his hands of the whole thing.

1920

6   SALOMON, MICHEL. "William James" in Portraits et paysages.
     Paris: Perrin et Cie.
          An appreciative survey written shortly after James's
     death. James was a Socratic philosopher.

7   SANTAYANA, GEORGE. Character and Opinion in the United States.
     New York: Charles Scribner's Sons.
          Contains an appreciation of James's thought and character.
     His excursions into philosophy were like "raids." For him,
     philosophy had a "Polish constitution." Nothing could pass
     if one vote was against it. His best known books are
     "somewhat incidental." His "best achievement" is The
     Principles of Psychology.

8   TALBERT, ERNEST L. "William James and the Professor's Salary,"
     School and Society, XI (March 27), 384-386.
          James is quoted on the value of poverty and wealth.

9   WAHL, JEAN. Les Philosophies pluralistes d'Angleterre et
     d'Amérique. Paris: Félix Alcan. English translation,
     The Pluralist Philosophies of England and America, trans-
     lated by F. Rothwell (London: Open Court, 1925).
          James is the first and last pluralist. His radical
     empiricism leads to pluralism, anti-intellectualism,
     temporalism, his views on freedom, and mysticism. Wahl
     traces the development of pluralism after James.

1921 A BOOKS - NONE

1921 B SHORTER WRITINGS

1   ANON. "William James as an Inspiration to His Family and
     Friends," Current Opinion, LXX (March), 366-368.
          Letters (1920) reveal James's "love for his family and
     friends."

2   BRETT, GEORGE SIDNEY. A History of Psychology, vol. III.
     London: George Allen & Unwin. Abridged and revised
     edition, Brett's History of Psychology, R. S. Peters, ed.
     (London: George, Allen & Unwin, 1962).
          James studied men rather than minds. He is deliberately
     unsystematic. The Principles of Psychology is a "survey
     of the possibilities of psychology." The text dealing
     with James was left intact in the revision.

3   DANA, CHARLES L. "The Anatomic Seat of the Emotions: A
     Discussion of the James-Lange Theory," Archives of
     Neurology and Psychiatry, VI, 634-639.
          Cases of anesthesia tend to disprove the theory.

4   ERSKINE, JOHN. "William James, Lover of Life," The Outlook,
     CXXIX (November 2), 355-356.
         Review of Letters (1920). James's letters in "literary
     art" are inferior to those of Emerson and others. But they
     reveal the man. James was first of all an "artist" de-
     lighting in the "quality of life."

5   JACKS, L. P. "William James and His Letters," The Atlantic
     Monthly, CXXVIII (August), 197-203.
         James's philosophy expresses his personality. He was
     unique and his power consisted in seeing the "queerness"
     of things. The letters introduce his pragmatism, his
     ethics, and his religion. James made philosophy interest-
     ing for everybody; his work led to greater interest in
     philosophy.

6   JOURDAIN, M. Review of Letters (1920), The International
     Journal of Ethics, XXXI (July), 445-446.
         James never completed his philosophy and this "informal
     biography" does not complete it. It reveals a "most indi-
     vidual and living personality."

7   JUNG, C. G. Psychologische Typen. Zürich: Rascher & Cie.
     English translation, Psychological Types, translated by
     H. Goodwin Baynes (New York: Harcourt, Brace, 1923).
         Discusses James's distinction between tendermindedness
     and toughmindedness. In Pragmatism, James is primarily
     concerned with intellectual qualities. His categories are
     too broad and, without much difficulty, one could show some
     of them to belong to the opposite type as well.

8   MARITAIN, JACQUES. "La Philosophie américaine et les
     continuateurs de James," La Revue Universelle, VII
     (October 1), 48-69. Excerpts reprinted as "William James
     and His Impetuous Philosophy," The Living Age, CCCXI
     (November 12), 392-396. Incorporated in Réflexions sur
     l'intelligence et sur sa vie propre (Paris: Nouvelle
     Librairie Nationale, 1924).
         James's reputation is greater than the value of his work.
     He is worth less than the American neo-realists who, at
     least, do not try to transform all philosophic values
     through the magic of pragmatism. His pluralism is vague,
     an emotional idea with little intellectual content, de-
     signed to restore the faith of simple souls.

9   MILLER, DICKINSON S. "Mr. Santayana and William James,"
     Harvard Graduates' Magazine, XXIX (March), 348-364.
         Review of Character and Opinion (1920). Contains some
     reminiscences of James and Santayana, but primarily

85

1921

(MILLER, DICKINSON S.)
attempts to contrast the two philosophies. Santayana
writes about James too patronizingly.

10 PERRY, BLISS. Life and Letters of Henry Lee Higginson.
Boston: The Atlantic Monthly Press.
Letters from and to James are included. Higginson acted
as James's banker and financial advisor.

11 RILEY, ISAAC WOODBRIDGE. "Le Bergsonisme," part III of "La
Philosophie francaise en Amérique," Revue Philosophique,
XCI, 75-107, 234-271.
Studies Bergson's reception in America. In A Pluralistic
Universe, James first announced that a great philosopher
had appeared in France. In the first installment, Pitkin's
article (1910) and Kallen's book (1914) are discussed at
some length.

12 SANTAYANA, GEORGE. "Professor Miller and Mr. Santayana,"
Harvard Graduates' Magazine, XXX (September), 32-36.
A reply to D. S. Miller (1921). Santayana arranges in
parallel columns extracts from Miller's review and from
Character and Opinion (1920).

13 SCHILLER, F. C. S. "William James," The Quarterly Review,
CCXXXVI, (July), 24-41. Reprinted in Must Philosophers
Disagree? (London: Macmillan, 1934).
An appreciation of James's personality based on Letters
(1920), emphasizes the contrast between James and the con-
ventional philosophy professor. Why did not some million-
aire free James from the drudgery of the Ph.D. factory?

14 SOREL, GEORGES. De l'utilité du pragmatisme. Paris: Marcel
Rivière.
In the preface, with many quotations, Sorel expounds
James's pragmatic method and theory of truth. The first
chapter is titled "De Kant à William James." Sorel claims
that James was mistaken in trying to identify various
European writers with pragmatism, gives some account of
James's defense against charges that pragmatism is sub-
jectivism, and discusses the fourteen categories mentioned
in Pragmatism.

15 THORNDIKE, EDWARD L. Review of Letters (1920), Science, NS
LIII (February 18), 165-167.
James is one of the great Americans. The letters show
that early James became interested in philosophy and that
most of his writing was due to outside pressures.

16   TUFTS, JAMES H. Review of Letters (1920), The Journal of
      Philosophy, XVIII (July 7), 381-387.
          James's letters correct many misconceptions, particularly
      that by 'practical' James understood something very narrow,
      that it excluded "imagination, science, friendship, and
      religion." The bulk of the review reports remarks alleg-
      edly made by various people when trying to understand
      James's personality.

17   ZULEN, PEDRO. Additions to Annotated Bibliography (1920).
      The Journal of Philosophy, XVIII (October 27), 615-616.
          List appears in the 1948 reprint. With one exception,
      lists translations.

1922 A BOOKS

1   BERTHELOT, RENÉ. Un Romantisme utilitaire: étude sur le
      mouvement pragmatiste. Vol. III, Le Pragmatisme religieux
      chez William James et chez les catholiques modernistes.
      Paris: Félix Alcan.
          James introduces the idea of a personal, limited God.
      His meliorism solves the problem of evil. His thought was
      affected by many influences: the protestant spirit,
      Swedenborgian mysticism, Carlyle's insistence upon action,
      British psychology, evolutionism, Hegelianism, and the
      neo-criticism of Renouvier.

1922 B SHORTER WRITINGS

1   DEWEY, JOHN. "Le Développement du pragmatisme américain,"
      Revue de Métaphysique et de Morale, XXIX (October-December),
      411-430. Reprinted in English, "The Development of Ameri-
      can Pragmatism" in Studies in the History of Ideas, vol.
      II (New York: Columbia University Press, 1925); also in
      Philosophy and Civilization (New York: Minton, Balch,
      1931).
          James took over and modified Peirce's principle. For
      general rules he substituted "particular consequences."
      James dropped the notion of habit and was much more a
      nominalist than Peirce. James developed pragmatism as a
      theory of truth.

2   KALLEN, HORACE M. "La Méthode de l'intuition et la méthode
      pragmatiste," Revue de Métaphysique et de Morale, XXIX
      (January-March), 35-62.
          For Bergson, ultimate reality is to be apprehended
      directly, the knower and the known are identified, con-
      ceptual knowledge deals with illusion and not reality.

1922

(KALLEN, HORACE M.)
Bergson remains close to traditional philosophy. James wanted to make philosophy scientific. He viewed conceptual knowledge instrumentally, as a means of leading to contact with objects.

3   KANOVITCH, ABRAHAM. The Will to Beauty. New York: Gold Rose Printing Co.
James is treated on pp. 117-121, "Bergson and William James." James is a mediocrity who "popularizes and cheapens" in his "obnoxious conversational style." Pragmatism gives one permission to "believe in any ideal," but no person "having emotion" needs permission, since we are "helpless against the human emotions."

4   LEROUX, EMMANUEL. Le Pragmatisme américain et anglais: étude historique et critique. Paris: Félix Alcan. The Bibliographie méthodique du pragmatisme américain, anglais et italien, was published separately (Paris: Félix Alcan, 1922). The two were published in a single volume in 1923.
James came to disassociate his justification of the role of feelings in belief from his pragmatic theory of truth. For James, the bibliography contains nothing otherwise unlisted.

5   LEWKOWITZ, ALBERT. "Zur Religionsphilosophie der Gegenwart," Monatsschrift für Geschichte und Wissenschaft des Judentums. LXVI (April-June), 97-115; (October-December), 249-268; LXVII (January-March, 1923), 1-26; (April-June), 81-110.
The fourth part, "Religiöse Erfahrung: Wundt, James, Otto, Scholz," deals with James. If Wundt studies religion by investigating groups, James tries to base religious psychology upon the experiences of individuals. He does not study primitive tribes, but the experiences of religious geniuses.

6   McGILVARY, EVANDER BRADLEY. "James, Bergson, and Determinism" in The Charles Mills Gayley Anniversary Papers. Berkeley: University of California Press.
Both denounce determinism, but in relation to the other, each is a determinist. For James indeterminism is the doctrine that out of many possibilities only a few are selected by chance to be actualized. For Bergson, things could not have been otherwise, but there is indeterminism, since the relation between antecedent and consequent cannot be expressed by a law. Both writers agree that the future is not completely calculable.

7   MACY, JOHN. "William James, Man of Letters" in The Critical
     Game. New York: Boni and Liveright.
          A favorable review of Letters (1920). James's thought
     is marked by balance. "To the over-credulous he preached
     caution; to the over-sceptical, faith."

8   MARON, N. C. "William James and the Harvard Tradition," The
     Nation, CXV (October 18), 412.
          A letter to the editor quoting "The True Harvard" (1903)
     to indicate how James would have responded to arguments
     that the admission of Jews to Harvard be restricted.

9   NICHOLS, HERBERT. "The Cosmology of William James," The
     Journal of Philosophy XIX (December 7), 673-683.
          James's "vision of the universe" was clouded by his
     "rationalism." While he wanted to be an empiricist, he
     could not escape the rationalism which permeated his time.

10   ROGERS, ARTHUR KENYON. English and American Philosophy Since
     1800. New York: Macmillan.
          James's insights cannot be combined into a system.
     Rogers makes brief critical comments about pragmatism as
     a method, the will to believe, James's demand for an open
     universe, and James's conception of knowledge.

11   WAHL, JEAN. "William James d'après sa correspondance,"
     Revue Philosophique, XCIII, 381-416; XCIV, 298-347.
     Reprinted in Vers le concret (Paris: J. Vrin, 1932).
          A biographical study based upon Letters (1920). There
     is a concluding section, breaking the chronological order
     followed by Wahl, titled "James et la nature."

1923 A BOOKS - NONE

1923 B SHORTER WRITINGS

1   DELATTRE, FLORIS. "William James bergsonien," Revue Anglo-
     Américaine, vol. I, no. 1 (October), 1-24; no. 2 (December),
     135-144. Reprinted as a pamphlet (Paris: Les Presses
     Universitaires de France, [n.d.].
          At first, they were simply participants in the modern
     revolt against rationalism, rejected scientific determin-
     ism, insisted on the primacy of consciousness, and tried
     to make psychology an empirical science. In the second
     period, they became brothers pursuing the same path. In
     Bergson, James found a firm foundation for his personal
     convictions.

1923

2   ROBERTSON, JOHN MACKINNON. Explorations. London: Watts.
         "Professor James's Plea for Theism," first published in
         1898, is an attack on The Will to Believe from the point
         of view of atheistical rationalism. The same arguments
         could be used by non-Christians against Christianity. In
         "Professor James on Religious Experience," Robertson
         argues that James is encouraging "commonplace conceit" by
         emphasizing the spiritual meaning of the Bible. His audi-
         ence forgets that "existentially" the Bible is nonsense.

1924 A BOOKS

1   DELATTRE, FLORIS and LE BRETON, MAURICE, eds. William James:
         extraits de sa correspondance. Paris: Payot.
         Translation of selected letters with a biographical
         introduction and notes.

1924 B SHORTER WRITINGS

1   BAUDOUIN, CHARLES. "William James' 'Talks to Teachers on
         Psychology'" in Contemporary Studies, translated by Eden
         and Cedar Paul. London: George Allen & Unwin.
         Originally appeared in La Feuille, Geneva, September 5,
         12, 26 and October 3, 1919. General sketch of James's
         psychology with emphasis on educational applications.
         James emphasizes the importance of action and the educa-
         tion of the will.

2   BERGSON, HENRI. Preface to F. Delattre and M. Le Breton,
         William James: extraits de sa correspondance (1924).
         Reprinted in Mélanges (1972).
         James's great originality lies in accepting the variety
         of the world.

3   BREMOND, HENRI. "L'Américanisme de William James," La Revue
         de France, VI (November 1), 181-188.
         James was a Yankee to the bone, both as a philosopher
         and as a man. He loved his country, but did not overlook
         its faults. He lacked the restraint of a European.

4   [DELATTRE, FLORIS and LE BRETON, MAURICE, eds.] "Lettres de
         William James à Théodore Flournoy," Bibliothèque
         Universelle et Revue Suisse, CXIV (May), 54-68.
         Letters to Flournoy taken from Delattre and Le Breton,
         William James: extraits de sa correspondance (1924). No
         editors are indicated for the selection.

5   HASTINGS, KATHARINE. William James of Albany, N. Y.
     (1771-1832) and His Descendants. [n.p., n.d.].
     An off-print from the New York Geneological and
     Biographical Record for 1924. This off-print has addi-
     tional illustrations and a name index. Contains a
     geneological list of the James family.

6   LEUBA, JAMES H. "The Immediate Apprehension of God According
     to William James and William E. Hocking," The Journal of
     Philosophy, XXI (December 18), 701-712.
        In Varieties, James seeks facts which support pluralism
     and religious faith. This leads him to regard as imme-
     diately given what in fact is not. The repose, safety,
     harmony claimed for mystical states are only interpreta-
     tions of a neutral experience. For Hocking, James is mis-
     taken about mysticism because James opposes the immediate
     to the conceptual.

7   MARSTON, WILLIAM M. "A Theory of Emotions and Affection
     Based Upon Systolic Blood Pressure Studies," The American
     Journal of Psychology, XXXV (October), 469-506.
        Attempts to develop theory of emotion to replace the
     James-Lange one. James's claims that "we are afraid be-
     cause we run away" and that emotions are sensations occur-
     ring during such flight, while usually identified, are
     quite different. The correct view of emotion could be
     expressed by the formula "we are afraid because we see we
     are not running away fast enough."

8   SUDRE, RENÉ. Introduction to W. James, Études et réflexions
     d'un psychiste, translated by E. Durandeaud. Paris:
     Payot.
        Surveys James's psychical research activities.

1925 A BOOKS - NONE

1925 B SHORTER WRITINGS

1   BIXLER, JULIUS SEELYE. "Mysticism and the Philosophy of
     William James," The International Journal of Ethics, XXXVI
     (October), 71-85. Incorporated into Religion in the Phi-
     losophy of William James (1926).
        Mysticism naturally supplements James's thought. James
     was torn between a life of action and risk and a desire
     for assurance and peace. Mysticism offers a practical
     reconciliation. Mysticism broadens James's pragmatism
     by expanding the range of experience and adds a social
     element to James's ethics.

1925

2   BIXLER, JULIUS SEELYE. "William James and Immortality," The
    Journal of Religion, V, 378-396.
        Studies James's views on immortality in his published
    letters.

3   BUSH, WENDELL T. "William James and Panpsychism" in Studies
    in the History of Ideas, vol. II. New York: Columbia
    University Press.
        Besides the naturalistic empiricism which insists upon
    the empirical character of relations, James advocated
    panpsychism. But his statements are "scattered, tentative
    and metaphorical."

4   GORDON, GEORGE A. My Education and Religion: An Autobiography.
    Boston: Houghton, Mifflin.
        Pp. 195-200 deal with James. Gordon studied under James
    in the 1880's. Four letters from James to Gordon are
    included.

5   HALL, ROBERT SPRAGUE. "The 'I': An Egoistic, Perhaps Ego-
    tistic Divagation," The Open Court, XXXIX (February),
    72-85.
        James is frequently quoted to show that psychologists
    should look "beneath consciousness" for the "real thinker."

6   HARRIS, MARJORIE S. "Comte and James," The Philosophical
    Review, XXXIV (March), 154-164.
        Comte shows "deeper insight" and is an "advance" over
    James. Both agree that men know only the phenomenal, but
    for Comte, the phenomenal is a world of law behind which
    stands an orderly reality. Both interpret thought instru-
    mentally, but Comte realizes that thought should not
    always be "confined by practical consequences" and has
    some "commerce with reality."

7   KALLEN, HORACE M. Introduction to The Philosophy of William
    James. New York: Random House, ©1925.
        James recognized the limits of philosophy. Because of
    this, after James, philosophy will continue to fail, but
    it will enjoy moments of "genuine efficacy and transform-
    ing power." James recognized a plurality of individuals
    and the spontaneity of things. Truth is an instrument in
    our "struggle to live."

8   MASSON, CHARLES. "La Personnalité religieuse de William James,"
    Revue de Théologie et de Philosophie, NS XIII, 126-139.
        Studies the religious side of James's personality, based
    on F. Delattre and M. Le Breton, William James, extraits
    de sa correspondance (1924).

9 WECHSLER, DAVID. "What Constitutes an Emotion?", The Psychological Review, XXXII (May), 235-240.
     By an "exciting fact," does James mean the "sensory
perception" of the object or does he also include our
interpretation of it? When James talks about bodily
changes, he never states clearly which he has in mind.

1926 A BOOKS

1 BIXLER, JULIUS SEELYE. Religion in the Philosophy of William
James. Boston: Marshall Jones Co.
     The conflict in James is not primarily between religion
and science but between two religious interests. There
are both active and passive moods, desires for a world of
risk and for a world of peace. Bixler quotes extensively
from unpublished letters from James to Thomas Davidson and
Mrs. William H. Prince.

1926 B SHORTER WRITINGS

1 BALDWIN, JAMES MARK. Between Two Wars. 2 vols. Boston:
Stratford.
     Autobiography includes eighteen letters from James to
Baldwin as well as references to James.

2 BRAHAM, ERNEST G. Personality and Immortality in Post-Kantian
Thought. London: George Allen and Unwin.
     At first, James was a dualist and distinguished the
psychical from the physical. Later, as a radical empiricist, he came to hold that the self is "turned out" of
pure experience. In Human Immortality, he makes belief
in immortality rest on feeling and offers no "constructive
theory."

3 DEWEY, JOHN. "William James in Nineteen Twenty-Six," The New
Republic, XLVII (June 30), 163-165. Reprinted in John
Dewey, Characters and Events, edited by Joseph Ratner
(New York: Henry Holt, 1929), vol. I.
     Review of Kallen's The Philosophy of William James
(New York: The Modern Library, ©1925). This fine book
gives rise to reflections about James as an interpreter of
American ideals. Did he express something permanent in
the American spirit or only give voice to characteristics
of his own time? There is such a sharp contrast between
James's pragmatism which insisted that thought have meaning for human life and the "current pragmatism" of a
society dominated by businessmen.

1926

4   LEROUX, EMMANUEL. "Le Plus humain des philosophes: William
        James d'après sa correspondance," Revue de Métaphysique et
        de Morale, XXXIII (April-June), 227-252.
        A study of James's personality based upon his letters.

5   MURRAY, DAVID LESLIE. "William James" in Scenes & Silhou-
        ettes. London: J. Cape.
        James was never understood by philosophers because he
        always remained "just a plain, natural man, unsophisticated
        by learning." His life and thought offer no riddle and
        were determined to a large extent by his ancestry and his
        times.

6   ORCUTT, WILLIAM DANA. In Quest of the Perfect Book. Boston:
        Little, Brown.
        Reminiscences by one of James's printers. James was
        especially concerned with design and with proof reading.
        Orcutt repeats much the same remarks in his Celebrities
        off Parade (Chicago: Wilett, Clark, 1935).

7   PERRY, RALPH BARTON. Philosophy of the Recent Past: An Out-
        line of European and American Philosophy since 1860. New
        York: Charles Scribner's Sons.
        Sketches James's thought and attempts to contrast James
        and Bergson. James came from the empiricist tradition and
        for him 'experience' is the most adequate term for reality.
        For Bergson, reality is 'activity'.

8   SCHNEIDER, HERBERT W. Review of H. M. Kallen, The Philosophy
        of William James (New York: The Modern Library, ©1925),
        The Journal of Philosophy, XXIII (November 25), 670-671.
        Kallen finds a more "catholic" James than is usual.
        However, we lose sense of development when various views
        are thus placed side by side.

9   STEIN, LEO. "William James," The American Mercury, IX
        (September), 68-70. Reprinted in The American Scholar,
        XVII (April 1948), 161-165.
        Most philosophers have imprecise thoughts which they
        try to express in more precise language. James did not
        attempt this, because he knew that his thought was impre-
        cise. James's thought grows out of the concrete.

1927 A BOOKS - NONE

1927 B SHORTER WRITINGS

1   CANNON, WALTER B. "The James-Lange Theory of Emotions: A Critical Examination and an Alternative Theory," The American Journal of Psychology, XXXIX (December), 106-124.
     The James-Lange theory is experimentally refuted.

2   EMERSON, EDWARD W. "William James" in Later Years of the Saturday Club, 1870-1920. Edited by M. A. DeWolfe Howe. Boston: Houghton, Mifflin.
     A biographical sketch with reminiscences of James's youth.

3   LEROUX, EMMANUEL. "Notes Toward the Completion of a Bibliography of the Writings of William James," The Journal of Philosophy, XXIV (April 14), 201-203.
     Lists several items by James and French translations not found in Perry's Annotated Bibliography (1920). The former have been included in McDermott (1967).

4   MARSTON, WILLIAM M. "Motor Consciousness as a Basis for Emotion," Journal of Abnormal and Social Psychology, XXII (July-September), 140-150.
     Marston agrees that emotion is the awareness of our reaction to a stimulus. But James also identifies emotion with sensation. The experiments of Sherrington, Cannon, and others were directed against the second theory and, thus, the first, has never been experimentally tested.

5   MILLER, DICKINSON, S. Review of J. S. Bixler, Religion in the Philosophy of William James (1926), The Journal of Philosophy, XXIV (April 14), 203-210.
     James had remarkable powers of analysis, yet Pragmatism suffers from an inadequate analysis of terms. Miller repeats his criticism of the will to believe. Schiller commented, "William James and the Will to Believe," XXIV (August 4, 1927), 437-440, regretting that Miller had not "moved an inch" from his "The Will to Believe and the Duty to Doubt" (1899) and was still tied to the conception of a static truth. Miller replied in "Dr. Schiller and Analysis," XXIV (November 10, 1927), 617-624; this was followed by Schiller's "William James and Empiricism," XXV (March 15, 1928), 155-162; by Miller's "'A Bird's-Eye View'," XXV (July 5, 1928), 378-383; and by Schiller's "The End of a Great Legend," XXVI (January 17, 1929), 43-46.

1927

6   SCHILLER, F. C. S.   Review of J. S. Bixler, Religion in the
      Philosophy of William James (1926), Mind, NS XXXVI
      (October), 509-511.
            Bixler makes out his case that the conflict in James's
      religious philosophy was between two aspects of James's
      religious nature. Religion is vital to James's pragmatism.
      The will to believe is not a "desperate dodge," but an
      important contribution to epistemology, one which casts
      even more light on science than on religion.

7   _____.   "William James and the Making of Pragmatism," The
      Personalist, VIII (April), 81-93. Reprinted in Must Phi-
      losophers Disagree? (London: Macmillan, 1934).
            Reminiscences about the founding of pragmatism and
      Schiller's contacts with James. According to a letter to
      Schiller from James's wife, James came to regret not adopt-
      ing Schiller's suggestion to use the name "humanism."

8   STUMPF, CARL.   "William James nach seinen Briefen: Leben,
      Charakter, Lehre," Kant-Studien, XXXII, 205-241. Reprinted
      as a pamphlet, (Berlin: Rolf Heise, 1928).
            Reminiscences of James by Stumpf are included.

9   TRUEBLOOD, CHARLES K.   "The Education of William James," The
      Dial, LXXXIII (October), 301-314.
            James's philosophy is an expression of his character.
      While in it we do not find logic, we "find discernment
      into humanity, the gifts of insight." Trueblood stresses
      James's relations with his father and Louis Agassiz.

1928 A BOOKS

1   KAUL, VISHWANATH.   Anti-Pragmatism. Gwalior, India, (n.p.).
            Kaul summarizes each lecture of Pragmatism. Pragmatism
      gives up all philosophical inquiry "as a hopeless task,"
      because of the presence of "human motives" and tells us
      to "take the cash in hand and waive the rest." It is
      "utilitarianism gone mad."

2   LE BRETON, MAURICE.   La Personnalité de William James.
      Bordeaux: Imprimerie de l'Université.
            Includes a general survey of the major aspects of James's
      thought. Le Breton emphasizes the influences which shaped
      James's personality, such as family, other philosophers,
      Cambridge surroundings.

1928 B SHORTER WRITINGS

1   CATTELL, J. McKEEN. "Early Psychological Laboratories,"
     Science, NS LXVII (June 1), 543-548.
          Attention is paid primarily to Wundt, with James receiv-
     ing relatively slight mention.

2   REYMERT, MARTIN L., ed. Feelings and Emotions: The Wittenberg
     Symposium. Worcester, Mass.: Clark University Press.
          Papers read at Wittenberg College, Springfield, Ohio,
     October 19-23, 1927. The James-Lange theory is frequently
     mentioned. It is discussed more extensively in papers by
     F. Aveling, Ed. Claparède, Knight Dunlap, and Walter B.
     Cannon.

1929 A BOOKS

1   JACCARD, BENJAMIN E. Étude sur quelques traits de la
     philosophie religieuse et sur la théorie de la sainteté
     de William James. (n.p., n.d.).
          Date has been estimated from internal evidence. For
     James, a final system of ethics would be possible only at
     the end of time. Hence, the idea of sainthood is indefin-
     able. For him, faith is the condition of a life of hardi-
     hood, a life which leads to holiness and higher joys. A
     copy can be found in the University of Michigan library,
     Ann Arbor.

1929 B SHORTER WRITINGS

1   BORING, EDWIN G. A History of Experimental Psychology. New
     York: The Century Co. Revised edition, 1950.
          James introduced experimental psychology into America
     although he was not an experimentalist. From his func-
     tional interpretation of mind, came functional psychology.

2   CANNON, WALTER B. Bodily Changes in Pain, Hunger, Fear and
     Rage. 2nd edition. New York: D. Appleton.
          First edition appeared in 1915. In the second edition,
     Chapter XVIII, "A Critical Examination of the James-Lange
     Theory of Emotions," has been added. The separation of
     the viscera from the central nervous system does not change
     emotional behavior; the viscera are too insensitive and
     change too slowly to be a source of emotion; appropriate
     visceral changes artificially induced do not produce
     strong emotions.

1929

3   EVANS, ELIZABETH GLENDOWER. "William James and His Wife,"
    The Atlantic Monthly, CXLIV (September), 374-387.
        Reminiscences by a life-long friend, widow of one of
    James's students, about James's home life. Excerpts of
    letters from James to Evans are included.

4   KELLER, HELEN. Midstream: My Later Life. Garden City, N. Y.:
    Doubleday, Doran.
        Pp. 316-317 describe James's visit in Keller's youth.

5   MURPHY, GARDNER. An Historical Introduction to Modern Psy-
    chology. New York: Harcourt, Brace. Revised edition,
    1949.
        While an "ardent empiricist," James disliked experimen-
    tation. His thought involves a conflict between "neuro-
    logical" explanations and a belief in a soul-like
    personality. Of major importance are James's theories of
    emotion, memory, and of the origin of necessary truths.

6   PERRY, RALPH BARTON, ed. "Correspondance de Charles Renouvier
    et de William James," Revue de Métaphysique et de Morale,
    XXXVI (January-March), 1-35; (April-June), 193-222.
        These letters, with many omissions, were used in Thought
    and Character (1935). Two additional letters were pub-
    lished separately by Perry (1935).

7   RILEY, ISAAC WOODBRIDGE. Men and Morals: The Story of Ethics.
    Garden City, N. Y.: Doubleday, Doran.
        The ethics of pragmatism is utilitarian, marked by
    practicality, "democracy and dynamism." It emphasizes
    self-sufficiency. James's special contribution was the
    adjustment of "religious aspirations" to science.

8   SIMONS, HI. "Why William James 'Stood by' God," The Open
    Court, XLIII, 77-86.
        James showed that religious beliefs compensate for
    deficiencies. A person who feels no deficiencies will
    need no religion. James also ignored the possibility of
    improvement through intelligence and social action.

9   SMITH, T. V. The Philosophic Way of Life. Chicago: The
    University of Chicago Press.
        James is a "guide" to the "scientific way of life,"
    although given his background, we would associate him with
    the religious. For James, philosophy was "such a state-
    ment of the method and attitude of science as made it
    available for fullness of living."

1930 A BOOKS - NONE

1930 B SHORTER WRITINGS

1 BOLTON, FREDERICK E. "William James," Progressive Education,
   VII (March), 82-88.
      James was among the first to apply psychology to educa-
   tion. He emphasized the importance of interest for educational progress.

2 MEAD, GEORGE HERBERT. "The Philosophies of Royce, James, and
   Dewey in Their American Setting," The International Journal
   of Ethics, XL (January), 211-231.
      James's philosophy was a "native American growth,"
   embodying American individualism, refined by culture. He
   wanted to make attitude in a crisis the test of the truth
   of the ideas of God and freedom, and this led him to an
   ambiguous notion of satisfaction.

3 WICKHAM, HARVEY. The Unrealists: James, Bergson, Santayana,
   Einstein, Bertrand Russell, John Dewey, Alexander and
   Whitehead. New York: Lincoln MacVeagh, The Dial Press.
      Einstein's theory of relativity is implicit in James
   since it is only an attempt to abolish standards. James
   tries to "damn" the absolute. This is fine if absolute
   means your own idea of the incomprehensible. But if you
   mean the fact that there is an absolute, "your damn is
   apt to fall back upon your own head--with disastrous
   results to the noodle."

1931 A BOOKS - NONE

1931 B SHORTER WRITINGS

1 KULOVESI, YRJÖ. "Psychoanalytische Bemerkungen zur James-
   Langeschen Affekttheorie," Imago, XVII, 392-398.
      Attempts to view the theory in the light of psycho-
   analysis. James went deeper than W. Wundt in the study
   of feelings and prepared the way for psychoanalysis.

2 PERRY, RALPH BARTON. "The Place of William James in the History
   of Empiricism," Proceedings of the Seventh International
   Congress of Philosophy. London: Oxford University Press.
      British empiricists held that experience is the only test
   of existence and that the essence of a thing is composed of
   the "content of sense-perception." James agreed, but held
   that this was not radical enough. James insisted that
   moral tests of truth be used where experiential ones are

1931

(PERRY, RALPH BARTON)
not available and that experience itself supplies materials for filling in the gaps between seemingly discontinuous entities.

3   TOWER, C. V. "Neutralism and Radical Empiricism," The Journal of Philosophy, XXVIII (October 22), 589-600.
An examination and criticism of the "analytic and pluralistic tendencies" in James's conception of neutral entities.

1932 A BOOKS

1   GRATTAN, CLINTON HARTLEY. The Three Jameses: A Family of Minds. New York: Longmans, Green.
Biographical, with emphasis on James's personality. An epilogue assesses the intellectual contributions of James, his father, Henry James, Sr., and his brother, Henry James, Jr.

1932 B SHORTER WRITINGS

1   BAUM, MAURICE. "The Attitude of William James Toward Science," The Monist, XLII, 585-604.
Critics have claimed that James's attitude towards science is inconsistent, but this is not true. James holds that while science attains results, it can do so only in limited fields. Aspects of the universe escape its methods of verification.

2   EHLERS, HUGO. Die Wirklichkeitsphilosophie in ihrem Verhältnis zum Pragmatismus. Berlin.
Criticizes pragmatism, particularly Schiller's, from the point of view of the "Wirklichkeitsphilosophie" of Heinrich Maier. If pragmatism elevates value above reality and even truth, Maier restores the primacy of reality.

3   HAZLITT, HENRY. "A Family of Minds," The Nation, CXXXV (November 9), 460-461.
Review of Grattan, The Three Jameses (1932). It is true, as Grattan says that James is a "shallow optimist." But we must not overlook the "penetrating incidental insights" and The Principles of Psychology, a work of genius.

4   MORRIS, CHARLES W. Six Theories of Mind. Chicago: The University of Chicago Press.

100

In "Relation and Function in James's View of Mind and Knowledge," Morris finds that James alternates between relational and functional theories.

1933 A BOOKS

1 BLAU, THÉODORE. William James: sa théorie de la connaissance et la vérité. Paris: Jouve & Cie.

For James, neither common sense, nor science, nor philosophy, can pretend to absolute knowledge. James's pramatism is not an attempt to find an absolute standard for truth, but simply an insistence upon its human character. Emphasis is placed on the distinction between conceptual and perceptual knowledge.

2 CORNESSE, MARIE. L'Idée de Dieu chez William James (Étude historique et critique). Grenoble: Allier Père et Fils.

James's conception of God has a mystical basis. It is deficient, for no reason for God's existence is given, the metaphysical attributes of God are not understood, and it is anthropomorphic. Cornesse emphasizes the development of James's God from the early suppression of mystical tendencies to their later full flowering.

3 _____. Le Rôle des images dans la pensée de William James. Grenoble: Allier Père et Fils.

James is a visualizer. Cornesse gives an elaborate classification of James's images. These images reveal James's personality. Both their biographical and philosophical meanings are analyzed. Thesis at the University of Grenoble.

4 MAIRE, GILBERT. William James et le pragmatisme religieux. Paris: Denoël et Steele.

James's philosophy is best understood as an expression of his life. It rests upon his experience of his mental crisis and of the power of his will. Maire surveys the major aspects of James's thought in view of this conviction. The deep individualism of his thought explains why James did not establish a school. An extensive bibliography of writings about James is included, most of the titles appear in the present list.

1933 B SHORTER WRITINGS

1 BAUM, MAURICE. "The Development of James's Pragmatism Prior to 1879," The Journal of Philosophy, XXX (January 19), 43-51.

1933

   (BAUM, MAURICE)
      In Pragmatism James asserts that Peirce's pragmatism lay
unnoticed till 1898. But James had quoted Peirce's remarks
in "Reflex Action and Theism" (1881) and "The Function of
Cognition" (1885). Furthermore, in "Quelques considérations
sur la méthode subjective" (1878), James himself had developed a similar method for establishing meanings.

2 HEIDBREDER, EDNA. Seven Psychologies. New York: Appleton-
     Century-Crofts.
      For James, psychology is a biological science. He
treated all ideas, including the fashionable psychologies,
democratically and with a "Yankee independence."

3 PERRY, RALPH BARTON. Letter to the editor, The Journal of
     Philosophy, XXX (February 16), 112.
      Comments on Baum's "The Development of· James's Pragma-
tism Prior to 1879" (1933). It is true that pragmatism
can be found in James's early thought, but this does not
mark the beginning of the pragmatic movement.

4   . "William James et M. Henri Bergson: Lettres (1902-
     1910)," Revue des Deux Mondes, 8th series, vol. XVII
     (October 15), 783-823.
      Chapters LXXXVI and LXXXVII of Thought and Character
(1935).

5 STIMSON, RUFUS W. "Professional Sanctions from William James,"
     Agricultural Education, V (January), 99-101.
      James's work contains thousands of "sanctions" of use to
a supervisor of "vocational education in agriculture."
When visiting a classroom, the supervisor should look for
"variety of learning activities," good presentations of
results, decisions made by students themselves, and the
like.

1934 A BOOKS

1 BURR, ANNA ROBESON, ed. Alice James: Her Brothers, Her
     Journal. New York: Dodd, Mead.
      An introduction by Barr, "Her Brothers," precedes an
edited text of Alice James's journal. The introduction
includes numerous letters particularly from the brothers,
William, Henry, Garth Wilkinson, and Robertson, to each
other and to Alice. Emphasis is on anecdotes of family
life.

1934 B SHORTER WRITINGS

1   BAUM, MAURICE. "William James' Philosophy of Higher Education,"
    School and Society, XXXIX (February 10), 161-166.
       While James wrote no treatise on education, his various
    addresses add up to a "genuine philosophy of education."
    James stressed method rather than content, insisted that
    education stimulate insight, emphasized experimentation.

2   BELL, ERIC TEMPLE. The Search for Truth. Baltimore: Williams
    & Wilkins.
       Pp. 59-66 contain a burlesque of a tavern discussion
    involving some students and James which Bell alleges he
    witnessed in California in 1906. Bell records that upon
    hearing James's name he asked "Who the hell's James?"
    and that he spent the two and one-half hours of James's
    lecture in a lavatory.

3   COMPTON, CHARLES H. Who Reads What? New York: H. W. Wilson.
    "Who Reads William James?" is found on pp. 91-100.
    Surveys readers of James's books in a large public library
    and concludes that many common people read James and that
    James's philosophy is "slowly permeating the masses."
    Compton wrote letters to readers and excerpts from some
    responses are included.

4   GOLDMARK, JOSEPHINE. "An Adirondack Friendship: Letters of
    William James," The Atlantic Monthly, CLIV (September)
    265-272; (October), 440-447.
       Reminiscences by one of the Goldmark sisters, who fre-
    quently vacationed near James's summer home in Keene
    Valley, N. Y. Part of the material appears in Perry's
    Thought and Character (1935).

5   HARTSHORNE, CHARLES and WEISS, PAUL, eds. Collected Papers
    of Charles Sanders Peirce. Cambridge, Mass.: Harvard
    University Press.
       Vol. V, Pragmatism and Pragmaticism, contains most of
    what Peirce wrote on pragmatism. However, in about 1907,
    Peirce was planning a letter to the Nation on the prag-
    matism controversy. Drafts have survived and portions
    are included in the Collected Papers. Richard S. Robin,
    Annotated Catalogue of the Papers of Charles S. Peirce
    (The University of Massachusetts Press, 1967), pp. 36-38,
    indicates that portions of the drafts in which Peirce
    defines his relations with James were not published.

1934

6 RUCKMICK, CHRISTIAN A. "McCosh on the Emotions," _The American Journal of Psychology_, XLVI (July), 506–508.
   Finds a hitherto unnoticed anticipation of the James-Lange theory of emotions in _The Emotions_ (1880) by James McCosh.

7 SCHILLER, F. C. S. "William James" in _Must Philosophers Disagree?_ London: Macmillan. Also published as "William James, The Maker of Pragmatism," _College of the Pacific Publications in Philosophy_, III (1934), 101–109.
   A popular lecture given in 1930, with personal reminiscences. James broke down the abstract separation of psychology from metaphysics. In psychology, he overthrew atomism and introduced the continuum. He also developed pragmatism which involved the breaking down of the distinction between theory and practiçe. James interpreted American life, but in its universal aspects. Actual life is everywhere pragmatic.

8 SOMERVILLE, JOHN. "The Strange Case of Modern Psychology," _The Journal of Philosophy_, XXXI (October 11), 571–577.
   The questions Locke refused to raise become central in James's psychology, for James wants to correlate mind with body. James asks not "what can I know," but "how do I know." This represents a major shift, although there are no signs that Locke's question has been answered. As James predicted, psychology has moved even further away from Locke.

9 TOWNSEND, HARVEY GATES. _Philosophical Ideas in the United States_. New York: American Book Co.
   James was a central figure in what should be called "neo-transcendentalism" in New England. He is in the line of descent from Emerson. James emphasized his connections with British empiricism, although he rejected its skepticism.

10 WELLS, HERBERT GEORGE. _Experiment in Autobiography_. 2 vols. London: Victor Gollancz.
   Vol. II, p. 538 contains an anecdote about James climbing over a garden wall in order to look at G. K. Chesterton.

1935 A BOOKS

1 PERRY, RALPH BARTON. _The Thought and Character of William James_. 2 vols. Boston: Little, Brown.
   The standard biography, with quotations from numerous letters and unpublished manuscripts.

1935 B SHORTER WRITINGS

1 BAUM, MAURICE. "William James and Psychical Research," The Journal of Abnormal and Social Psychology, XXX (April-June), 111-118.
    James's interest in psychical research was serious, "cautious and scrupulous." Surveys James's writings in this field.

2 BRADLEY, FRANCIS HERBERT. Collected Essays. 2 vols. Oxford: Clarendon.
    Besides the writings on simple resemblance (1893) and "A Disclaimer," (1910), abstracted separately, the collection contains criticism of James's views on moral responsibility, his notion of consent, and other references.

3 CURTI, MERLE. The Social Ideals of American Educators. New York: Charles Scribner's Sons.
    In Varieties, James idealized poverty but he himself never experienced it and remained insensitive to the poor. His teachings on instinct and habit have conservative social implications. He interpreted social conflicts psychologically and never understood their deeper roots.

4 DEARBORN, GEORGE VAN NESS. "William James's Scientific Integrity," The Journal of Abnormal and Social Psychology, XXX (July-September), 262-264.
    Praises article by Baum (1935). How could James not be interested in psychical research, when survival is one of the most interesting questions of life? Dearborn served as James's assistant and was a friend for "twenty-five years."

5 HOOK, SIDNEY. "Our Philosophers," Current History, XLI (March), 698-704.
    Characterizes major American philosophers. James remained a "sensitive European" who paid little attention to the social. He populated the universe with "spooks," adopting a will to believe "incompatible with his own psychology."

6 _____. "William James," The Nation, CXLI (December 11), 684, 686-687.
    Review of Perry's Thought and Character (1935). James is more remarkable as an "intellectual force" than as a "systematic thinker." The work is important because it reveals James's political and social views.

1935

7   MATHER, FRANK JEWETT, JR. "A Champion of Lost Causes," The
        Saturday Review of Literature, XIII (November 30), 3-4,
        14.
            Review of Perry's Thought and Character (1935). James
        is interpreted in terms of his Irish background, relations
        with his father, and neurasthenia. James was an "outsider"
        trying to become an "insider."

8   PERRY, RALPH BARTON. "The Common Enemy: ·Early Letters of
        Oliver Wendell Holmes, Jr., and William James," The
        Atlantic Monthly, CLVI (September), 293-303.
            Chapter XXX of Thought and Character (1935).

9   _____, ed. "Un Échange de lettres entre Renouvier et
        William James," Revue de Métaphysique et de Morale, XLII
        (July), 303-318.
            Additional letters, one from James to Renouvier
        (December 1879) and the reply (January 18, 1880). Both
        are long and philosophical.

1936 A BOOKS

1   LAPAN, ARTHUR. The Significance of James' Essay. New York:
        Law Printing Co.
            A doctoral dissertation at Columbia University on
        James's "Does 'Consciousness' Exist?" (1904). James's
        shift from 'consciousness' to 'experience' amounts to a
        shift from the traditional separation of man from nature
        towards their reunion.

1936 B SHORTER WRITINGS

1   ANON. "A Pragmatical Romantic: The Conflict in William
        James," The Times Literary Supplement, vol. XXXV, no. 1811
        (October 17), 821-822.
            Review of Perry's Thought and Character (1935). Perry
        lacked nothing but a pair of scissors.

2   BERGSON, HENRI. Letter to J. Chevalier in Harvard et la
        France. Paris: La Revue d'Histoire Moderne. Reprinted
        in Écrits et Paroles (Paris: Presses Universitaires de
        France, 1959) and Mélanges (1972).
            Praises Chevalier (1936). Chevalier should have said
        that Bergson knew James personally. For Bergson, meeting
        James was one of the great joys. Bergson repeats anec-
        dotes about his meeting with James. James is comparable
        to the great philosophers. He used introspection and
        made it a fruitful method. The center of his thought was
        his direct contact with spirit.

WILLIAM JAMES: A REFERENCE GUIDE

3 BURKE, KENNETH. "William James: Superlative Master of the Comparative," Science and Society, I, 122-125.
   Review of Perry's Thought and Character (1935). James regarded the intellect as a "non-moral" power, while Peirce made logic a branch of ethics. As a result, James had to engraft moral exhortations upon his pragmatism.

4 CHEVALIER, JACQUES. "William James et Bergson" in Harvard et la France. Paris: La Revue d'Histoire Moderne.
   Studies the relations between James and Bergson in light of the thesis that their philosophies, from different starting points and using different methods, converge towards a common center.

5 DEWEY, JOHN. Review of Perry, Thought and Character (1935), The New Republic, LXXXVI (February 12), 24-25.
   James is fortunate in finding a biographer who permits him to speak for himself. Contains reminiscences of James.

6 EASTWOOD, DOROTHY MARGARET. The Revival of Pascal: A Study of His Relation to Modern French Thought. Oxford: Clarendon.
   In Varieties, James developed a sympathetic secular approach to religion and mysticism. James helped prepare for the revival of Pascal by viewing ascetisism sympathetically, by removing the taint of morbidity and fanaticism. Also included is a chapter on "Moral Pragmatism and Pascal's Wager."

7 GRATTAN, C. HARTLEY. Review of Perry, Thought and Character (1935), The North American Review, CCXLI (March), 174-181.
   A history of the James family should form an important part of the history of American families. Perry contributes to this. James was an "eupeptic for philosophers," "shallow," but a consolation to sick souls, a contributor to "inspirational literature." He was a "great and noble human being."

8 GROOS, KARL. Die Unsterblichkeitsfrage. Berlin: Junker und Dünnhaupt.
   Includes chapters on Fechner, Hans Driesch, and James. James treats immortality on a personal level. He rejects the idea of the soul as substance and accepts the hypothesis of a world-soul acting on us.

9 HOUSE, FLOYD NELSON. The Development of Sociology. New York: McGraw-Hill.
   James was the first American to hold that men have instincts. Instinct was made the basis of sociology by

1936

(HOUSE, FLOYD NELSON)
Wilfred Trotter, Instincts of the Herd in Peace and War
(London: T. F. Unwin, 1916), and was used by William
McDougall. The idea of instinct gave rise to an individ-
ualistic social psychology in America.

10 HOWE, M. A. DeWOLFE, ed. "John Jay Chapman to William James:
A Packet of Letters," Harpers Monthly Magazine, CLXXIV
(December), 46-54. Included in M. A. DeWolfe Howe, John
Jay Chapman and His Letters (Boston: Houghton, Mifflin,
1937).
No letters from James to Chapman are included. One let-
ter relates how a woman came out of the lectures on prag-
matism and said "Ah, Fragmentism--such a good name too."

11 KRAUSHAAR, OTTO F. "Lotze's Influence on the Psychology of
William James," The Psychological Review, XLIII (May),
235-257.
Lotze's influence on James is to be understood as
"Socratic midwifery." Both stressed the "dynamic and
functional" elements in mental life. James's doctrine of
space perception owes much to Lotze. In his Medizinische
Psychologie (1852), Lotze developed a theory of emotion
like James's.

12 MARHENKE, PAUL. "The Constituents of Mind," University of
California Publications in Philosophy, XIX, 171-208.
Consciousness does exist and the theory in "Does
'Consciousness' Exist?" (1904) that the constituents of
mind are its objects is weak. When expanded into a theory
of knowledge, the identification of knower and known results in difficulties concerning error.

13 MARTIN, NEWELL. "Two Great Adirondack Guides," High Spots
(Adirondack Mountain Club), XIII (January), 29-30.
In 1877, James was in a group of "dignified Harvard men"
fearful that a Yale group would try to buy a house the
Harvard men wanted for themselves.

14 MILLER, DICKINSON S. "James's Philosophical Development;
Professor Perry's Biography," The Journal of Philosophy,
XXXIII (June 4), 309-318.
Perry portrays an "indisputable" James. James's commit-
ment to the "fulness and richness and satisfaction of
human life" led him to adopt theoretical positions not
really required by it. James's work was not analytical
enough. Rather than ask whether freedom exists, he should
have tried to find its meaning.

15 MÜLLER, GUSTAV E. <u>Amerikanische Philosophie</u>. Stuttgart:
    Fr. Frommann.
        Contains an account of James which emphasizes his influ-
    ence on the new realists and George Santayana.

16 ROBINSON, EDWARD S. Review of Perry's <u>Thought and Character</u>
    (1935), <u>The Yale Review</u>, NS XXV (March), 616-620.
        James prepared the way for Freudian psychology and
    behavorism. His repudiation of "logical nicety" reflects
    the "pandemonium of nineteenth-century America." Perry
    has contributed to the history of American thought and the
    art of biography.

<u>1937 A BOOKS - NONE</u>

<u>1937 B SHORTER WRITINGS</u>

1   BAYM, MAX I. "William James and Henry Adams," <u>The New England
    Quarterly</u>, X (December), 717-742.
        A study of the marginalia in Adams' copy of <u>The Prin-
    ciples of Psychology</u>.

2   BRETT, GEORGE SIDNEY. "William James and American Ideals,"
    <u>University of Toronto Quarterly</u>, VI (January), 159-173.
        A review of Perry's <u>Thought and Character</u> (1935).
    Perry has produced a "picture of American life."

3   DEWEY, JOHN. "The Philosophy of William James," <u>The Southern
    Review</u>, II, 447-461. Reprinted in <u>Problems of Men</u>, (New
    York: Philosophical Library, 1946).
        Comments on the interplay between James's personality
    and thought based upon Perry's <u>Thought and Character</u> (1935).
    What James's critics decried as disrespect for logic was
    an experience of James's greater "intellectual conscien-
    tiousness." He did not wish to impose a system greater
    than what the facts warranted.

4   KALLEN, HORACE M. "Remarks on R. B. Perry's Portrait of
    William James," <u>The Philosophical Review</u>, XLVI (January),
    68-78.
        In <u>Thought and Character</u> (1935), Perry's analysis of
    James into four personalities distorts him for James was
    "so essentially integrated a personality." He was "book-
    ish" and did not prefer "achievement to contemplation."
    James did not hate "exact thought," he only renounced cer-
    tain logical techniques through "painstaking study."
    Kallen discusses the relation of James's philosophy to that
    of James's father and Bergson. C. S. Peirce's originality

1937

(KALLEN, HORACE M.)
was limited and his reputation, the result of James's
interest.

5   RAYMOND, MARY E. "Memories of William James," The New England
Quarterly, X (September), 419-429.
Reminiscences by James's student at Radcliffe College.
Contains letters from James to Raymond.

6   SIDGWICK, ALFRED. Review of Perry, Thought and Character
(1935), Mind, NS XLVI (January), 67-74.
Summarizes contents. James's pragmatism has no "special
connexion" with the will to believe. It is concerned with
"reasoning in general" rather than religious faith.

1938 A BOOKS

1   BAUMGARTEN, EDUARD. Der Pragmatismus: R. W. Emerson, W. James,
J. Dewey. Vol. II of Die geistigen Grundlagen des
amerikanischen Gemeinwesens. Frankfurt am Main: Vittorio
Klostermann.
The larger work interprets the spirit of America. The
treatment is primarily cultural and not philosophical. A
biographical sketch is followed by an account of James's
doctrines of man and of science.

2   MOORE, JOHN MORRISON. Theories of Religious Experience with
Special Reference to James, Otto and Bergson. New York:
Round Table Press.
The term religious experience is vague and has outlived
its usefulness. What counts as religious experience
varies from culture to culture.

3   PERRY, RALPH BARTON. In the Spirit of William James. New
Haven: Yale University Press.
Contrasts James and Royce, especially in their relations
to American culture. Separate chapters deal with James's
empiricist theory of knowledge, his metaphysics of experience, the right to believe, and James as a militant liberal.

1938 B SHORTER WRITINGS

1   FORD, WORTHINGTON CHAUNCEY, ed. Letters of Henry Adams.
Vol. II. Boston: Houghton, Mifflin.
Covers 1892-1918, contains several letters to James.

2   HANSEN, VALDEMAR. "Un Grand livre sur William James,"
Theoria, IV (Part II), 176-180.

Perry's Thought and Character (1935) is a rich work
which deepens our understanding of James.

3 KALLEN, HORACE M. "Mussolini, William James, and the Rational-
   ists," The Social Frontier, IV (May), 253-256.
      Comments on the controversy between Sidney Hook and
   Brand Blanshard over the connection between rationalism
   and totalitarianism and between James and Mussolini.
   Mussolini mentioned James only for publicity. When Kallen
   asked him what of James's Mussolini had read, the latter
   was visibly irritated and made no reply. Kallen reported
   this interview in "Fascism: for the Italians," The New
   Republic, LIX (January 1927), 211-212.

4 KRAUSHAAR, OTTO F. "What James's Philosophical Orientation
   Owed to Lotze," The Philosophical Review XLVII (September)
   517-526.
      While there are many similarities, Lotze is not the
   primary influence on James. Both wanted to defend "spiritual experience" from "mechanistic principles." For both,
   philosophy arose out of deep intellectual need and was
   neither a science nor a game. Both mistrusted Hegel and
   "pan-logism." Kraushaar surveys James's reading of Lotze.

1939 A BOOKS - NONE

1939 B SHORTER WRITINGS

1 ANDERSON, PAUL RUSSELL and FISCH, MAX HAROLD. Philosophy in
   America: From the Puritans to James. New York:
   D. Appleton-Century Co.
      James was cosmopolitan and did not try to develop an
   American philosophy. His other interests were subordinated
   to the moral.

2 BURTT, EDWIN A. Types of Religious Philosophy. New York:
   Harper and Brothers. Revised edition, 1951.
      James is neither a modernist nor a humanist. He retains
   "supernaturalism" and is attracted to mysticism. His major
   contribution is the argument for faith. The section on
   James was dropped from the revised edition.

3 CARPENTER, FREDERIC I. "William James and Emerson," American
   Literature, XI (March), 39-57.
      A study of the marginalia in the 9 volumes of Emerson's
   works from James's library preserved in the Houghton
   Library of Harvard University. Emerson is part of James's
   "intellectual heritage" and that of pragmatism.

1939

4 KRAUSHAAR, OTTO F. "Lotze as a Factor in the Development of
      James's Radical Empiricism and Pluralism," The Philosoph-
      ical Review, XLVIII (September), 455-471.
         The dualism of thought and object adopted by James to
      about 1900 is defined in reference to Lotze. But his
      breaking away towards radical empiricism owes little to
      Lotze. In marginal notes, James noted traces of pluralism
      in Lotze. However, since Lotze remained a monist, James's
      pluralism avoids the "ineptitudes" of monism with special
      reference to Lotze.

5 NEWHALL, JANNETTE E. "Wobbermin und William James" in Luther,
      Kant, Schleiermacher in ihrer Bedeutung für den
      Protestantismus. Berlin: Arthur Collignon.
         A contribution to the celebration of Georg Wobbermin's
      70th birthday. Wobbermin translated Varieties and was
      personally acquainted with James. Without attempting to
      trace influences, Newhall holds that both begin with ego-
      psychology, use moral arguments to establish religion,
      and face the question of materialism.

1940 A BOOKS - NONE

1940 B SHORTER WRITINGS

1 BROOKS, VAN WYCK. New England: Indian Summer, 1865-1915.
      New York: E. P. Dutton.
         A history of literature with references to James.

2 DEWEY, JOHN. "The Vanishing Subject in the Psychology of
      James," The Journal of Philosophy, XXXVII (October 24),
      589-599. Reprinted in Problems of Men (New York: Philo-
      sophical Library, 1946).
         In The Principles of Psychology James commits himself
      to epistemological dualism. But in his analysis of par-
      ticular topics, the self tends to vanish and become a
      "subject," an organism interacting with its environment.
      Even the "spiritual" self, consisting of acts and emotions,
      is interpreted biologically.

3 DuBOIS, W. E. BURGHARDT. Dusk at Dawn. New York: Harcourt,
      Brace.
         Contains reminiscences of James. DuBois was a student
      at Harvard. James had agreed to serve on the advisory
      board of an "Encyclopaedia Africana" being organized by
      DuBois in 1909.

4   GABRIEL, RALPH HENRY.   The Course of American Democratic
      Thought. New York: The Ronald Press Co.
         James drew back from Royce's "sophisticated collectivism"
      to a "primitive individualism reminiscent of the American
      frontier." He personified the best of American
      nationalism.

5   KRAUSHAAR, OTTO F.   "Lotze's Influence on the Pragmatism and
      Practical Philosophy of William James," Journal of the
      History of Ideas, I (October), 439-458.
         It would be a mistake to exaggerate Lotze's influence on
      James. James studied Lotze in two waves. The first,
      lasted into the 1890's, the second, much weaker, to James's
      death. Lotze held that things are what they are known as,
      knowledge is instrumental, the practical reason is primary.
      In practical philosophy, Lotze interpreted mechanism in
      teleological terms and emphasized individuality.

1941 A BOOKS - NONE

1941 B SHORTER WRITINGS

1   FLACK, CHARLES R.   "The Incidence of William James," Education,
      LXII (October), 67-76.
         Biographical with emphasis on the contemporary conditions
      which could have formed James's thought. Also studies
      James's influence.

2   LEVINSON, RONALD B.   "Gertrude Stein, William James, and
      Grammar," The American Journal of Psychology, LIV, 124-128.
         Stein's violations of the rules of grammar puts into
      practice James's views on the use of language. Levinson
      traces them to James's view that relations are given with
      the terms.

3   LOWE, VICTOR.   "William James and Whitehead's Doctrine of
      Prehensions," The Journal of Philosophy, XXXVIII
      (February 27), 113-126.
         The study of James helps us to understand Whitehead,
      particularly his "peculiar empiricism." James's doctrine
      of "felt transition" is like Whitehead's notion of
      "prehension."

4   McGOVERN, WILLIAM MONTGOMERY.   From Luther to Hitler: The His-
      tory of Fascist-Nazi Political Philosophy. Boston:
      Houghton, Mifflin.
         James is part of the current of irrationalism out of
      which Fascism developed. He would have been "aghast" at
      the use made of his views.

1941

5   NATHANSON, JEROME. <u>Forerunners of Freedom: The Re-creation</u>
    <u>of the American Spirit</u>. Washington, D.C.: American
    Council on Public Affairs.
        Americans believe that the world is there to be changed
    and James expresses that spirit. James's pragmatism is
    itself not a way of life, but a rule for choosing between
    ways of life.

6   PARKES, HENRY BAMFORD. "William James" in <u>The Pragmatic Test:</u>
    <u>Essays on the History of Ideas</u>. San Francisco: The Colt
    Press.
        James accepted scientific method as long as it was com-
    patible with freedom. He believed in the primacy of
    action, holding that a "contemplative life was pathologi-
    cal." His major insights were expressed before 1880.

7   SCHUETZ, ALFRED. "William James' Concept of the Stream of
    Thought Phenomenologically Interpreted," <u>Philosophy and</u>
    <u>Phenomenological Research</u>, I (June), 442-452. Reprinted
    in <u>Collected Papers</u>, vol. III. (The Hague: Nijhoff,
    1966).
        James's conception of psychology as a natural science is
    not acceptable to a phenomenologist. No attempt need be
    made to reduce James to a precursor of phenomenology. But
    there are important similarities. The "stream of thought"
    contains much phenomenology.

<u>1942 A BOOKS</u>

1   ALDRICH, ELIZABETH PERKINS. <u>As William James Said</u>. New York:
    The Vanguard Press.
        Selections from James's published writings, with a
    biographical introduction.

2   BLANSHARD, BRAND and SCHNEIDER, HERBERT W., eds. <u>In Commemora-</u>
    <u>tion of William James: 1842-1942</u>. New York: Columbia
    University Press.
        Contains a foreword by Horace M. Kallen and papers by
    Henry James, Horace M. Kallen, Dickinson S. Miller,
    Edwin B. Holt, John Dewey, Julius Seelye Bixler, Ralph
    Barton Perry, George Sidney Brett, Donald Cary Williams,
    Herbert W. Schneider, Jacob R. Kantor, Victor Lowe,
    Charles Morris, Eugene W. Lyman, Arnold Metzger, and
    Walker H. Hill. These are listed separately.

3   OTTO, MAX C., and others. <u>William James: The Man and the</u>
    <u>Thinker</u>. Madison: University of Wisconsin Press.

114

1942

Papers at the University of Wisconsin on the centenary
of James's birth. Those by Max C. Otto, D. S. Miller,
Norman Cameron, John Dewey, Boyd H. Bode, and J. S. Bixler
are listed separately. Also contains George C. Sellery,
"William James and Wisconsin" and Clarence A. Dykstra,
"Introductory Remarks."

4   ROBACK, A. A. William James: His Marginalia, Personality and
    Contribution. Cambridge, Mass.: Sci-Art Publishers.
        Contains quotations from marginalia and letters. Some
    of the topics covered: the room where James kept his
    books, reading of H. S. Chamberlain and W. Wundt, attitude
    towards Jews, handwriting. There is a name and subject
    index.

1942 B SHORTER WRITINGS

1   AMENT, WILLIAM S. "William James as a Man of Letters," The
    Personalist, XXIII (Spring), 199-206.
        James was not interested in elegance.

2   ANON. The Centenary of William James: January 11, 1842-1942.
    Waterville, Maine: Colby College Library.
        Notes for the exhibition at Colby College. Describes
    holdings of James's letters to Katharine Prince and tran-
    scripts of letters to Thomas Davidson and Théodule Ribot.
    The originals of the Ribot letters were lost during World
    War II.

3   BIXLER, JULIUS SEELYE. "Two Questions Raised by William
    James's Essay 'The Moral Equivalent of War,'" The Harvard
    Theological Review, XXXV (April), 117-129. Also appeared
    in In Commemoration of William James (1942).
        James professes to be an empiricist and a pragmatist,
    but in his essay, he sets up certain ideals, ideals of
    cooperation, and asks that we simply accept them. James
    espouses individualism, yet in this essay, he approaches
    socialism. Thus, an "individualistic philosophy" is not
    an appropriate framework for James's "spiritual insights."

4   _____. "William James as Religious Thinker" in William James:
    The Man and the Thinker (1942).
        James's approach to religion is radical for he emphasizes
    the creative role of men even where we tend to view men in
    terms of submission. "Interest" and "purpose" are every-
    where and they are "trustworthy."

5   BODE, BOYD H. "William James in the American Tradition" in
    William James: The Man and the Thinker (1942).

1942

(BODE, BOYD H.)
Pragmatism insists that men themselves must fashion their
standards of value. James expresses the American traditions which looks not towards the past, but emphasizes
"self-reliance," "struggle," and "mastery over the
environment."

6   BOODIN, JOHN ELOF. "William James as I Knew Him," The
Personalist, XXIII (Spring), 117-129; (Summer), 279-290;
(Autumn), 396-406.
Anecdotes about the origins of The Will to Believe,
Varieties, and Thomas Davidson's role in arranging James's
marriage. Letters from James to Boodin are included.

7   BORING, EDWIN G. "Human Nature vs. Sensation: William James
and the Psychology of the Present," The American Journal
of Psychology, LV (July), 310-327.
Reflections on psychology, in light of the opposition
between values and facts. James disliked the experimental
movement, because he disliked pretense and there was much
sham science. James wanted a "functional" psychology which
would interpret our moral and religious life. In later
psychology, we find similar conflicts.

8   BRETT, GEORGE SIDNEY. "The Psychology of William James in
Relation to Philosophy" in In Commemoration of William
James (1942). Abstract in The Journal of Philosophy,
XXXVIII (December 4, 1941), 673.
James's views of activity, relations, consciousness, and
"psychic experience," developed in his psychology, form
the basis of James's philosophy.

9   BROTHERSTON, BRUCE W. "The Wider Setting of 'Felt Transition,'"
The Journal of Philosophy, XXXIX (February 12), 97-104.
Dewey and others want to remove from James all traces of
"metaphysics" and place James on the side of "biological
behaviorism." The paper tries to show that biological
behaviorism and the notion of "felt transition" are not
incompatible but support each other.

10   BUCHLER, JUSTUS. "The Philosopher, the Common Man and William
James," The American Scholar, XI (October), 416-426.
Few philosophers have found the common man as intelligible or have been so well understood by him as James. He
expresses every man's "bewilderment in a stubborn universe."
James's relations to America have been too much regarded
in a biographical way, and not enough in a philosophical.

11 BUCKHAM, JOHN WRIGHT. "William James, 1842-1942," The
    Personalist, XXIII (Spring), 130-149.
        The central notion in James is "experience." The per-
    ceptual realm is the world we have in common, filled with
    novelty, and the realm of action. James's philosophy
    fails in "making men and women seem sufficiently worth
    while."

12 CAMERON, NORMAN. "William James and Psychoanalysis" in
    William James: The Man and the Thinker (1942).
        American abnormal psychology due to Freud has moved
    away from James. A "hidden world" has been invented and
    replaces the real one.

13 DEWEY, JOHN. "William James and the World Today" in William
    James: The Man and the Thinker (1942).
        Democracy, the counterpart of pluralism, has not yet
    discovered how to fill in the "empty spaces" between indi-
    viduals. James and others have done little to point out
    "concrete intermediaries," but James indicates how this
    is to be done.

14 _____. "William James as Empiricist" in In Commemoration of
    William James (1942).
        The Principles of Psychology transformed empiricism.
    James had scientific resources not available to earlier
    empiricists. The will to believe is not concerned with
    the truth of scientific statements but rather with the
    "momentousness" of philosophical principles.

15 EDMAN, IRWIN. "William James: 1842-1942," The Nation, CLIV
    (January 17), 67-68.
        James was a poet who "restored men to the innocencies of
    their more immediate experience." He lacked a social
    philosophy, but was an acute "social critic."

16 EWER, BERNARD C. "The Influence of William James upon Psy-
    chology," The Personalist, XXIII (Spring), 150-158.
        James did not so much influence specific doctrines, as
    "the general direction and force" of American psychology.

17 FLEWELLING, RALPH TYLER. "James, Schiller and Personalism,"
    The Personalist, XXIII (Spring), 172-181.
        Letters from F. C. S. Schiller to an unidentified
    correspondent containing numerous references to James.
    Pragmatism was personalistic, and later turned towards
    materialism.

1942

18   HILL, WALKER H. "The Founder of Pragmatism" in <u>In Commemora-</u>
      <u>tion of William James</u> (1942).
              Peirce did not found pragmatism. Pragmatism begins with
      James's "Remarks on Spencer's Definition of Mind as Corre-
      spondence" (1878).

19   HOLT, EDWIN B. "William James as Psychologist" in <u>In Commemo-</u>
      <u>ration of William James</u> (1942).
              In <u>The Principles of Psychology</u> while James abandoned
      the notion of a soul, he retained dualism under the head-
      ing of "consciousness." In his radical empiricism, the
      dualism was reduced further but still survived in the
      notion of experience. The elimination of dualism yields
      materialism. James did not take this step. The dualism
      was eliminated by later psychology, particularly by
      "radically <u>motor</u> psychology."

20   JAMES, HENRY. "Remarks on the Occasion of the Centenary of
      William James" in <u>In Commemoration of William James</u> (1942).
              James's son explains the continuing vitality of James's
      thought.

21   KALLEN, HORACE M. Foreword to <u>In Commemoration of William</u>
      <u>James</u> (1942).
              Bronislaw Malinowski died before he could prepare his
      paper on "The Moral Equivalent of War" for publication.

22   _____. "Remembering William James" in <u>In Commemoration of</u>
      <u>William James</u> (1942).
              For James, philosophy is the ability to envisage alter-
      natives. If you examine any of the political totalitar-
      ianisms, you will find philosophical absolutism.

23   KANTOR, JACOB R. "Jamesian Psychology and the Stream of
      Psychological Thought" in <u>In Commemoration of William</u>
      <u>James</u> (1942).
              James tried to make psychology a natural science by
      correlating mental with physiological states. He remained
      a dualist and failed to turn psychology into a science.
      He did take important preliminary steps.

24   LOWE, VICTOR. "William James's Pluralistic Metaphysics of
      Experience" in <u>In Commemoration of William James</u> (1942).
              James's is a pluralistic metaphysics of experience. His
      views culminated in a pluralism which insisted both upon
      the independence and the "power to fuse" of separate
      centers of experience.

25   LYMAN, EUGENE W. "William James, Philosopher of Faith," The
      Journal of Religion, XXII (July), 233-250. Reprinted in
      In Commemoration of William James (1942).
          For James, faith must be congenial to our knowing and
      our active powers. This "focus" can be understood
      biographically.

26   McCORMICK, JOHN F. "The Pragmatism of William James," The
      Modern Schoolman, XX (November), 18-26.
          James himself never developed a whole philosophy and our
      efforts to view him as a whole are bound to be tentative,
      especially, since James accepted pluralism. McCormick
      examines James's theories of truth, meaning, and radical
      empiricism.

27   METZGER, ARNOLD. "William James and the Crisis of Philosophy"
      in In Commemoration of William James (1942).
          Hume's contention that we know no eternal order in
      things brought about a crisis in philosophy. James's skep-
      ticism in this respect is more radical than Hume's.
      James's insistence upon the primacy of the practical rea-
      son offers a resolution.

28   MILLER, DICKINSON S. "James's Doctrine of 'The Right to
      Believe'," The Philosophical Review, LI (November),
      541-558.
          A criticism of "The Will to Believe" by one of James's
      students who very much wished to be a disciple. James
      confuses the "probability" with the value of a belief;
      does not distinguish between faith and hypothesis, between
      belief and will. He confuses formal reason with reason
      in general.

29   _____. "William James, Man and Philosopher" in William James:
      The Man and the Thinker (1942).
          Contains reminiscences. James tried to find signifi-
      cance in every contribution. His new method for philoso-
      phy was that of "Social Co-operation in thought," a method
      akin to the experimental.

30   MORRIS, CHARLES. "William James Today" in In Commemoration of
      William James (1942).
          Because of emphasis on the social and behavioral, we
      tend to ignore views marked by individualism and based on
      introspection. James's central problem remains important.
      He tried to interpret science so that it would not weaken
      the "dynamic impulses" of men. The technical problem is
      that of the cognitive status of moral and religious
      utterances.

1942

31 MUELDER, WALTER G. "William James and the Problems of Religious Empiricism," The Personalist, XXIII (Spring),
159-171.
James gave theology greater freedom by making it independent of idealism. In making room for faith, he opened
the way for "credulous irrationalism."

32 NAGEL, ERNEST. "William James, 1842-1910," The Scientific
Monthly, LV (October), 379-381.
James's "voluntaristic naturalism," "empiricism," and
distrust of claims to finality have become a part of
everyone's thought. In spite of his acceptance of theism,
he stimulated the development of a "biological naturalism."

33 OTTO, MAX C. "The Distinctive Philosophy of William James" in
William James: The Man and the Thinker (1942).
For James, the true world view would express the combined
experiences of all experiencers. He believed that imagination and feeling also lead to truth. He tended to be un-
aware of economic factors.

34 PERRY, RALPH BARTON. "If William James Were Alive Today" in
In Commemoration of William James (1942).
James would be an opponent of the totalitarian state.
Bigness and absolutes violated his individualism.

35 SCHNEIDER, HERBERT W. "William James as a Moralist" in In
Commemoration of William James (1942). Abstract in The
Journal of Philosophy, XXXVIII (December 4, 1941), 674-675.
James's early decision to become a pure scientist led
to a crisis when he realized that he needed a theory of
action. The crisis was overcome by James's "free and
spontaneous" temperament. The sources of James's moral
philosophy were Goethe's emphasis on individuals, Darwin's
spontaneous variations, French and German Neo-Kantians, and
his colleagues Peirce and Royce. Peirce freed him from
the empiricism of Chauncey Wright.

36 SPOERL, HOWARD DAVIS. "Abnormal and Social Psychology in the
Life and Work of William James," The Journal of Abnormal
and Social Psychology, XXXVII (January), 3-19.
James's contributions to social and abnormal psychology
were restricted by his "devotion" to individuality which
may well have arisen out of his relations with his brother,
Henry James, and his father.

37 WIGGINS, FORREST ORAN. "William James and John Dewey," The
Personalist, XXIII (Spring), 182-198.

James is imbued with the science of the middle 19th century which saw the world in terms of atoms indifferent to human needs. A place for these needs had to be found in the inner world. Dewey was formed by late 19th century biology which found no break between man and nature.

38 WILLIAMS, DONALD CARY. "William James and the Facts of Knowledge" in In Commemoration of William James (1942). Abstract in The Journal of Philosophy, XXXVIII (December 4, 1941), 673-674.
James seems very distant. Few philosophers have been more immersed in their own times. James lived in a comfortable world, not in "our present fantastic universe." His "great moral passion" was to save young men from drink. Yet, somehow he can still reach us. In his philosophy, James hesitated between a panpsychist representationism and a neutral objectivism.

1943 A BOOKS

1 NASSAUER, KURT. Die Rechtsphilosophie William James'. Bern: Gustav Grunau & Cie.
Studies the significance of James's thought for social philosophy. Benjamin Franklin and Emerson are discussed as predecessors of James. Nassauer looks for the sources of James's thought in family influences, British psychology, and Renouvier.

1943 B SHORTER WRITINGS

1 ALLPORT, GORDON W. "The Productive Paradoxes of William James," The Psychological Review, L (January), 95-120. Reprinted in The Person in Psychology. (Boston: Beacon Press, 1968).
Six puzzles face every psychologist. James struggled with all six and in each case offered several inconsistent solutions. The resolution of the paradoxes should be sought in James's pragmatism and pluralism.

2 AMES, EDWARD SCRIBNER. "William James Still Lives," The Christian Century, LX (February), 134.
A review of William James: The Man and the Thinker (1942) and In Commemoration of William James (1942).

3 ANGELL, JAMES R. "Toastmaster's Speech," The Psychological Review, L (January), 83-86.
Angell would have introduced the speakers at the meeting of the American Psychological Association commemorating the hundreth anniversary of James's birth, but because of the war the meeting was not held.

1943

4 ANGIER, ROSWELL P. "Another Student's Impressions of James at the Turn of the Century," The Psychological Review, L (January), 132-134.
An account of James's class-room manner. On pp. 136-139, facsimile copies of portions of two letters by James to Carl Stumpf and Münsterberg are published.

5 ANON. "Native Philosopher," Fortune, XXVII (March), 114-115.
One of a series of "Notes on Americans Whose Careers are Relevant Today." James insisted that things be judged by their fruits, deciding the question as to which are "rotten" and which "ripe" by the "principles of inclusiveness," "by taking thought of the other person's point of view."

6 BARZUN, JACQUES. "William James As Artist," The New Republic, CVIII (February 15), 218-220.
James's view that each man carves out a portion of experience in accordance with his temperament needs but slight modification to become the "creed of the artist." James showed that life is a "work of art."

7 BENTLEY, ARTHUR F. "The Jamesian Datum," Journal of Psychology, XVI (July), 35-79. Reprinted in Arthur F. Bentley, Inquiry into Inquiries, edited by Sidney Ratner (Boston: The Beacon Press, 1954).
The celebrators of James's centenary ignore the central point of his thought. Bentley lists ten writers, most of whom have misinterpreted James. For Bentley, crucial in James is his discovery of the "datum," or of neutral experience.

8 _____. "Truth, Reality, and Behavioral Fact," The Journal of Philosophy, XL (April 1), 169-187.
James's great discovery was that of the datum, called "pure," "neutral," "immediate," or "concrete" experience. This is not a metaphysical guess at the "world-stuff," but simply means "concrete fact."

9 DELABARRE, EDMUND B. "A Student's Impressions of James in the Late '80's," The Psychological Review, L (January) 125-127.
James freely admitted his "uncertainties and doubts." He disliked laboratory work.

10 EDMAN, IRWIN. "For a New World," The New Republic, CVIII (February 15), 224-228.
Excerpts from a lecture given at the National University of Mexico and published in Filosofia y Lettras in Mexico City. James tried to keep hold of the "immediately given." His thought expresses the better side of Americanism. He

had faith in the "common man" and a sense of being in a
new world with "new hope."

11 GURWITSCH, ARON. "William James' Theory of the 'Transitive
    Parts' of the Stream of Consciousness," Philosophy and
    Phenomenological Research, III (June), 449-477. Reprinted
    in Studies in Phenomenology and Psychology (Evanston, Ill.:
    Northwestern University Press, 1966).
        James's stream of consciousness was to solve problems of
    the "immediately experienced continuity of consciousness."
    Gurwitsch examines this to elucidate problems of interest
    to contemporary phenomenology.

12 KAZIN, ALFRED. "'Our Passion is our Task'," The New Republic,
    CVIII (February 15), 215-218.
        Surveys the relations between James and his brother,
    Henry James. There was neither "envy nor indifference,"
    but "fraternity" which, however, brought "little mutual
    understanding."

13 LARRABEE, HAROLD A. Review of In Commemoration of William
    James (1942); William James: The Man and the Thinker
    (1942); William James: His Marginalia, Personality and
    Contribution (1942); As William James Said (1942), The
    Journal of Philosophy, XL (November 25), 657-667.
        James's "influence" has passed through two stages and is
    now beginning a third. Up to World War I, James was pri-
    marily a spokesman for his own age. Then, his reputation
    suffered an eclipse, because of the emphasis on "objective
    and behavioristic studies." The fate of the current re-
    vival depends upon the fate of romantic individualism.

14 MILLER, DICKINSON S. Comment on J. S. Moore (1943), The
    Philosophical Review, LII (January), 70.
        In disbelief, the matter is dropped, but in suspension
    of judgement, the investigation is continued. Pragmatism
    added to but did not alter James's earlier doctrines.

15 MOORE, JARED S. "James's Doctrine of 'The Right to Believe',"
    The Philosophical Review, LII (January), 69-70.
        A criticism of Miller's "James's Doctrine of the 'Right
    to Believe'" (1942). The "right" to believe is only one
    of four claims James makes in "The Will to Believe." He
    also insists on the "duty" to believe, the "necessity of
    choice," and the "superior value of belief over disbelief."
    The third is the critical point. Pragmatism denies that
    the intellect has any authority and for this merits severe
    criticism.

1943

16 OTTO, MAX C. "On A Certain Blindness in William James,"
    Ethics, LIII (April), 184-191.
        James ignored economic conditions in the formation of
    character because for him social life was secondary,
    "ministerial," and not "fundamental."

17 PERRY, RALPH BARTON. "James the Psychologist -- As a Philoso-
    pher Sees Him," The Psychological Review, L (January),
    122-124.
        The problems of James's psychology center around the
    dualism of knowledge and being. James never lost sight
    of the "total man" and refused to reduce the higher to the
    lower. He rejected the subjection of facts to technique;
    if the technique did not work, he discarded it and kept
    the facts.

18 PILLSBURY, W. B. "Titchener and James," The Psychological
    Review, L (January), 71-73.
        E. B. Titchener's students usually thought that Titchener
    did not think highly of James. There seems to have been a
    general feeling that James did not belong to the "true
    experimental tradition."

19 STARBUCK, EDWIN D. "A Student's Impressions of James in the
    Middle '90's," The Psychological Review, L (January),
    128-131.
        While a member of James's class, Starbuck developed a
    questionnaire on religion, material from which was used
    in Varieties.

20 THORNDIKE, EDWARD L. "James' Influence on the Psychology of
    Perception and Thought," The Psychological Review, L
    (January), 87-94.
        James influenced psychology through The Principles of
    Psychology rather than teaching. His most important dis-
    covery was the discovery of the "fringes" of mental states.
    Thorndike compares James's work with that of his contem-
    poraries. He had a great influence on education.

21 VIVAS, ELISEO. "Henry and William (Two Notes)," The Kenyon
    Review, V, 580-594.
        Temperamentally, the two brothers were quite different.
    They were alike in the way they conceived the process
    whereby mind enters into relations with the world.

1944 A BOOKS - NONE

1944 B SHORTER WRITINGS

1   HERMAN, THELMA. "Pragmatism: A Study in Middle Class Ideol-
    ogy," Social Forces, XXII (May), 405-410.
        Pragmatism is optimistic about human nature, insists
    that logic and morality are only "adjustments" to expe-
    rience, and emphasizes the interdependence of means and
    ends. This reflects experiences of the American middle
    class.

2   HOFSTADTER, RICHARD. Social Darwinism in American Thought.
    Philadelphia: University of Pennsylvania Press.
        James's thought is partly a reaction against Herbert
    Spencer whose evolutionism led him to expect "automatic
    progress." James insisted that human effort was needed.

1945 A BOOKS - NONE

1945 B SHORTER WRITINGS

1   READ, HERBERT. "The Significance of William James" in A Coat
    of Many Colours. London: Routledge & Kegan Paul.
        Mussolini's use and Lenin's rejection of James both were
    probably based on misunderstanding. James has been for-
    gotten, but he was important in the transition from abso-
    lutism and scientific dogmatism to "relativity," "the
    analytical method in psychology," and "empirical study
    of religion."

1946 A BOOKS - NONE

1946 B SHORTER WRITINGS

1   DEWEY, JOHN and KILPATRICK, WILLIAM H. Introduction to Talks
    to Teachers. New York: Henry Holt.
        This edition omits the talks to students. James strips
    psychological principles of everything not required by the
    teacher. There are, however, some "backward" looking ele-
    ments, James's acceptance of the fact that schools will be
    dull at times, that teachers have to force students to
    learn.

2   MAES, ANDRÉ. "La Notion de vérité chez W. James," Revue
    Philosophique de Louvain, XLIV (August), 416-428.
        A criticism of the thesis of E. Leroux (1922) that in
    the genuine pragmatic conception of truth there is no room
    for sentiment.

1946

3   MILLER, DICKINSON S. "William James" in Great Teachers: Por-
    trayed by those Who Studied Under Them. New Brunswick:
    Rutgers University Press.
        Reminiscences of James's classroom manner in around 1890
    when Miller studied under James.

4   SCHNEIDER, HERBERT W. A History of American Philosophy. New
    York: Columbia University Press.
        The development of major aspects of James's thought is
    viewed in relation to his critics and allies. James devel-
    oped two psychologies, a "phenomenology of the emotional
    life" and a "biology of intelligence." The first edition
    lists writings about James; a list of recent publications
    was substituted in the second edition (1963).

5   WIENER, PHILIP P. "Peirce's Metaphysical Club and the Genesis
    of Pragmatism," Journal of the History of Ideas, VII
    (April), 218-233.
        A revised version is included in Evolution and the
    Founders of Pragmatism (1949).

1947 A BOOKS - NONE

1947 B SHORTER WRITINGS

1   CATER, HAROLD DEAN, ed. Henry Adams and His Friends: A Collection
    of His Unpublished Letters. Boston: Houghton, Mifflin.
        Includes several letters to James.

2   LEVINSON, RONALD B. "A Note on One of James's Favorite Meta-
    phors," Journal of the History of Ideas, VIII (April),
    237-239.
        Surveys James's use of the phrase "salto morale." In
    his earlier writings, James saw knowledge as a leap, while
    later, he emphasized continuity.

3   _____. "Sigwart's Logik and William James," Journal of the
    History of Ideas, VIII (October), 475-483.
        Christoph Sigwart's Logik (1872-1879) offered to James
    a "voluntaristic idealism" within which James's own prag-
    matism could be formed. The paper is in part based on
    James's annotated set of the two volumes of the Logik sold
    at a sale of James's books in 1922.

4   MORRIS, LLOYD. Postscript to Yesterday; America: The Last
    Fifty Years. New York: Random House.
        With Pragmatism, James became a spokesman for American
    ideas. For him life is an "experiment."

5   RAHV, PHILIP, ed. Discovery of Europe. Boston: Houghton,
        Mifflin.
        Four letters by James, taken from Letters (1920), are
        included in a collection of documents by travelers in
        Europe.

6   RUGG, HAROLD. Foundations for American Education. Yonkers-on-
        Hudson: World Book Co.
        The Principles of Psychology became the basis of progres-
        sive education in America. James recognized the importance
        of "body-response."

1948 A BOOKS

1   PERRY, RALPH BARTON. The Thought and Character of William
        James: Briefer Version. Cambridge, Mass.: Harvard
        University Press.
        An abridgment of Thought and Character (1935), with some
        additional material.

1948 B SHORTER WRITINGS

1   BROWN, ROLLO WALTER. Harvard Yard in the Golden Age. New
        York: Current Books.
        James was one of the great minds, willing to examine
        everything.

2   CASTELL, ALBUREY. "The Humanism of William James," Introduc-
        tion to Essays in Pragmatism, edited by A. Castell. New
        York: Hafner.
        James was on the side of humanity and against the
        "prophets of death." Any adequate philosophy must satisfy
        both theoretical and practical needs.

3   DEWEY, JOHN. "William James' Morals and Julien Benda's,"
        Commentary, V (January), 46-50.
        Defends James against charges that his pragmatism is
        opportunism leveled by Benda, "The Attack on Western
        Morality," Commentary, IV (November 1947), 416-422.

4   LAZAREFF, ADOLPHE. Vie et connaissance. Paris: J. Vrin.
        Translated from the Russian.
        Two essays are devoted to James, "Le Destin philosophique
        de William James" and "Le Pragmatisme." James was an anti-
        rationalist, but the enemy was within him. Pragmatism is
        to be understood as a way of dealing with religious ques-
        tions rather than as a method.

1948

5   MATTHIESSEN, F. O. The James Family: Including Selections from
    the Writings of Henry James, Senior, William, Henry, &
    Alice James. New York: Alfred A. Knopf.
        Consists primarily of quotations, with brief biographical
    introductions. There is a postscript comparing the charac-
    ters of James and his brother.

6   MAYHALL, JANE. "William James and the Modern Mood," The
    Antioch Review, VIII (September), 291-305.
        James gave us as "practicable a philosophy of the human
    predicament as one can have." He gave us the two centers
    of "will and belief."

7   PERRY, RALPH BARTON. Introduction to Psychology. Cleveland:
    World Publishing Co.
        James was one of the first to extend scientific methods
    to the study of the mind. He did not sharply distinguish
    philosophy from psychology.

1949 A BOOKS - NONE

1949 B SHORTER WRITINGS

1   HARPER, ROBERT S. "The Laboratory of William James," Harvard
    Alumni Bulletin, LII (November 5), 169-173.
        James began laboratory instruction in psychology at
    Harvard as early as 1875. Summarizes the history of psy-
    chology at Harvard during the James years.

2   LEITHAUSER, JOACHIM G. "William James und der Barwert der
    Philosophie," Der Monat, vol. I, no. 11 (August), 26-33.
        To understand his thought, one should understand how
    through an act of the will James overcame his crisis.

3   LOWE, VICTOR. "The Influence of Bergson, James and Alexander
    on Whitehead," Journal of the History of Ideas, X (April),
    267-296.
        James had little influence on Whitehead, although
    Whitehead read James with "appreciation and sympathy."

4   MURPHY, GARDNER. "William James and Psychical Research," The
    Journal of the American Society for Psychical Research,
    XLIII (July), 85-93. Incorporated into the Introduction
    to William James on Psychical Research (1960).
        James's interest in psychical research flows naturally
    out of his life and philosophical convictions.

5   PERRY, RALPH BARTON. "The Influence of a First-Hand Mind,"
     The New Republic, CXXI (October 17), 11-14.
          Primarily on Dewey. James's ancestry is to be traced to
     the British empiricists, while Dewey's, to Kant. For
     James, discursive thought is preliminary to intuition,
     for Dewey, thought is "the very life of knowledge." Thus,
     in James we find "experientialism," in Dewey,
     "operationalism."

6   _____. "William James and American Individualism" in
     Characteristically American. New York: Alfred A. Knopf.
          Both in his thought and in his life, James was a perfect
     expression of American individualism.

7   WERKMEISTER, W. H. A History of Philosophical Ideas in Amer-
     ica. New York: The Ronald Press Co.
          A survey of major points in James's thought. James
     expresses the spirit of his age.

8   WIENER, PHILIP P. Evolution and the Founders of Pragmatism.
     Cambridge, Mass.: Harvard University Press.
          James's thought is dominated by the desire to discover
     empirically the limits of science and make room for faith
     in the human individual. Thus, he was attracted to Darwin's
     notion of spontaneous variation since that suggests an
     indeterminate universe. But in opposition to Darwin, he
     tended to hold that these variations survive even when
     they have no survival value.

1950 A BOOKS

1   KNIGHT, MARGARET. William James: A Selection From His Writ-
     ings on Psychology. Harmondsworth, England: Penguin
     Books.
          Excerpts from The Principles of Psychology and Psychology,
     with a biographical introduction by Knight.

2   MORRIS, LLOYD. William James: The Message of a Modern Mind.
     New York: Charles Scribner's Sons.
          A general, popular survey of the major aspects of James's
     thought. James's philosophy provided the framework for
     the New Deal and the philosophy of law of Oliver Wendell
     Holmes, Jr.

1950

1950 B SHORTER WRITINGS

1   BLANSHARD, BRAND. "The Great Pragmatist," The Saturday Review
    of Literature, XXXIII (November), 11.
        Review of Lloyd Morris, William James: The Message of a
    Modern Mind (1950). Blanshard traces James's pragmatism
    to James's view that philosophers neither could nor should
    keep their personalities out of philosophy.

2   CAPEK, MILIC. "Stream of Consciousness and 'Durée Réelle,'"
    Philosophy and Phenomenological Research, X (March),
    331-353.
        James and Bergson, working independently, turned philos-
    ophers towards temporality. James's stream of conscious-
    ness is a more empirical, psychological conception, while
    Bergson's "durée réelle" is more the product of metaphysical
    analysis.

3   COMMAGER, HENRY STEELE. The American Mind: An Interpretation
    of American Thought and Character Since the 1880's. New
    Haven: Yale University Press.
        James's pragmatism is a philosophy of "expedience." It
    is democratic, optimistic, and adventurous, and in this
    way expressive of American character.

4   HARLOW, VIRGINIA. Thomas Sergeant Perry: A Biography.
    Durham, N. C.: Duke University Press.
        Includes letters from James to Perry.

5   HARPER, ROBERT S. "The First Psychological Laboratory,"
    Isis, XLI (July), 158-161.
        Compares the development of the Harvard laboratory with
    others.

6   McCREARY, JOHN K. "William James and Modern Value Problems,"
    The Personalist, XXXI (Spring), 126-134.
        For James, pluralism offered action and risk, monism,
    peace and security. This conflict exists today, but we
    need not adopt James's solution of taking an "aggressive
    attitude towards life." A "naturalistic monism" is a
    possible alternative.

7   PERSONS, STOW, ed. Evolutionary Thought in America.
    New Haven: Yale University Press.
        No extended discussion of James, but many references.

8   ROSENSTOCK-HÜSSY, EUGEN. "William James: Der Philosoph des
    amerikanischen Lebens," Thema. Zeitschrift für die
    Einheit der Kultur, no. 8, pp. 3-5.

Men should abandon narrow nationalism and live in the spirit of freedom and hope, in the spirit of James.

1951 A BOOKS

1 JOST, JOSEF. Die James-Langesche Gefühlstheorie und ihre Auswirkungen: unter besonderer Berücksichtigung der "Principles" von James. Zürich: Kommerzdruck und Verlags AG.

   The theory of emotion has its roots in the psychology of Hermann Lotze and Wilhelm Wundt's theory of emotion. Jost treats Lotze and Wundt, and then separately presents the views of James and Lange. Their theory of emotion needs correction particularly in the light of recent phenomenology.

1951 B SHORTER WRITINGS

1 CHARLTON, D. G. "An Unpublished Letter of William James," The Philosophical Quarterly (St. Andrews), I (October), 439-443.

   Letter to Joseph Milsand, February 5, 1885.

2 COPE, JACKSON I. "William James's Correspondence with Daniel Coit Gilman, 1877-1881," Journal of the History of Ideas, XII (October), 609-627.

   James's letters to and from Gilman. James, as part of his effort to move away from physiology, was trying to obtain a position at Johns Hopkins, of which Gilman was president. Includes letters of recommendation written in support of James's application and notes about James's lecturing at Johns Hopkins.

3 HENLE, PAUL. Introduction to selections from W. James in Classic American Philosophers. Edited by Max H. Fisch. New York: Appleton-Century-Crofts.

   The center of James's thought is his theory of meaning. A statement is meaningful if it or belief in it has experiential consequences. James's religious philosophy has few followers, but his theory of meaning and radical empiricism remain important.

4 Schmid, Karl Anton. "William James und der Glaube," Neues Abendland, VI, 182-183.

   A notice of Essays über Glaube und Ethik, translated by W. Flottmann (Gütersloh: Bertelsmann, 1948). The essays give insight into a characteristic American point of view, the defense of faith.

1951

5   SMITH, CARLETON SPRAGUE. "William James in Brazil" in Four
     Papers Presented in the Institute for Brazilian Studies,
     Vanderbilt University. Nashville, Tenn.: Vanderbilt
     University Press.
          An account of James's travels with the Thayer expedition.
     Contains excerpts from his diary and letters and reproduces
     some of James's sketches.

1952 A BOOKS - NONE

1952 B SHORTER WRITINGS

1   BLAU, JOSEPH L. Men and Movements in American Philosophy.
     Englewood Cliffs, N. J.: Prentice-Hall.
          James identifies the true with the useful. His view is
     "practicalism."

2   BRODBECK, MAY. "Philosophy in America, 1900-1950" in American
     Non-Fiction 1900-1950. Chicago: Henry Regnery.
          In James's work, poet and philosopher struggle. Decisive
     was James's belief in free will. Pragmatism is a generali-
     zation of the right to believe.

3   DAVIDSON, ROBERT F. Philosophies Men Live By. New York: The
     Dryden Press.
          James brought philosophy down from its "ivory tower."
     He confused the truth of an idea with our knowledge of
     that truth.

4   FEN, SING-NAN. "Has James Answered Hume?" The Journal of
     Philosophy, XLIX (February 28), 159-167.
          Relations are real. There can be "a knowledge of
     acquaintance as well as a knowledge about" relations. This
     solves Hume's difficulty and shows how we can dispense with
     Kant's apparatus.

5   HORTON, ROD W. and EDWARDS, HERBERT W. Backgrounds of American
     Literary Thought. New York: Appleton-Century-Crofts.
          James holds that to have free will we need only believe
     in it. To a people who had subdued a continent, this
     would appear to be "only the plainest common sense."

6   ROBACK, A. A. History of American Psychology. New York:
     Library Publishers.
          James had the Midas touch, what he touched turned into
     "psychic gold." He contributed few new ideas, but few
     psychologists have understood the issues as well.

132

7   SHOUSE, J. B. "David Hume and William James: A Comparison,"
    Journal of the History of Ideas, XIII (October), 514-527.
        While Hume is a skeptic, skepticism is not all-important
    to him. It is not important for "actual living" and here
    we need belief. In this regard, he is much like James.

8   SMITH, JAMES WARD. "Pragmatism, Realism and Positivism in the
    United States," Mind, NS LXI (April), 190-208.
        While the intent is systematic, the views of James,
    Peirce, and Dewey on truth and meaning are discussed.

9   WEIGAND, PAUL. "Psychological Types in Friedrich Schiller and
    William James," Journal of the History of Ideas, XIII
    (June), 376-383.
        James's tough-minded and tender-minded resemble the
    psychological types given in Schiller's Über naive und
    sentimentalische Dichtung (1795-96). James had read
    Schiller, but there is no evidence that he ever read this
    work.

1953 A BOOKS - NONE

1953 B SHORTER WRITINGS

1   BOISEN, ANTON T. "The Present Status of William James's
    Psychology of Religion," The Journal of Pastoral Care,
    VII (Fall), 155-157.
        While interest in psychology of religion is undergoing
    a recession, James's role as a pioneer is just beginning
    to be recognized.

2   BURGELIN, PIERRE. "L'Expérience religieuse comme problème,"
    Études Théologiques et Religieuses, vol. XXVIII, no. 2,
    pp. 85-109.
        James's approach is not objective but is guided by his
    own presuppositions. This becomes especially clear when
    we consider that James does not mention sacrifice, the
    feeling of otherness, and other elements essential to
    religion.

3   CAPEK, MILIC. "The Reappearance of the Self in the Last
    Philosophy of William James," The Philosophical Review,
    LXII (October), 526-544.
        James both denies the self and insists that "personal
    activity" is a "genuine and irreducible fact." These
    views were reconciled only in A Pluralistic Universe, by
    the doctrine of the "reality of subconsciousness."

1953

4   DUNHAM, BARROWS. Giant in Chains. Boston: Little, Brown and Co.
    James is the most "adorable" of philosophers. His theory of truth, stated in terms drawn from a commercial culture, was that truth satisfied some immediate need.

5   EDEL, LEON. Henry James: The Untried Years (1843-1870). Philadelphia: J. B. Lippincott. Other volumes, all published by Lippincott: Henry James: The Conquest of London (1870-1881) (1962), Henry James: The Middle Years (1882-1895) (1962), Henry James: The Treacherous Years (1895-1901) (1969), Henry James: The Master (1901-1916) (1972).
    Edel holds that the two brothers were rivals, with Henry James, as the younger, seeking James's approval, but often being rejected. William did not allow Henry to play with him, he critized Henry's novels and Henry's decision to buy a house in England.

6   GALLUP, DONALD C., ed. The Flowers of Friendship: Letters Written to Gertrude Stein. New York: Alfred A. Knopf.
    Contains letters from James.

7   ISHAM, CHAPMAN. "William James and The Ego Problem," American Journal of Psychotherapy, VII, 217-224.
    Discusses James's notion of the self with frequent references to Freud.

8   JOHNSON, PAUL E. "William James: Psychologist of Religion," The Journal of Pastoral Care, VII (Fall), 137-141.
    James sought to resolve the "contest" between "naturalistic determinism and supernatural mysticism."

9   KNIGHT, MARGARET. "The Permanent Contribution of William James to Psychology," British Journal of Educational Psychology, XXIII, 77-86.
    James made a non-professional audience aware of psychology. He emphasized the relations between psychology and physiology, pioneered in experimentation, rejected associationism, and stressed applied psychology.

10 LE CLAIR, ROBERT C. "William James to Theodore Flournoy of Geneva: Some Unpublished Letters," The New England Quarterly, XXVI (December), 512-532.
    These letters are included in Le Clair (1966).

11 MILLER, SAMUEL H. "The Influence of William James From the Viewpoint of a Parish Minister," The Journal of Pastoral Care, VII (Fall), 142-147.

James's conception of truth plays into the hands of
practical men. America followed him and lost "transcen-
dental values."

12 OVERHOLSER, WINFRED. "A Psychiatrist's Comments on the Impor-
tance of William James," The Journal of Pastoral Care,
VII (Fall), 153-154.
Varieties is one of the most important books.

13 POLLOCK, ROBERT C. "James: Pragmatism" in The Great Books:
A Christian Appraisal. vol. IV. Edited by Harold C.
Gardiner. New York: Devin-Adair.
James's thought originates in the "ripening of age-old
tendencies" towards subjectivity. It was a protest
against deductive procedures in favor of an empirical view
of knowledge. He understood experience in a much wider
sense than others and insisted on the noetic importance of
the affective side of human nature.

.14 RUYSSEN, THEODORE "Le Rôle de la conscience subliminale dans
la psychologie religieuse de William James," Études
Théologiques et Religieuses, vol. XXVIII, no. 2,
pp. 110-136.
Studies the role of the subliminal consciousness in
James's conception of conversion and of the religious life
generally. Emphasis is placed on James's life, especially
upon his crisis.

15 SANTAYANA, GEORGE. "Three American Philosophers," The American
Scholar, XXII (Summer); 281-284.
James was inclined towards British empiricism but also
had inherited a mystical strain.

16 SPERRY, WILLARD L. "The Importance of William James," The
Journal of Pastoral Care, VII (Fall), 148-152.
In Varieties, James attempted to interpret psychologically the human side of religion, the relations between
men and God.

17 STAFFORD, WILLIAM T. "Emerson and the James Family," American
Literature, XXIV (January), 433-461.
Views on Emerson expressed by three Jameses: Henry
James, Sr., Henry James, the novelist, and James.

1954 A BOOKS - NONE

1954

1954 B SHORTER WRITINGS

1   CAPEK, MILIC. "James's Early Criticism of the Automaton
        Theory," Journal of the History of Ideas, XV (April),
        260-279.
            Around 1880, James began to oppose the mechanistic view
        of mind because it is impossible to explain purposeful
        adjustment in mechanical terms. James came to view con-
        sciousness as a free power of selection. There is an ex-
        tended footnote comparing James's views with those of
        Peirce.

2   COHEN, MORRIS RAPHAEL. American Thought: A Critical Sketch.
        Glencoe, Ill.: The Free Press.
            While James was familiar with philosophy as technique,
        he was primarily interested in philosophy as vision.

3   COTTON, JAMES HARRY. Royce on the Human Self. Cambridge,
        Mass.: Harvard University Press.
            There is not much difference between James and Peirce.
        Peirce coined 'pragmaticism' not in response to James, but
        to the literary use of 'pragmatism.' Cotton also examines
        Royce's criticism of James on the question of truth.

4   DAVIS, ELISABETH LOGAN. Mothers of America: The Lasting
        Influence of the Christian Home. Westwood, N. J.:
        F. H. Revell.
            "Mary James, Mother of Thinkers," sketches James's
        mother.

5   DELEDALLE, GÉRARD. Histoire de la philosophie américaine.
        Paris: Presses Universitaires de France.
            James is a theoretician of experimentation and a realist.
        Realism is apparent in his earlier writings. It is most
        prominent in "Does 'Consciousness' Exist?" (1904).

6   LOVETT, SIDNEY. "A Boy's Recollections of William James," The
        Yale Review, XLIII (June), 525-533.
            Recollections by a friend of Francis Alexander Robertson
        James, James's son. Lovett met "Alec's 'Uncle Henry'" who
        was wearing a "decidedly loud waistcoat," had a boil lanced
        by James, and heard from Alec his father's "earthy" stories.

7   LUKACS, GEORG. Die Zerstörung der Vernunft. Berlin:
        Aufbau-Verlag.
            In the preface, a number of pages are given to James's
        pragmatism. James is an extreme irrationalist. He gives
        no objective refutation of materialism, but simply claims
        that it is not as useful as belief in God.

8   MADDEN, EDWARD H.   "Wright, James, and Radical Empiricism,"
     The Journal of Philosophy, LI (December 23), 868-874.
        Little attention has been paid to Chauncey Wright as a
     source for James's notion of pure experience. Wright held
     that phenomena are originally neutral, neither physical
     nor mental.

9   WELLS, HARRY K. Pragmatism: Philosophy of Imperialism.
     New York: International Publishers, ©1954. .
        Criticizes pragmatism from a Marxist point of view.
     James's The Principles of Psychology are the foundation
     of the pragmatist "theory of knowledge." Bourgeois ideolo-
     gists conceal its contents so as not to "give the show
     away." James's psychology leads to solipsism and to
     "believing what one wills to believe."

1955 A BOOKS - NONE

1955 B SHORTER WRITINGS

1   CORY, DANIEL, ed. The Letters of George Santayana. New York:
     Charles Scribner's Sons.
        Contains some letters to James.

2   DELEDALLE, GÉRARD. "William James et son père: essai de
     caractérologie philosophique," Les Études Philosophiques,
     NS X (October-December), 634-646.
        James's character is emotive, not active, with non-
     persistent impressions, in the sense given these terms
     by characterology. The philosophies of father and son are
     linked by similarities in the characters of their authors.

3   DURKHEIM, ÉMILE. Pragmatisme et sociologie. Paris: J. Vrin.
        Lectures delivered at the Sorbonne in 1913-1914.
     Pragmatism is a method and a theory of truth, although
     only the latter is distinctive of it. With sociology,
     pragmatism shares the historical attitude towards human
     beliefs. However, pragmatism is individualistic while
     sociology sees beliefs evolving in the whole of human
     history.

4   KAPLAN, SIDNEY. "Taussig, James and Peabody: A 'Harvard
     School' in 1900?", American Quarterly, VII (Winter),
     315-331.
        Compares the views on social reform of Frank Taussig,
     James, and Francis G. Peabody. They favored gradualism
     and were optimistic.

1955

5   MATHUR, G. B.   "Hume and Kant in Their Relation to the Prag-
         matic Movement," Journal of the History of Ideas, XVI
         (April), 198-208.
           Hume distinguished theoretical from practical certainty
         and held that some beliefs are adopted from purely prac-
         tical motives. Kant recognized the working of the
         categories.

6   OLSHANSKY, SIMON S.   "William James on Phantom Limbs," The New
         England Journal of Medicine, CCLIII (July 14), 70-71.
           A summary of "The Consciousness of Lost Limbs" (1887).

7   PARAMPANTHI, SWAMI PURAGRA.   "William James on Religion," The
         Vedanta Kesari, XLII (September), 223-227.
           In "faith-state" there is an "inflow of actual energy"
         from some divine source. We can commune with a greater
         self and find our "greatest peace."

1956 A BOOKS - NONE

1956 B SHORTER WRITINGS

1   BARZUN, JACQUES.   "William James and the Clue to Art" in The
         Energies of Art: Studies of Authors Classic and Modern.
         New York: Harper & Brothers.
           The neo-Romantic movement was directly preceded by The
         Principles of Psychology. James did away with the "machine-
         inspired" conception of mind and re-established the "mind
         as myth-maker and artist."

2   BUSH; VANNEVAR.   "Can Men Live Without War?" The Atlantic
         Monthly, CXCVII (February), 35-38.
           James's proposed substitute for war is too limited. We
         also need dignified competition and the cooperation of
         scientific research.

3   CHILDS, JOHN L.   American Pragmatism and Education. New York:
         Henry Holt.
           Studies the influence of American pragmatism upon
         education. The more extended treatment of James is devoted
         to his religious views.

4   MASIH, Y.   "Metapsychology of James and Freud," Journal of
         Bihar University, I, 61-69.
           In many respects, Freud's metapsychology of religion is
         a continuation of James's theories.

5   WILKINS, BURLEIGH TAYLOR. "James, Dewey, and Hegelian Ideal-
    ism," Journal of the History of Ideas, XVII (June),
    332-346.
        James's pragmatism was pluralistic, Dewey's monistic.
    James reached pragmatism through British Empiricism, while
    Dewey, through Hegelian idealism.

1957 A BOOKS

1   COMPTON, CHARLES H. William James: Philosopher and Man.
    New York: The Scarecrow Press.
        "Quotations and references in 652 books." There is
    little overlap between Compton and the present list.

1957 B SHORTER WRITINGS

1   BUDMEN, KARL OSCAR. "The Religious Philosophy of William
    James," Phi Delta Kappan, XXXVIII (April), 291-292.
        James accepted the possibility that the traditional
    faith may be true, but his conclusions place him outside
    the "Judeo-Christian" tradition. James rejected a per-
    sonal God and tried to justify faith by reason, whereas
    religion is an act of faith alone.

2   CARRINGTON, HEREWARD. Letters to Hereward Carrington From
    Famous Psychical Researchers, Scientists, Mediums &
    Magicians. Mokelume Hill, Cal.: Health Research.
        Mimeographed. Contains letters from James to Carrington.

3   GURWITSCH, ARON. Théorie du champ de la conscience. Paris:
    Desclée de Brouwer. English translation, The Field of
    Consciousness (Pittsburgh: Duquesne University Press,
    1964).
        For James, the field of consciousness is divided into
    focus and margin. The organization of the field is a
    product of interest and attention. James's distinction
    between topic and object of thought is also discussed.

4   PASSMORE, JOHN. A Hundred Years of Philosophy. London:
    Gerald Duckworth.
        James represents the more radical form of the revolt
    against Cartesian intellectualism. James's sources were
    Kant's doctrine of the practical reason and Renouvier's
    defense of free will. The main motive of James's philoso-
    phy was to separate empiricism from determinism.

5   SCHRADER, GEORGE. "Der Pragmatismus von James und Dewey,"
    Kant-Studien, XLVIII, 425-436.

1957

    (SCHRADER, GEORGE)
        If pragmatism is a reflection of America, America is a
    reflection of pragmatism. The move from pragmatism to
    present day positivism is easy to understand.

6   SCHRICKEL, KLAUS. "Über den pragmatistischen Freiheitsbegriff
        bei W. James, R. B. Perry, J. Dewey und S. Hook," Deutsche
        Zeitschrift für Philosophie, V, 144-186.
        A criticism of the pragmatic conception of freedom from
    the Marxist point of view. James's pragmatism is the
    official philosophy of American imperialism.

7   WOLFE, DON M. The Image of Man in America. Dallas: Southern
        Methodist University Press.
        For James, great men are chance physiological mutations.
    Geniuses are not products of their environment, but have
    lives of their own full of "spontaneous variations."

1958 A BOOKS - NONE

1958 B SHORTER WRITINGS

1   BARZUN, JACQUES. Forward to Varieties. New York: New Amer-
        ican Library.
        James considered variety more fundamental than unity.

2   CLARK, WALTER HOUSTON. The Psychology of Religion. New York:
        Macmillan.
        Contains numerous references to James.

3   DeCAMP, LYON SPRAGUE. "William James: Leader of American
        Psychology," Science Digest, XLIII (January), 86-91.
        James, "a flaming idealist," was repelled by the "dry
    cynicism" of Oliver Wendell Holmes, Jr. James taught
    Theodore Roosevelt, who tried to pick disputes with him.
    James's pragmatism carries the germ of "unscrupulous
    opportunism."

4   HUTIN, SERGE. La Philosophie anglaise et américaine, Paris:
        Presses Universitaires de France.
        Pp. 101-104 contain a summary of James's thought.

5   KENNEDY, GAIL. "Pragmatism, Pragmaticism, and the Will to
        Believe -- A Reconsideration," The Journal of Philosophy,
        LV (July 3), 578-588.
        We must distinguish the right to believe in the absence
    of complete evidence from the will to believe, from the
    fact that the belief is needed to bring about some fact.

140

This latter follows from James's evolutionary conception of mind as an instrument of survival. Dewey and Peirce did not notice this distinction and disassociated themselves from James needlessly.

6   MURPHY, GARDNER. "Our Pioneers. III: William James," Journal of the Society for Psychical Research, XXXIX (December), 309-314. Incorporated into the Introduction to William James on Psychical Research (1960).
     James gave psychical research "respectability." He was instrumental in organizing the American society and discovered Mrs. Piper, the major psychical research tool at the time. However, his major contribution was his intense interest in facts.

7   ROSENZWEIG, SAUL. "The Jameses' Stream of Consciousness," Contemporary Psychology, III, 250-257.
     Traces the notion of the stream of consciousness in the James family. It resembles the "Method of Impression" of J. Garth Wilkinson, a close family friend. It is possible that Freud was influenced by James's formulation.

8   SCOTT, FREDERICK J. D. "William James and Maurice Blondel," The New Scholasticism, XXXII (January), 32-44.
     Based on James's unpublished notes on Blondel and Blondel's comments about James. Three letters from James to Blondel preserved in the Blondel Archives are published.

9   WOODRING, PAUL. Introduction to Talks to Teachers. New York: W. W. Norton.
     James's Talks were among the earliest to apply psychology to education. Much of what is best in "Progressive Education" can be found in Talks.

1959 A BOOKS

1   SCHMIDT, HERMANN. Der Begriff der Erfahrungskontinuität bei William James und seine Bedeutung für den amerikanischen Pragmatismus. Heidelberg: Carl Winter. (Supplementary volume to the Jahrbuch für Amerikastudien).
     The first chapter, treats the stream of consciousness as the basis of a conception of experience; the second, views radical empiricism as an attempt to ground the phenomena of consciousness in the continuity of experience; the third, treats the pragmatic conception of truth; the fourth, examines moral duty on the basis of pure experience.

1959

1959 B SHORTER WRITINGS

1   AMES, VAN METER. "William James and Zen," <u>Psychologia: An International Journal of Psychology in the Orient</u>, II, 114-119.
James and Zen defend experience against "philosophy." Both realize that "life is for life," that "this moment is the most real reality."

2   BASTIEN, HERMAS. <u>Philosophies et philosophes américains</u>. Montreal: Les Frères des Écoles Chrétiennes.
Pp. 177-183, contain a biographical treatment of James. James drew the attention of the general public to pragmatism.

3   BIXLER, JULIUS SEELYE. "The Existentialists and William James," <u>The American Scholar</u>, XXVIII (Winter), 80-90.
James has much in common with exentialists, but is more deserving of our attention. Philosophy should deal with "our love, our fears and our hopes." The existentialists are pessimists, while James finds in human freedom an opportunity for creativity.

4   BLIVEN, BRUCE. "The Adventure of Being Human," <u>Reader's Digest</u>, LXXV (August), 41-48.
The implications of James's psychology for mental health and self-improvement.

5   BRINNIN, JOHN MALCOLM. <u>The Third Rose: Gertrude Stein and Her World</u>. Boston: Little, Brown.
Contains an account of Gertrude Stein's studies under James.

6   COLLINS, JAMES. <u>God in Modern Philosophy</u>. Chicago: Henry Regnery.
James's pluralistic theism is examined against the background of John Stuart Mill. Collins examines the pragmatic grounds of belief in a finite God and James's criticism of absolutism.

7   KNIGHT, MARGARET. "William James" in <u>The Function of Teaching: Seven Approaches to Purpose, Tradition and Environment</u>. Edited by A. V. Judges. London: Faber and Faber.
James held that human behavior can be studied scientifically. Knight discusses James's views on memory, habits, and the arousal of interest and shows their educational importance.

8   MARCUSE, LUDWIG. Amerikanisches Philosophieren: Pragmatisten, Polytheisten, Tragiker. Hamburg: Rowohlt.
    The treatment of James centers around his "Williamcy." He was an untrained, wild-growing philosopher. Marcuse draws many comparisons between James and Nietzsche.

9   STAFFORD, WILLIAM T. "William James as Critic of His Brother Henry," The Personalist, XL (Autumn), 341-353.
    James was his brother's critic for forty years. He raised the same issues as did "his age": questions of "social realism," "morality," "Americanism," of style and technique.

10 STEVICK, ROBERT D. "Robinson and William James," The University of Kansas City Review, XXV (Summer), 293-301.
    E. A. Robinson drew upon James while writing "The Man Against the Sky." There is no external evidence, but many "parallels."

11 THARP, LOUISE HALL. Adventurous Alliance: The Story of the Agassiz Family of Boston. Boston: Little, Brown.
    Extended references to James during the Thayer expedition headed by L. Agassiz to Brazil, including quotations from letters and diaries.

1960 A BOOKS

1   MURPHY, GARDNER and BALLOU, ROBERT O., eds. William James on Psychical Research. New York: The Viking Press.
    Most of James's writings on the subject are included. The introduction by Murphy traces James's interest in psychical research and related subjects such as mental healing.

1960 B SHORTER WRITINGS

1   BECK, LEWIS WHITE. Six Secular Philosophers. New York: Harper and Brothers.
    Discusses the contributions to religion by philosophers who are independent of accepted religions. James was both a pragmatist concerned with the grounds of religious belief and a spiritualistic pluralist whose study of religious experience led him towards polytheism.

2   CLIVE, GEOFFREY. The Romantic Enlightenment. New York: Meridian Books.
    The chapter on James is titled "The Breakdown of Empirical Certainty: William James and the Leap." James is

1960

(CLIVE, GEOFFREY)
often placed in the empiricist tradition with Hume, but this is only a half-truth. James was involved in "the Kantian quest" for answers to "ultimate questions."

3   JONES, EVAN, ed. The Father: Letters to Sons and Daughters. New York: Rinehart.
Contains letter to James's daughter, taken from Letters (1920).

4   KALLEN, HORACE M. "The Modern World, the Intellectual and William James," The Western Political Quarterly, XIII (December), 863-879.
James would be a model modern intellect, willing to emerse himself in the world of affairs, an individualist judging all ideologies by their fruits.

5   LASSWELL, HAROLD D. "Approaches to Human Personality: William James and Sigmund Freud," Psychoanalysis and the Psycho-analytic Review, XLVII (Fall), 52-68.
The many similarities and differences between James and Freud can be explained by reference to their "personality structures" and "social situations." James was more the organizer of knowledge, Freud, the original theorizer. James never set out to shock as did Freud. Much of James's personality can be understood in terms of his relations with his father.

6   NOCK, ARTHUR DARBY. Introduction to Varieties. London: The Fontana Library.
James presents numerous case histories arranged in a convenient way.

7   PADOVER, SAUL K. The Genius of America. New York: McGraw-Hill.
As a pluralist, James rejects the "antidemocratic" view that history is the work of great men, but recognizes the need for intelligent leadership. James's writings on war are his most important contributions to social thought.

8   SPIEGELBERG, HERBERT. The Phenomenological Movement: A His-torical Introduction. The Hague: Martinus Nijhoff.
Studies the influence of James's psychology on the phenomenology of Carl Stumpf and on Edmund Husserl. Spiegelberg traces in detail Husserl's knowledge of James's thought.

9   VAN WESEP, H. B. Seven Sages: The Story of American Philoso-phy. New York: Longmans, Green.

144

James is a "primitive pragmatist" who subjected American
ideals to a "professional overhauling." He realized that
"help your neighbor, and keep your powder dry" was advice
applicable not only to the frontier.

1961 A BOOKS

1   BRENNAN, BERNARD P. The Ethics of William James. New York:
    Bookman Associates.
        No single aspect of James's thought, neither anti-
    intellectualism, nor voluntarism, nor radical empiricism,
    by itself provides an adequate center for organizing
    James's thought. Each aspect must be taken in a general
    framework and in relation to others.

2   HARDWICK, ELIZABETH. The Selected Letters of William James.
    New York: Farrar, Straus and Cudahy. The introduction
    was reprinted in A View of My Own (New York: Farrar,
    Straus and Cudahy, 1962) and appeared as "William James:
    An American Hero," Mademoiselle, LI (June 1960), 60-61,
    106-108.
        Several letters have not been published elsewhere. The
    introduction is biographical.

3   MOORE, EDWARD C. American Pragmatism: Peirce, James, and
    Dewey. New York: Columbia University Press.
        James was first attracted to pragmatism because it
    promised to settle the question of God's existence. For
    James, the problem of truth is a special case of the
    problem of knowledge.

1961 B SHORTER WRITINGS

1   ALLPORT, GORDON. Introduction to Psychology. New York:
    Harper Torchbooks.
        Freudianism and behaviorism had eclipsed James's psy-
    chology, but now there is a revival. It is unfortunate
    that James treated the self phenomenologically, that he
    did not objectify it.

2   LARRABEE, HAROLD A. "William James' Impact upon American
    Education," School and Society, LXXXIX (February 25),
    84-86.
        James challenged formalism in education. Considering
    the popular repute of pragmatism, some will be surprised
    to learn that James considered "a sense for human superi-
    ority" a mark of an educated man.

1961

3   MADSEN, TRUMAN G. "William James: Philosopher-Educator,"
     Brigham Young University Studies, IV (Autumn), 81–105.
          Discusses James as a teacher. Based in part on letters
     to the author by James's former students, Edgar A. Singer,
     Charles M. Bakewell, B. A. G. Fuller, Levi Edgar Young,
     H. V. Kaltenborn, James R. Angell, and H. M. Kallen.

4   NIEBUHR, REINHOLD. Introduction to Varieties. New York:
     Collier Books.
          Not even genius can keep a work from becoming out of
     date. James's optimism expressed the mood of his day. His
     chapter on saintliness overlooks the "ambiguity of good and
     evil." He does not recognize as a defect the mystical ten-
     dency to flee the responsibilities of history.

5   STROUT, CUSHING. "The Unfinished Arch: William James and the
     Idea of History," American Quarterly, XIII (Winter),
     505–515.
          If James had had the time to complete his philosophy, he
     would have moved towards a philosophy of history. He
     would have seen in history "the place where man makes him-
     self in actions and institutions."

1962 A BOOKS

1   ROBERTS, JAMES DEOTIS. Faith and Reason. Boston: Christopher
     Publishing House.
          A comparison of Pascal, Bergson, and James. James was
     led to emphasize "supra-rational knowledge" by his dis-
     covery of the limits of the "rational method."

1962 B SHORTER WRITINGS

1   AIKEN, HENRY DAVID. "American Pragmatism Reconsidered: II.
     William James," Commentary, XXXIV (August), 120–130;
     (September) 238–246.
          The second segment deals with James. James was basically
     tough-minded, in contrast with Peirce, who was tender-
     minded. James viewed all questions as primarily questions
     of conduct. Truth is to be defined as that which we ought
     to believe.

2   CAPEK, MILIC. "La Signification actuelle de la philosophie de
     James," Revue de Métaphysique et de Morale, LXVII
     (July-September), 291–321.
          James's pragmatism and theory of knowledge are now of
     little interest. His real contributions are to be sought
     in psychology and metaphysics. He attacked the mechanistic
     conception of the world and adopted pluralism.

3   HOFFMAN, FREDERICK J. "William James and the Modern Literary
      Consciousness," Criticism, IV (Winter), 1-13.
          James has greatly affected modern intellectual history.
      For him, the self was not a substance, but a process.
      This change is reflected in modern literature. Unhappy
      without a self, James resorted to a voluntaristic solu-
      tion. The self exists because "it must be" and this again
      is duplicated in literature.

4   HOLE, MYRA CADWALADER. "Rhymed Proverbs Interpreting James"
      in Emerson, James and Dewey in Rhyme. Chicago: Estate
      of Myra C. Hole.
          Topics covered are Action, Decisions, Endurance, War,
      Great Men, Materialism, Surprises, Self-Reliance, The
      World, Pragmatism. Proverb for action: "To know a pro-
      cess you must put it to use and see the results it will
      produce."

5   WHITE, MORTON and WHITE, LUCIA. "Pragmatism and Social Work:
      William James and Jane Addams" in The Intellectual Versus
      the City. Cambridge, Mass.: Harvard University Press and
      the M. I. T. Press.
          James is delighted in city life and "spurred on" a move-
      ment for the reform of cities. The chapter emphasizes the
      work of Jane Addams, James's "worshipper."

1963 A BOOKS

1   CLARK, GORDON H. William James. Philadelphia: Presbyterian
      and Reformed Publishing Co.
          Written to "help the defense and development of Chris-
      tian theism." Logic leads to the rejection of monism and
      the acceptance of theism. James finds theism so intoler-
      able that he repudiates logic. This is "intellectual
      suicide." James's choice, between nonentity and an un-
      certain salvation dependent upon human effort, ignores the
      preferable alternative, certain salvation.

2   MARTLAND, THOMAS R., JR. The Metaphysics of William James and
      John Dewey: Process and Structure in Philosophy and
      Religion. New York: Philosophical Library.
          Philosophy and religion converge in that both revolve
      around the poles of change and stability. This thesis is
      proved through the analysis of several religions and the
      naturalism of James and Dewey.

1963

1963 B SHORTER WRITINGS

1 BLAU, JOSEPH L. Introduction to Pragmatism and Other Essays. New York: Washington Square Press.
James's thought could reconcile the scientific conception of the world with an emotional attachment to God. James's pragmatism differs from Peirce's in that James considers not only the consequences of a statement but also the consequences of believing it.

2 HALL, ROLAND. "O.E.D. Antedatings From William James," Notes and Queries, CCVIII (September), 341-346.
A series of sentences from James to illustrate meanings of words, where these sentences are earlier than the illustrative sentences cited in the main body of the Oxford English Dictionary.

3 JEROME, VICTOR J. "Accident and History," Philologica Pragensia, VI, 337-342.
Criticizes James's accidentalist philosophy of history. Contrary to James's view, communities have a "self-movement" which impels them in a certain direction. Men are only instruments of history. James heavily influenced "American bourgois ideologies" and had repercussions among "philosophers and politicos abroad."

4 KAUFMAN, MARJORIE R. "William James's Letters to a Young Pragmatist," Journal of the History of Ideas, XXIV (July-September), 413-421.
James letters to Howard V. Knox, a British military officer who became an enthusiastic defender of pragmatism. Notes and connecting commentary are provided.

5 LOVEJOY, ARTHUR ONCKEN. The Thirteen Pragmatisms and Other Essays. Baltimore: The Johns Hopkins Press.
Three papers are listed separately (1908), (1911). "James's Does Consciousness Exist?" appears for the first time. James's arguments for the non-existence of consciousness prove that there are no "contents" of consciousness, that we perceive the physical objects themselves.

6 MADISON, CHARLES A. "Skirmishes With a Publisher," The Saturday Review of Literature, XLVI (November 16), 24-25.
Included with extensive changes in The Owl Among Colophons (New York: Holt, Rinehart and Winston, ©1966).
Relations between James and Henry Holt, with emphasis on the years when James was writing The Principles of Psychology and the controversy over the publication of Talks to Teachers. Includes quotations from letters.

148

7   MARRA, WILLIAM A. "The Five-Sided Pragmatism of William James,"
    The Modern Schoolman, XLI (November), 45-61.
        Pragmatism insists that any intellectual activity must
    be linked with experience and action. James's statement
    of pragmatism is very "flexible" and reveals "different
    articulations or sides": an orthodox side linking James
    with Peirce; a fanciful side legitimatizing daydreams; the
    "creative faith" side; the "determination of value" side;
    and a side which insists that abstract terms be interpreted
    concretely.

8   MAVRODES, GEORGE I. "James and Clifford on 'The Will to
    Believe,'" The Personalist, XLIV (Spring), 191-198.
        In The Will to Believe James is mistaken about the point
    of his dispute with William Kingdon Clifford. James holds
    that in the case of forced options suspension of belief is
    impossible, whereas Clifford denies that there are forced
    options.

9   RATNER, JOSEPH. Introduction to Varieties. Hyde Park, N. Y.:
    University Books.
        Varieties is not a psychology of religion because, for
    James, there is no special religious experience, only
    human experience directed towards special objects. At
    Edinburgh, James attempted to shock his clerical audience
    by comparing religious and non-religious experience.
    Ratner compares James's religious views with Freud's.

10 REMLEY, DAVID A. "William James: The Meaning and Function of
    Art," Midcontinent American Studies Journal, vol. IV,
    no. 2 (Fall), 39-48.
        James thought that the enjoyment of pleasure, including
    aesthetic, for its own sake would injure one's character.
    Aesthetic pleasure is valuable when it stimulates "con-
    structive ethical action."

11 SMITH, JOHN E. The Spirit of American Philosophy. New York:
    Oxford University Press.
        James wanted to develop an "immediately relevant philos-
    ophy." He was the most "outspoken" of the pragmatists.
    His thought is a "fresh distillation" of experience.
    James sought to show the value of religion by seeking its
    roots in experience and its "fruits in morality."

12 WATSON, ROBERT I. The Great Psychologists. Philadelphia:
    J. B. Lippincott.
        While James became the leading American psychologist,
    he considered himself a philosopher. Watson outlines
    James's views on selected topics in psychology.

WILLIAM JAMES: A REFERENCE GUIDE

1964

1964 A BOOKS - NONE

1964 B SHORTER WRITINGS

1 ALLEN, GAY WILSON. "William James's Determined Free Will" in
   Essays on Determinism in American Literature. Edited by
   Sydney J. Krause. Kent, Ohio: Kent State University
   Press.
       James's belief in free will was determined by his
   background.

2 BOLLER, PAUL F., JR. "Freedom in the Thought of William James,"
   American Quarterly, XVI (Summer), 131-152.
       James accepted freedom as unobstructed self-realization.
   He rejected freedom as "bondage to the highest." He held
   that freedom as free-will was a necessary postulate in a
   world with an uncertain future.

3 EDEL, LEON, ed. The Diary of Alice James. New York: Dodd,
   Mead.
       Complete text, edited from the manuscript and a pri-
   vately printed version. Edel restores the cuts made by
   Burr (1934). An introductory "Portrait of Alice James" by
   Edel is included.

4 FISCH, MAX H. "Philosophical Clubs in Cambridge and Boston:
   From Peirce's Metaphysical Club to Harris's Hegel Club,"
   Coranto (University of Southern California), vol. II,
   no. 1 (Fall), 12-23; vol II, no. 2 (Spring 1965), 12-25;
   vol. III, no. 1 (Fall 1965), 16-29.
       A history of three clubs based on letters and diaries
   at many points correcting accounts given by James, George
   Herbert Palmer, and G. Stanley Hall. Emphasis is given
   to James's relations with Thomas Davidson, James Elliot
   Cabot, and the origins of pragmatism.

5 MILLS, C. WRIGHT. Sociology and Pragmatism. New York:
   Paine-Whitman.
       James was a popularizer of pragmatism. He proposed to
   define issues in terms of practicality, but 'practical'
   meant 'personal' and 'moral'. He had no developed social
   theory. His attitude was "psychological liberalism."

6 SAN JUAN, E., JR. "William James as Prose Writer," The Cen-
   tennial Review of Arts and Science (Michigan State),
   VIII, 323-336.
       Examines James's prose as an "expressive medium of
   experience."

7 SCHNEIDER, HERBERT W. Sources of Contemporary Philosophical
   Realism in America. Indianapolis: Bobbs-Merrill.
   Two excerpts from A History of American Philosophy
   (1946).

8 WHITTEMORE, ROBERT CLIFTON. Makers of the American Mind.
   New York: William Morrow.
   James identifies the true with the sensed. Other empir-
   icisms "candidly pronounce" the falsity of metaphysical
   and ethical statements. Pragmatism reserves the right to
   hope that they may be true.

9 WINETROUT, KENNETH. "William James and F. C. S. Schiller,"
   Educational Theory, XIV (July), 158-167.
   Many letters are quoted, all from published sources.
   Schiller has been much neglected.

1965 A BOOKS

1 ANDERSON, M. LUKE. The Concept of Truth in the Philosophy of
   William James. Rome [n.p.].
   A dissertation at the Pontificia Studiorum Universitas
   A. Sancto Thoma Aquinate in Urbe. James's view of truth
   is not "totally untraditional." For James, an idea "is a
   form to the likeness of which things are made," ontological
   truth is dependent upon the creating mind.

2 MOORE, EDWARD C. William James. New York: Washington Square
   Press.
   A popular introduction. The will to believe and pragmatism have been given an exaggerated place in James's
   thought and some balance should be restored.

1965 B SHORTER WRITINGS

1 ALLEN, GAY WILSON. "James's Varieties of Religious Experience
   as Introduction to American Transcendentalism," The
   Emerson Society Quarterly, no. 39, pp. 81-85.
   Varieties is the best introduction to the teaching of
   American transcendentalism. James was not a transcenden-
   talist, but has many points in common with them.

2 CLARK, WALTER HOUSTON. "William James: Contributions to the
   Psychology of Religious Conversion," Pastoral Psychology,
   XVI (September), 29-36.
   James insisted on experience, focused on the individual,
   studied extreme cases and respected the unconscious.

1965

3   EDIE, JAMES M. "Notes on the Philosophical Anthropology of
    William James" in An Invitation to Phenomenology. Edited
    by James M. Edie. Chicago: Quadrangle Books.
      Presents James's "philosophy of man" as the "natural
    center and focal point." Similarities and differences
    between James and phenomenology are pointed out, as part
    of the current re-evaluation of James.

4   FISHER, JOHN J. "Santayana on James: A Conflict of Views on
    Philosophy," American Philosophical Quarterly, II
    (January) 67-73.
      Santayana criticized James's "lack of discernment" in
    allowing everyone to speak about religious experience.
    The paper uses marginalia in Santayana's copy of Varieties.

5   MEYER, DONALD. The Positive Thinkers: A Study of the American
    Quest for Health, Wealth and Personal Power from Mary Baker
    Eddy to Norman Vincent Peale. Garden City, N. Y.:
    Doubleday.
      In a postscript, "William James as the Authority," Meyer
    criticizes James's analysis of healthy-mindedness. James
    has been quoted as an authority by advocates of mind cure,
    including Norman Vincent Peale.

6   RATHER, L. J. "Old and New Views of the Emotions and Bodily
    Changes: Wright and Harvey versus Descartes, James and
    Cannon," Clio Medica, I (November), 1-25.
      Thomas Wright (fl. 1600) and William Harvey held that
    emotions are mental activities which cause bodily changes.
    Descartes, James, and Walter B. Cannon reversed the causal
    relation.

7   REID, ALFRED S. "Emerson and Bushnell as Forerunners of
    Jamesian Pragmatism," Furman Studies issue of the Furman
    University Bulletin, NS XIII (November), 18-30.
      Emerson's role in the development of pragmatism is well
    known, Horace Bushnell's is not. James probably knew
    nothing of Bushnell, but Bushnell was a "rudimentary"
    pragmatist.

8   ROTH, ROBERT J. "Is Peirce's Pragmatism Anti-Jamesian?"
    International Philosophical Quarterly, V (December),
    541-563.
      Incorporated into American Religious Philosophy (1967).
    The differences between James and Peirce should not be
    exaggerated. Peirce too sought justification for man's
    higher aspirations in the subjective realm.

9 _____. "William James and Alcoholics Anonymous," _America_, CXIII (July 10), 48-50.
The founder of AA read _Varieties_ and was inspired.

10 SMITH, JOHN E. "Radical Empiricism," _Proceedings of the Aristotelian Society_, NS LXV, 205-218.
James insists upon the empirical character of relations. Experience initially is neutral, neither mental nor physical. James did not realize that experience does not contain within itself all we need for its interpretation.

11 THIELE, J. "William James und Ernst Mach: Briefe aus den Jahren 1884-1905," _Philosophia Naturalis_, IX, 298-310.
Letters from and to James, with introduction and notes. Most of the letters are in English.

12 WILD, JOHN. "William James and Existential Authenticity," _Journal of Existentialism_, V (Spring), 243-256.
James has worked out an empirical concept of "self-becoming" very similar to that of the existential philosophers in their efforts to elucidate the transition from "unauthentic" to "authentic" existence.

1966 A BOOKS

1 LE CLAIR, ROBERT C. _The Letters of William James and Théodore Flournoy_. Madison: The University of Wisconsin Press.
Contains some 130 letters from and to James, some not published elsewhere. The correspondence begins in 1890.

1966 B SHORTER WRITINGS

1 ALLPORT, GORDON W. "William James and the Behavioral Sciences," _Journal of the History of the Behavioral Sciences_, II (April), 145-147.
Remarks at the installation of James's portrait in William James Hall, Harvard University.

2 BEARD, ROBERT W. "James's Notion of Rationality," _Darshana International_, VI (July), 6-12.
The notion of rationality in James's early reviews underlies his will to believe and pragmatism. Besides the cognitive, men have many other interests. The view which satisfies more interests will be more rational.

1966

3   BEARD, ROBERT W. "'The Will to Believe' Revisited," Ratio,
    VIII (December) 169-179. A German version was published
    in the German edition of Ratio.
        The right to believe applies only to genuine options
    and these are rare. Independent of this is the view that
    we can go beyond the evidence where belief is needed to
    obtain evidence. This is the meaning of the will to
    believe.

4   FAIRBANKS, MATTHEW. "Wittgenstein and James," The New
    Scholasticism, XL, 331-340.
        Wittgenstein often referred to James. Both insisted on
    the inadequacy of idealism and empiricism, were aware of
    "vagueness" in communication and sought to avoid it by
    looking at "practical circumstances or contextual use."

5   FOX, JUNE T. "Peirce and the Pragmatists: A Study in Con-
    trasts," Educational Theory, XVI (July), 262-270.
        The pragmatism of James and Dewey is not derived from
    Peirce. Peirce was a realist and not a nominalist, con-
    cerned with meanings and not actions, a conservative for
    whom ethical theory had little bearing on social action.

6   HOFFMAN, MICHAEL J. "Gertrude Stein and William James," The
    Personalist, XLVII (Spring), 226-233.
        Studies how James's thought "can illuminate Gertrude
    Stein's abstract style."

7   KENNA, J. C. "Ten Unpublished Letters from William James,
    1842-1910 to Francis Herbert Bradley, 1846-1924," Mind,
    NS LXXV (July), 309-331.
        The originals of the letters are in the Bradley Archives,
    Merton College, Oxford. Perry in Thought and Character
    (1935) published only fragments of James's letters to
    Bradley. Letters from Bradley to James can be found in
    Perry.

8   ROTH, ROBERT J. "The Religious Philosophy of William James,"
    Thought, XLI (Summer), 249-281.
        Reprinted in American Religious Philosophy (1967).

1967 A BOOKS

1   ALLEN, GAY WILSON. William James. New York: Viking Press.
        A biography based in part upon sealed family letters in
    Houghton Library at Harvard, and letters and diaries in
    the hands of James's heirs. Information from the sealed
    letters was provided by the family.

2   RECK, ANDREW J. Introduction to William James: An Essay and
    Selected Texts. Bloomington: Indiana University Press.
    Originally published in French, William James et l'attitude
    pragmatiste (Paris: Seghers, 1967).
        Intended for a non-professional audience.

1967 B SHORTER WRITINGS

1   BEARD, ROBERT W. "James and the Rationality of Determinism,"
    Journal of the History of Philosophy, V (April), 149-156.
        The best reply to the charge that James abhorred "exact
    thought" is to indicate the "logical essentials" of a
    paper by James. In the paper chosen, the crucial notion
    is rationality, the criteria of which are both theoretical
    and practical.

2   BORING, EDWIN G. "Psychologists' Letters and Papers," Isis,
    LVIII (Spring), 103-107.
        Included is a brief description of the James Collection
    in Houghton Library at Harvard.

3   CHILDS, KENNETH W. "Reality in Some of the Writings of Robert
    Frost and William James," Proceedings of the Utah Academy
    of Sciences, Arts, and Letters, vol. XLIV, pt. 1, 150-158.
        Both James and Robert Frost "share a theory of knowledge
    that illustrates a duality in empiricism."

4   COMSTOCK, W. RICHARD. "William James and the Logic of
    Religious Belief," The Journal of Religion, XLVII (July),
    187-209.
        James tried to make religion viable in a scientific age.
    He did not advocate license, but formulated rules for
    belief. There is a "technical rigor."

5   EARLE, WILLIAM JAMES. Article on William James in The Encyclo-
    pedia of Philosophy. Edited by Paul Edwards. New York:
    Macmillan.
        James's work adds up to a "serious philosophical posi-
    tion" worthy of study.

6   FEATHERSTONE, JOSEPH. "William James as Sage," The New
    Republic, CLVII (October 14), 18-21.
        A favorable review of Allen, William James (1967) and
    McDermott, The Writings of William James (1967). James
    was the last of the sages typical of the nineteenth cen-
    tury. His thought is alive today because he described how
    we think.

1967

7 GATES, ARTHUR I. "Talks to Teachers," NEA Journal, LVI
   (October), 34-35.
      Talks to Teachers is introduced in a series of educational
   classics.

8 KAUFMANN, WALTER. "Philosopher for the Tender-minded," The
   Saturday Review of Literature, L (August 12), 31-32.
      A review of Allen's William James (1967). The work is
   crammed with facts, but Allen is not interested in ideas.
   James was not "prophetic" and could not foresee the
   "realities of the later twentieth century." He was a
   "wonderful human being."

9 KOCKELMANS, JOSEPH J. Edmund Husserl's Phenomenological Psy-
   chology: A Historico-Critical Study. Pittsburgh:
   Duquesne University Press. Translated from the Dutch by
   Bernd Jager and revised by the author.
      A brief section outlines James's psychology.

10 McDERMOTT, JOHN J. "Introduction" to The Writings of William
   James: A Comprehensive Edition. New York: Random House.
      A general survey of James's thought, with particular
   emphasis on James's vision of the world, his radical empiricism and pluralism. James's crisis of 1870 was decisive
   in forming his thought. James rejected suicide in favor
   of life "unsupported by certitude" and worked out a doctrine
   to support this belief. The bibliography is a revision of
   Perry's (1920). It is the best published, although incomplete and with errors.

11 MACLEOD, WILLIAM J. "James's 'Will to Believe': Revisited,"
   The Personalist, XLVIII (Spring), 149-166.
      A criticism of John Hick Philosophy of Religion
   (Englewood Cliffs, N.J.: Prentice-Hall, 1963). Hick
   confuses 'faith' with 'working-hypothesis', does not
   consider James's audience, and ignores James's notion of
   a genuine option.

12 MAYER, FREDERICK. The Great Teachers. New York: The Citadel
   Press.
      James's philosophy of education is presented with
   extended quotations. James emphasized "functional training
   in laboratory work" rather than the study of the classics.

13 ROTH, ROBERT J. American Religious Philosophy. New York:
   Harcourt, Brace & World.
      James's knowledge of theology and religious philosophy
   was poor and his criticisms often were superficial. He can
   teach us the "need of a deep interior life." James's

pragmatism "inevitably" leads to belief in God as the only
belief that can make the world rational.

14 RUSSELL, BERTRAND. The Autobiography of Bertrand Russell:
    1872-1914. Boston: Little, Brown.
        Includes one letter from James and references to him.

15 SIMON, ROBERT I. "Great Paths Cross: Freud and James at
    Clark University, 1909," The American Journal of Psychiatry,
    CXXIV (December), 831-834.
        Describes the meeting of James and Freud and speculates
    as to what their relations would have been if James had
    not died.

16 STROUT, CUSHING. "Pragmatism in Retrospect: The Legacy of
    James and Dewey," The Virginia Quarterly Review, XLIII
    (Winter), 123-134.
        Pragmatism does not worship the "bitch goddess success."

1968 A BOOKS

1 AYER, A. J. The Origins of Pragmatism: Studies in the Philosophy of Charles Sanders Peirce and William James. San
   Francisco: Freeman, Cooper.
        James recognizes truths of fact, a priori, and moral and
   aesthetic truths, each with appropriate standards. For
   James, "pure experience" is the stuff out of which a subject arises who then differentiates between himself and
   the external world.

2 BRENNAN, BERNARD P. William James. New York: Twayne.
        An introduction for the "beginner." James demands "pro-
   found changes" and marks a "radical turning-point."

3 LINSCHOTEN, JOHANNES. On the Way Toward a Phenomenological
   Psychology: The Psychology of William James. Edited by
   Amedeo Giorgi. Pittsburgh: Duquesne University Press.
   Translated from the Dutch (Utrecht, 1959).
        Studies the whole of James's thought. James never
   developed a phenomenological psychology; he was on the way
   towards one. James recognized that subjectivity is responsible for the way the world appears and that it is impossible to go "behind experience." James lacked an adequate
   concept of intentionality.

4 WILSHIRE, BRUCE. William James and Phenomenology: A Study
   of 'The Principles of Psychology.' Bloomington: Indiana
   University Press.

1968

    (WILSHIRE, BRUCE)
        In The Principles of Psychology, James sets himself a
    dualistic program. When this breaks down, James moves
    towards phenomenology. James and Husserl are compared.

1968 B SHORTER WRITINGS

1   ARNOLD, WALTER. "Why William James?", The Catholic World,
       CCVII (July), 172-177.
         James's "insights" seem appropriate to our age. However,
       his work is not without its dangers. He comes close to
       irrationalism and "psychologism."

2   BEISNER, ROBERT L. Twelve Against Empire: The Anti-
       Imperialists, 1898-1900. New York: McGraw-Hill.
         Discusses James's general social views, the background of
       his opposition to American policy.

3   CONKIN, PAUL K. Puritans and Pragmatists: Eight Eminent
       American Thinkers. New York: Dodd, Mead.
         James's philosophy can be found in his psychology. Sec-
       tions are devoted to voluntarism, ontology, pragmatism,
       and James's practical concerns.

4   EDIE, JAMES M. "William James and the Phenomenology of
       Religious Experience" in M. Novak, ed., American Philosophy
       and the Future (1968).
         James's methodology of religious experience is often
       phenomenologically sounder than those of writers directly
       affected by Husserl. James did not interpret texts and
       symbols, but turned to the naive religious experience.

5   ERIKSON, ERIK H. Identity: Youth and Crisis. New York:
       W. W. Norton.
         James's life provides a "source of insight into the
       development of identity." Rosenzweig, "Erik Erikson on
       William James's Dream" (1970), corrects Erikson on James's
       "terminal dream."

6   FISHMAN, STEPHEN M. "James and Lewes on Unconscious Judgment,"
       Journal of the History of the Behavioral Sciences, IV
       (October), 335-348.
         In The Principles of Psychology, James presents ten
       arguments against the doctrine of unconscious judgment
       as stated by George Henry Lewes and others. Fishman
       examines five and questions their adequacy.

7   GOLDSTEIN, MELVIN L. "Physiological Theories of Emotion: A
    Critical Historical Review from the Standpoint of Behavior
    Theory," Psychological Bulletin, LXIX (January), 23-40.
        Summarizes the James-Lange theory and discusses experi-
    ments bearing on it.

8   GRAY, PHILIP HOWARD. "Prerequisite To An Analysis of Behavior-
    ism: The Conscious Automaton Theory from Spalding to
    William James," Journal of the History of the Behavioral
    Sciences, IV (October), 365-376.
        Gives no account of James's views. James would have made
    fewer mistakes in his attack on automatism had he realized
    that this theory does not rule out a "descriptive" study
    of mind. The materialists only refuse to treat the mind
    as a cause.

9   HARE, PETER H. and MADDEN, EDWARD H. "William James, Dickinson
    Miller & C. J. Ducasse on the Ethics of Belief," Trans-
    actions of the Charles S. Peirce Society, IV (Fall),
    115-129.
        Correspondence between Miller and Ducasse on The Will to
    Believe.

10 JONCICH, GERALDINE. The Sane Positivist: A Biography of
    Edward L. Thorndike. Middletown, Conn.: Wesleyan Univer-
    sity Press.
        Includes quotations from James's letters to Thorndike.
    Discusses Thorndike's offer to revise James's psychology
    texts.

11 KOLAKOWSKI, LESZEK. The Alienation of Reason. Translated by
    N. Guterman. Garden City, N.Y.: Doubleday. Originally
    published in Polish in 1966.
        James's conception of truth is utilitarian. It is
    "epistemological Jesuitism." He expressed the attitude of
    those who simply wanted to get on in life. But James is
    important because he shows that an empiricist metaphysics
    can be developed.

12 McDERMOTT, JOHN J. "To Be Human is to Humanize: A Radically
    Empirical Aesthetic" in M. Novak, ed., American Philosophy
    and the Future (1968).
        Art has undergone a revolution. James and Dewey give
    a "fruitful" statement of the meaning of modern art.
    McDermott emphasizes the resemblances between the impres-
    sionism of Claude Monet and James's "metaphysics of
    relations."

1968

13   McGRATH, MICHAEL. "Peirce and James: Epistemological Perspec-
     tives," Educational Theory, XVIII (Fall), 376-379, 387.
        Criticism of Fox, "Peirce and the Pragmatists: A Study
     in Contrasts" (1966). Fox would not have concluded that
     pragmatism does not originate with Peirce if she had con-
     sidered the theory of truth rather than educational
     implications.

14   MARX, OTTO M. "American Psychiatry Without William James,"
     Bulletin of the History of Medicine, XLII (January-
     February), 52-61.
        The American Journal of Insanity and the Journal of
     Nervous and Mental Diseases up to 1910 contain few refer-
     ences to James. The Journal of Abnormal Psychology, was
     founded in 1906 by persons associated with James. However,
     it is not known how much influence James had.

15   MURPHEY, MURRAY G. "Kant's Children: The Cambridge Prag-
     matists," Transactions of the Charles S. Peirce Society,
     IV (Winter), 3-33.
        Pragmatism is part of an "idealistic" attempt to harmon-
     ize science and religion. James himself is heavily indebted
     to Kant. The Principles of Psychology raised issues solved
     in pragmatism and radical empiricism. It forces one to
     abandon the copy theory of truth and leads to the view
     that experience is neutral, neither mental nor physical.

16   NETHERY, WALLACE. "Pragmatist to Publisher: Letters of
     William James to W. T. Harris," The Personalist, XLIX
     (Autumn), 489-508.
        Letters from James with explanatory notes.

17   NOVAK, MICHAEL, ed. American Philosophy and the Future. New
     York: Charles Scribner's Sons.
        Essays by John J. McDermott, P. M. Van Buren, James M.
     Edie, and R. W. Sleeper are abstracted separately. Of the
     others, Robert C. Pollock, "Dream and Nightmare: The
     Future as Revolution," refers to James extensively.

18   PETRAS, JOHN W. "Psychological Antedecents of Sociological
     Theory in America: William James and James Mark Baldwin,"
     Journal of the History of the Behavioral Sciences, IV
     (April), 132-142.
        James's role in the development of American sociology has
     been neglected. He contributed habit, instinct, and the
     social self. James's "unelaborated" ideas "became
     centralized" in Baldwin's theories.

19   RAMAKRISHNA RAO, K. Gandhi and Pragmatism. Calcutta: Oxford
     & Ibh Publishing Co.
         Compares similar modes of thought arising in different
     cultures. James's practicalism leads to "practical
     idealism," a position similar to Gandhi's.

20   RIEPE, DALE. "A Note on William James and Indian Philosophy,"
     Philosophy and Phenomenological Research, XXVIII (June),
     587-590.
         James knew something of Indian thought, but what he knew
     of it was not particularly "congenial" to him.

21   ROSENZWEIG, SAUL. "William James and the Stream of Thought"
     in Historical Roots of Contemporary Psychology. Edited
     by B. B. Wolman. New York: Harper and Row. French
     translation, "William James et le courant de conscience,"
     Bulletin de Psychologie, XXIII (1969-1970), 1001-1009.
         An expansion of "The Jameses' Stream of Consciousness"
     (1958), with emphasis on the connection between the stream
     of consciousness and Freud's free association.

22   SHIELDS, ALLAN. "On A Certain Blindness in William James --
     and Others," The Journal of Aesthetics and Art Criticism,
     XXVII (Fall), 27-34.
         James expressed a strong distaste for aesthetics although
     he was sensitive to art. James's case may help us to
     understand why other philosophers share the same blindness.

23   SLEEPER, R. W. "Pragmatism, Religion, and 'Experienceable
     Difference'" in M. Novak, ed., American Philosophy and the
     Future (1968).
         For Peirce, pragmatism was a theory of meaning rather
     than of truth. He emphasized laws while James was inter-
     ested in "particular events and outcomes." Both held that
     beliefs are rules of action.

24   SMITH, JOHN E. "William James as Philosophical Psychologist,"
     Midway, VIII (Winter), 3-19.
         James was a philosophical psychologist. He never ignored
     the background from which he had abstracted some item for
     analysis. He accepted the responsibility of interpreting
     human existence in a comprehensive way.

25   STROH, GUY W. American Philosophy from Edwards to Dewey: An
     Introduction. Princeton, N.J.: D. Van Nostrand.
         Surveys major aspects of James's thought. With James,
     pragmatism becomes a "life-philosophy."

1968

26   STROUT, CUSHING. "Ego Psychology and the Historian," History
      and Theory, VII, 281-297.
          James mediates between the idealism of R. G. Collingwood
      and the naturalism of Freud.

27   _____. "William James and the Twice-Born Sick Soul," Daedalus,
      XCVII (Summer), 1062-1082.
          James saw life as a struggle in which the self is trans-
      formed. James's own life illustrates this.

28   THAYER, HORACE S. Meaning and Action: A Critical History of
      Pragmatism. Indianapolis: Bobbs-Merrill.
          Covers American, English, French, and Italian pragmatism.
      James is viewed primarily in his relations with Peirce,
      his interpretation of Peirce's pragmatic maxim and his
      extension of pragmatism into a theory of truth. An
      extensive bibliography is provided.

29   VAN BUREN, PAUL M. "William James and Metaphysical Risk" in
      M. Novak, ed., American Philosophy and the Future (1968).
          For modern theology, the central aspect of James's
      thought should be his avowal of metaphysical risk.

1969 A BOOKS

1   MACLEOD, ROBERT B., ed. William James: Unfinished Business:
     Washington, D. C.: American Psychological Association.
         Papers by David Kretch, Harry F. Harlow, Ernest R.
     Hilgard, and Rollo May are indexed separately. Partici-
     pants in discussions are listed with the main papers.
     Contains an unsigned introduction "James as Phenomenologist."

2   ROTH, JOHN K. Freedom and the Moral Life: The Ethics of
     William James. Philadelphia: Westminster Press.
         Man's moral life combines uncertainty, risk, and hope.
     Roth traces the development of James's conception of the
     self and of freedom. James's ethical views give rise to
     an "existential norm": "Act so as to maximize freedom and
     unity."

3   WILD, JOHN DANIEL. The Radical Empiricism of William James.
     Garden City, N.Y.: Doubleday.
         James is an important early phenomenologist. In a broad
     sense, phenomenologists seek to discover structure in
     experience itself. James avoids "verbal construction" and
     looks for structures in the "brute facts of experience."
     Emphasis is placed on The Principles of Psychology.

1969 B SHORTER WRITINGS

1 ALLEN, GAY WILSON. "William James: Pragmatism, A New Name for Some Old Ways of Thinking" in Landmarks of American Writing. Edited by Hennig Cohen. New York: Basic Books.
For James, "only the test of experience can prove the reliability of assumptions." Americans are said to be pragmatists, but even now they often "rationalize the larger issues."

2 BLOMBERG, JAAKKO. "James on Belief and Truth," Ajatus XXXI, 171-187.
James is treated from an analytical point of view with reference to the criticisms of G. E. Moore (1908). James is dealing with the truth of beliefs rather than propositions. For him, utility distinguishes not true from false beliefs, but true beliefs from those the truth-value of which is unknown.

3 CARDNO, J. A. "'The Birds Are Rather Big for Ducks': Criterion and Material in History," Journal of the History of the Behavioral Sciences, V (January), 68-73.
A criticism of the view advanced by J. W. Fay, American Psychology Before William James (Brunswick, N.J.: Rutgers University Press, 1939), that T. C. Upham had anticipated the James-Lange theory.

4 CUNNINGHAM, G. WATTS. "On Reason's Reach: Historical Observations," American Philosophical Quarterly, VI (January), 1-16.
James revolts against reason as traditionally understood, but offers his own conception of rationality centering around the "beautiful or good." Cunningham surveys conceptions of rationality following the classification in A Pluralistic Universe.

5 DECONCHY, JEAN PIERRE. "La Définition de la religion chez William James: dans quelle mesure peut-on l'opération-aliser?" Archives de Sociologie des Religions, XXVII, 51-70.
James's definition of religion and his methods are examined at great length. James erred in separating religion from institutions and in ignoring its sociological context, since observational methods are applicable to the group. James shows few signs of methodological worries.

6 EDIE, JAMES M. "Necessary Truth and Perception: William James on the Structure of Experience" in New Essays in Phenomenology. Edited by J. M. Edie. Chicago: Quadrangle Books.

(EDIE, JAMES M.)
James insists upon the primacy of perception; "categorical thought" is "founded" upon the structures of perception. But he avoids "psychologism" and does not identify the two orders.

7   EHMAN, ROBERT R.   "William James and the Structure of the Self" in New Essays in Phenomenology. Edited by J. M. Edie. Chicago: Quadrangle Books.
Ehman analyses James's conception of "mineness," his theory of the central "core" of the self, and his view of personal identity. James's view are inadequate, but lead to a richer conception of the self than others.

8   GREENLEE, DOUGLAS. Review of A. J. Ayer The Origins of Pragmatism (1968) and H. S. Thayer Meaning and Action (1968), Journal of the History of Ideas, XXX (October–December), 603–608.
Thayer correctly views James's pragmatism as an attempt to mediate between the new science and the old religion and morals, but errs in applying this to all pragmatists. James's theory of truth involves many absurdities and neither Thayer nor Ayer explain why James tolerated them.

9   HARLOW, HARRY F.   "William James and Instinct Theory" in R. B. MacLeod, ed., William James (1969).
In The Principles of Psychology, James relied heavily upon instincts. Through the work of John Broadus Watson, psychology came to abandon this notion. The main paper is followed by Sidney W. Bijou, "Modern Meaning of Instincts" and Ogden R. Lindsley, "The Secret Life of William James."

10   HILGARD, ERNEST R.   "Levels of Awareness: Second Thoughts on Some of William James' Ideas" in R. B. MacLeod, ed., William James (1969).
The main problem can be divided into three parts: that of "levels of attention," that of the stream of thought and how many streams there are, that of the "unconscious and subconscious levels." Hilgard compares James with later psychologists. The main paper is followed by Paul Bakan, "Thoughts on Hilgard's Paper on 'Levels of Awareness'" and Jerome L. Singer, "Some Experimental Studies of the Stream of Thought."

11   KERSTEN, FRED.   "Franz Brentano and William James," Journal of the History of Philosophy, VII (April), 177–191.
James's earlier theory of "multiple realities" and his later radical empiricism can be shown to be not inconsistent by the study of Brentano's influence upon James.

James's thought moves towards the abandonment of the
"primacy of the mere presentendeness of reality" and
towards intentionality.

12 KRECH, DAVID. "Does Behavior Really Need a Brain? In Praise
of William James: Some Historical Musings, Vain Lamenta-
tions, and a Sounding of Great Expectations" in
R. B. MacLeod, ed., William James (1969).
James valued brain research. Had psychology followed
him, it would be further advanced. But Edward Bradford
Titchener and John Broadus Watson joined forces to banish
brain research from psychology. The main paper is followed
by. George Mandler, "Acceptance of Things Past and Present:
A Look at the Mind and the Brain," and Peter Milner, "Do
Behaviorists Really Need a Brain Drain?"

13 McCOOL, GERALD A. "Philosophy and Christian Wisdom," Thought,
XLIV (Winter), 485-512.
Catholic philosophers find James's humanism attractive.
However, James is hostile to the metaphysics which sustains
Christian wisdom.

14 MASON, GABRIEL RICHARD and BURTON, ARTHUR. William James and
Religion. New York: Diana Press.
A pamphlet. James ignored conflicting religious faiths,
the brutality of believers, and the faith and hope provided
by science.

15 MAY, ROLLO. "William James' Humanism and the Problem of Will"
in R. B. MacLeod, ed., William James (1969).
Discusses James's humanism, relations with existentialism,
and concepts of the will. The will is treated in relation
to intentionality to show how "we can build upon it for our
day." The paper is followed by James F. T. Bugental,
"Intentionality and Ambivalence," Nevitt Sanford, "I Know
How It Is Done but I Just Can't Do It," and Silvan S.
Tomkins, "Free Will and the Degrees-of-Freedom Principle."

16 MEYERS, ROBERT G. "Natural Realism and Illusion in James's
Radical Empiricism," Transactions of the Charles S. Peirce
Society, V (Fall), 211-223.
In the end, James prefers naive realism to phenomenalism.
James and G. E. Moore in claiming that observers viewing an
object from different perspectives have "numerically distinct contents" are both mistaken. James errs about "per-
spectival illusions," but his argument can be reconstructed
into a view of immediate perception like Moore's.

1969

17   MILLS, EUGENE S.   George Trumbull Ladd: Pioneer American
     Psychologist.   Cleveland: Press of Case Western Reserve
     University.
          Includes two letters from James to Ladd.

18   MYERS, GERALD E.   "William James's Theory of Emotion," Trans-
     actions of the Charles S. Peirce Society, V (Spring),
     67-89.
          Criticism led James to modify his theory.   Myers discusses
     these modifications and philosophical arguments for and
     against the theory.

19   ROTH, JOHN K.   Introduction to The Moral Philosophy of William
     James.   New York: Thomas Y. Crowell.
          A man's moral task is to find a place in an uncertain
     world.   James held that moral values are closely connected
     with free choices.   He never elaborated a moral system.

20   SCHIRMER, DANIEL B.   "William James and the New Age," Science
     and Society, XXXIII (Fall-Winter), 434-445.
          Surveys James's social thought with emphasis on anti-
     imperialism and war.   Through the influence of H. G.
     Wells, James came to accept Fabian socialism.   In his last
     years, he was gathering material for a book on The Psychol-
     ogy of Jingoism.

21   SCHRAG, CALVIN O.   "Struktur der Erfahrung in der Philosophie
     von James und Whitehead," Zeitschrift für philosophische
     Forschung, XXIII, 479-494.
          James and Whitehead both overcome the subject-object
     analysis of experience.

22   WILD, JOHN DANIEL.   "William James and the Phenomenology of
     Belief" in New Essays in Phenomenology.   Edited by J. M.
     Edie.   Chicago: Quadrangle Books.
          James was "phenomenologically oriented."   He tried to
     describe "empirical structures as we live them through."
     James's description of belief contains inaccuracies.

23   WILSHIRE, BRUCE.   "Protophenomenology in the Psychology of
     William James," Transactions of the Charles S. Peirce
     Society, V (Winter), 25-43.
          In The Principles of Psychology, James tries to correlate
     mental with bodily states.   But this program breaks down
     and gives rise to a second dualism, between thought and
     its object, which leads James to the view that the two are
     identical, a step towards radical empiricism and
     phenomenology.

1970 A BOOKS

1   ALLEN, GAY WILSON. <u>William James</u>. Minneapolis: University of
    Minnesota Press. University of Minnesota Pamphlets on
    American Writers. Reprinted in Ralph Ross, ed., <u>Makers of</u>
    <u>American Thought: An Introduction to Seven American</u>
    <u>Writers</u>, (Minneapolis: University of Minnesota Press,
    1974).
       Provides summaries of the major works.

1970 B SHORTER WRITINGS

1   BIXLER, JULIUS SEELYE. "James Family Letters in Colby College
    Library," <u>Colby Library Quarterly</u>, IX (March), 35-47.
       Letters by James are included.

2   CLENDENNING, JOHN, ed. <u>The Letters of Josiah Royce</u>. Chicago:
    University of Chicago Press.
       Contains letters to James.

3   EDIE, JAMES M. "William James and Phenomenology," <u>The Review</u>
    <u>of Metaphysics</u>, XXIII (March), 481-526.
       A review of Linschoten, <u>On the Way Toward a Phenomenologi-</u>
    <u>cal Psychology</u> (1968), Wilshire, <u>William James and</u>
    <u>Phenomenology</u> (1968), Wild, <u>The Radical Empiricism of</u>
    <u>William James</u> (1969). These studies have established the
    facts concerning James's influence on phenomenology and
    show it to have been important.

4   . "William James and the Phenomenological Thesis of the
    Primacy of Perception," <u>Proceedings of the XIVth Interna-</u>
    <u>tional Congress of Philosophy</u> (Vienna: Herder), V, 88-95.
       A short version of "Necessary Truth and Perception"
    (1969).

5   FEHR, FRED S. and STERN, JOHN A. "Peripheral Physiological
    Variables and Emotion: The James-Lange Theory Revisited,"
    <u>Psychological Bulletin</u>, LXXIV (December), 411-424.
       Surveys the experimental literature with an extensive
    bibliography.

6   FEINSTEIN, HOWARD M. "William James on the Emotions," <u>Journal</u>
    <u>of the History of Ideas</u>, XXXI (January-March) 133-142.
       Traces the development of James's theory of emotion.
    <u>The Principles of Psychology</u> contain a conflict between
    materialistic method and James's personal spiritualistic
    bias, particularly in the theory of emotion. This theory
    is similar to certain views expressed by Darwin.

1970

7   GOBAR, ASH. "The Phenomenology of William James," <u>Proceedings</u>
     <u>of the American Philosophical Society</u>, CXIV (August),
     294-309.
          Traces the development of the phenomenological strain
     through distinct phases, interrupted by years when the
     phenomenological strain was dormant.

8   GOULD, JAMES A. "R. B. Perry on the Origin of American and
     European Pragmatism," <u>Journal of the History of Philosophy</u>,
     VIII (October), 431-450.
          In letters to the author, Perry argued that James goes
     back to British empiricism while European pragmatism
     originates in pragmatic interpretation of Kant's <u>a priori</u>.
     This thesis is not correct. Gould compares James with
     Locke, Charles Renouvier, and Hans Vaihinger.

9   LARRABEE, HAROLD A. "The Fourth William James," <u>Colby Library</u>
     <u>Quarterly</u>, IX (March), 1-34.
          Sketch of the life of William James (1797-1868), James's
     half-uncle, with an account of the will of William James
     of Albany, James's grandfather.

10   LINDEMAN, JACK. "William James and the Octopus of Higher Edu-
     cation," <u>School and Society</u>, XCVIII (October), 365-367.
          James would be shocked by our gigantic universities. He
     believed that practical concerns should lie outside the
     university. In the spirit of James, we may hope that uni-
     versities become the home of scholarship and help create
     a "natural aristocracy."

11   MARCELL, DAVID W. "John Fiske, Chauncey Wright, and William
     James: A Dialogue on Progress," <u>Journal of American</u>
     <u>History</u>, LVI (March), 802-818.
          Parts incorporated in <u>Progress and Pragmatism</u> (1974).
     Traces the development of the idea of progress in the three
     thinkers.

12   MORRIS, CHARLES. <u>The Pragmatic Movement in American Philosophy</u>.
     New York: George Braziller.
          Morris states the basic ideas of Peirce, James, Mead,
     and Dewey, and shows their similarities to each other.
     Treated at greater length are James's relations with
     Peirce, with the Chicago School, his formulation of the
     pragmatic maxim, theory of truth, and radical empiricism.

13   NÉDONCELLE, MAURICE. "Une Lettre inédite de Friedrich von
     Hügel à William James," <u>Studi Internazionali di Filosofia</u>,
     II (Summer-Fall), 117-130.

168

French translation of letter sent by von Hugel to James
with a copy of von Hugel's The Mystical Element of Religion
(1908), May 10, 1909.

14 REEVE, E. GAVIN. "William James on Pure Being and Pure
Nothing," Philosophy, XLV (January), 59-60.
     James's criticism of Hegel's contention that being and
nothing are identical overlooks the fact that Hegel holds
the two to be also opposed. Using James's terms, Hegel
takes the concepts both statically and dynamically.

15 ROSENZWEIG, SAUL. "Erik Erikson on William James's Dream:
A Note of Correction," Journal of the History of the
Behavioral Sciences, VI (July), 258-260.
     In Identity: Youth and Crisis (1968), Erikson interprets
James's dream, related in "A Suggestion About Mysticism"
(1910), as a case of "'terminal despair' centering in an
'identity confusion'." Erikson thinks that James died in
1906; in fact, the dream occured in 1906, one of the most
creative periods of James's life. On p. 260 appears
Erikson's rejoinder that the mistake does not invalidate
his interpretation.

16 ROSS, RALPH. Introduction to The Meaning of Truth. Ann Arbor:
The University of Michigan Press.
     Explains why James was so misunderstood on the question
of truth.

17 STROUT, CUSHING. "All the King's Men and the Shadow of William
James," The Southern Review, NS 6 (Autumn), 920-934.
     Robert Penn Warren claimed that he drew from James in
developing the character of Willie Stark, a southern
demagogue, in All the King's Men. Warren develops certain
themes of James's philosophy and reveals the dangers of
pragmatism when that is "abstracted from the moral sense
and metaphysics that James notably had."

18 STRUNK, ORLO, JR. "Humanistic Religious Psychology: A New
Chapter in the Psychology of Religion," The Journal of
Pastoral Care, XXIV (June), 90-97.
     James, its founder, gave psychology of religion a
humanistic tone which has survived attacks by "insipid
scientism."

1971

1971 A BOOKS

1   EISENDRATH, CRAIG R. The Unifying Moment: The Psychological
        Philosophy of William James and Alfred North Whitehead.
        Cambridge, Mass.: Harvard University Press.
            James describes the "creation of the self" and how it
        guides "perception and action." Whitehead accepts this
        analysis and works out theories of space, time, and per-
        ception. Together, they offer an alternative both to
        phenomenology and positivism. Materials for the study of
        James's influence on Whitehead are not available.

1971 B SHORTER WRITINGS

1   BLANSHARD, BRAND. "The Ethics of Belief," Philosophic
        Exchange, vol. I, no. 2 (Summer), 81-93.
            James mistakenly holds that belief in some cases is
        justified even where knowledge is lacking. Men have other
        duties besides that of action and happiness which results
        from illusion has little value.

2   BROWN, WILLIAM R. "William James and the Language of Personal
        Literature," Style, V (Spring), 151-163.
            Proposes a "more precise genre designation" for writing
        in which the author is present in the style more than in
        other genres. James is used as an illustration.

3   CHAMBERLAIN, GARY L. "The Drive for Meaning in William James'
        Analysis of Religious Experience," The Journal of Value
        Inquiry, V (Summer), 194-206.
            James tried to explain how we discover meaning in life.
        He used a "mechanistic horizontal model" with expressions
        such as 'fringe,' 'width,' 'beyond' rather than the
        "superego-ego-id" model derived from Freud.

4   DELANEY, C. F. "Recent Work on American Philosophy," The
        New Scholasticism, XLV (Summer), 457-477.
            Ayer's The Origins of Pragmatism (1968) is the most sig-
        nificant work on classical figures.

5   EDIE, JAMES M. Preface to William James: The Essential
        Writings. Edited by Bruce Wilshire. New York: Harper &
        Row.
            Some treat James as an historical figure, others, as an
        expression of American culture. He should be regarded as
        a philosopher whose work is worth developing.

6   FURLONG, E. J. "On Moving One's Arm," Hermathena, no. 111
     (Spring), 65-73.
         Continues discussion by G. N. A. Vesey, "Volition,"
     Philosophy, XXXVI (October 1961), 352-365; Robert A. Imlay,
     "Do I Ever Directly Raise My Arm?," Philosophy, XLII
     (April 1967), 119-127; and Vesey, "Do I Ever Directly
     Raise My Arm?," Philosophy, XLII (April 1967), 148-149,
     in which a case discussed in The Principles of Psychology
     (1890), II, 492 served as an illustration. The problem
     is whether or not volition can be eliminated from the
     descriptions.

7   GILMORE, LYMAN. "What Teachers Have to Learn from William
     James -- A Payment or Neglect," Journal of Education, CLIV
     (December), 7-14.
         James is relevant to a changing world because he in-
     sisted that education train our ability to cope.

8   HALE, NATHAN G. Freud and the Americans: The Beginnings of
     Psychoanalysis in the United States, 1876-1917. New York:
     Oxford University Press.
         James developed a pre-Freudian view of the unconscious
     and took psychopathology seriously. About sexuality,
     James was "conservative and rebellious." He ridiculed
     excessive modesty.

9   _____. James Jackson Putnam and Psychoanalysis: Letters
     Between Putnam and Sigmund Freud, Ernest Jones, William
     James, Sandor Ferenczi, and Morton Prince, 1877-1917.
     Cambridge, Mass.: Harvard University Press.
         Letters between James and Putnam. In the Introduction,
     Hale quotes a letter by Freud in which Freud describes
     Keene Valley, N. Y., where Freud was Putnam's guest.

10   HERTZ, RICHARD A. "James and Moore: Two Perspectives on
     Truth," Journal of the History of Philosophy, IX (April),
     213-221.
         Moore viewed truth from a divine perspective, James,
     from a human. While they argued at cross-purposes, James
     identified some important points.

11   HULL, BYRON D. "'Henderson the Rain King' and William James,"
     Criticism, XIII (Fall), 402-414.
         In his Henderson the Rain King, Saul Bellow refers to
     James's Psychology and this provides a clue to understand-
     ing the character, Dahfu. Dahfu acts as a psychotherapist
     using James's ideas.

1971

12   LA RUE, HOMER C. "W. E. B. Du Bois and the Pragmatic Method
      of Truth," Journal of Human Relations, XIX, 82-96.
         Du Bois understood that negro life could not be inter-
      preted by science alone, that a poetic understanding was
      needed. Du Bois learned this two-fold approach from
      James's pragmatism. A number of passages in which Du Bois
      refers to James are quoted.

13   MATHUR, D. C. Naturalistic Philosophies of Experience:
      Studies in James, Dewey and Farber Against the Background
      of Husserl's Phenomenology. St. Louis, Mo.: Warren H.
      Green.
         James is an important precursor of "naturalistic
      phenomenology." He differs from Husserl's idealistic
      phenomenology by his empiricism and emphasis on the per-
      sonal and changing character of knowledge.

14   MEYERS, ROBERT G. "Meaning and Metaphysics in James," Philos-
      ophy and Phenomenological Research, XXXI (March), 369-380.
         James's theory of meaning seems close to the positiv-
      istic and yet he holds metaphysical statements to be mean-
      ingful. This has led to views that James is confused.
      The problem vanishes when we distinguish tests of meaning
      from reasons for holding a belief.

15   MULLER, HERBERT J. In Pursuit of Relevance. Bloomington:
      Indiana University Press.
         James's thought is relevant to the problems raised by
      the student revolt. James was a democratic thinker who
      could do justice to ordinary people without neglecting
      culture.

16   MURPHY, GARDNER. "William James on the Will," Journal of the
      History of the Behavioral Sciences, VII (July), 249-260.
         James distinguished hard from soft determinism, but held
      neither, insisting on free will. James's choice is itself
      a case of soft determinism. James analyzed "voluntary
      processes" into effort, attention, selection, holding in
      mind, and "ideo-motor action." This is an "experimentable
      theory."

17   MYERS, GERALD E. "William James on Time Perception," Philoso-
      phy of Science, XXXVIII (September), 353-360.
         James mistakenly held that "time is a sensation."

18   PANCHERI, LILLIAN U. "James, Lewis and the Pragmatic A Priori,"
      Transactions of the Charles S. Peirce Society, VII (Summer),
      135-149.

172

C. I. Lewis' "conceptualistic pragmatism" is usually
traced to James, but Lewis' notion of the pragmatic a
priori also could come from James.

19 PHILLIPS, D. C. "James, Dewey, and the Reflex Arc," <u>Journal
of the History of Ideas</u>, XXXII (October-December),
555-568.
Surveys the history of the reflex theory with emphasis
on its development in James and James's influence on
H. Münsterberg and Dewey. The theory seems to conflict
with freedom. To resolve this, James developed the view
that consciousness selects a response from a range of
responses.

20 PLATT, DAVID. "Is Empirical Theology Adequate?" <u>International
Journal for Philosophy of Religion</u>, II (Spring), 28-42.
James tried to develop an empirical theology and his
efforts are instructive.

21 RECK, ANDREW J. "The Philosophical Psychology of William
James," <u>Southern Journal of Philosophy</u>, IX (Fall),
293-312.
The task of philosophical psychology is to analyze the
fundamental concepts of psychology. Reck surveys James's
views on the methods of psychology, the mind-body relation,
consciousness, and the self.

22 ROTH, JOHN K. Introduction to <u>Moral Equivalent of War and
Other Essays</u>. Edited by John K. Roth. New York: Harper
& Row.
James can help Americans understand themselves during
this critical period of American history. Meliorism is
the fundamental "dimension of his thought." Roth discusses
James's views on war, education, health, and "man's search
for meaning."

23 _____. "William James, John Dewey, and the 'Death-of-God,'"
<u>Religious Studies</u>, VII (March), 53-61.
James holds that God, when properly understood, is
compatible with an "empirical and naturalistic orientation," in contrast with Dewey and radical theology.

24 SINGER, MARCUS G. "The Pragmatic Use of Language and the Will
to Believe," <u>American Philosophical Quarterly</u>, VIII
(January), 24-34.
Analytic philosophy has overlooked the pragmatic use of
language. This use is illustrated by the will to believe.

1971

25   SPICKER, STUART F. "William James and Phenomenology," The
     Journal of the British Society for Phenomenology, vol. II,
     no. 3 (October), 69-74.
         A review of Wilshire, William James and Phenomenology
     (1968). Wilshire has little knowledge of Husserl and
     fails to relate James to phenomenology. Wilshire replies
     on pp. 75-80, while Spicker ends the exchange on p. 80.

26   STROUT, CUSHING. "The Pluralistic Identity of William James:
     A Psychohistorical Reading of The Varieties of Religious
     Experience," American Quarterly, XXIII (May), 135-152.
         Varieties marks James's passage from the early to the
     mature phase. It can be clarified by understanding
     James's "development as a person."

27   TIBBETTS, PAUL. "The Philosophy of Science of William James:
     An Unexplored Dimension of James's Thought," The Personal-
     ist, LII (Summer), 535-556.
         James is one of several authors who paved the way for a
     new conception of science.

28   _____. "William James and the Doctrine of 'Pure Experience,'"
     University of Dayton Review, VIII (Summer), 43-58.
         James's conception of experience developed from "sensa-
     tionism," to "phenomenalism," to pure experience. He was
     influenced by Ernst Mach and Wilhelm Wundt.

29   VANDEN BURGT, ROBERT. "William James on Man's Creativity in
     the Religious Universe," Philosophy Today, XV (Winter),
     292-301.
         The conception of an "open universe" awaiting "man's
     creative touch" pervades James's thought.

30   WEINSTEIN, MICHAEL A. "Life and Politics as Plural: James
     and Bentley on the Twentieth Century Problem," Journal of
     Value Inquiry, V (Winter), 282-291.
         James viewed politics pluralistically, applying his
     nominalism to the analysis of government. James's ideas
     were developed by Arthur F. Bentley.

31   WILSHIRE, BRUCE W. Introduction to William James: The Essen-
     tial Writings. New York: Harper & Row.
         James belonged to no school, but rather with a "pre-
     Socratic naivete" saw problems "as if for the first time."

1972 A BOOKS - NONE

1972 B SHORTER WRITINGS

1   ÅKERBERG, HANS. "The Significance of William James's Psychology
     of Religion Today," Studia Theologica, XXVI, 141-158.
          James provides the basis of a humanistic psychology of
     religion. Also noteworthy is his treatment of the sick
     soul and of conversion.

2   ALLEN, GAY WILSON. Introduction to A William James Reader.
     Edited by G. W. Allen. Boston: Houghton, Mifflin.
          Comments on selections in the anthology.

3   BARZUN, JACQUES. Letter to the editor, Times Literary Supple-
     ment, September 15, 1972, p. 1060.
          Includes letter from James to Robert U. Johnson, June 17,
     1905, on James's rejection of membership in the Academy of
     Arts and Letters. This letter is part of a controversy
     about the relations between James and Henry James sparked
     by Edel (1953). Burzun commented in the New York Times
     Book Review, April 16, 1972, p. 36. Edel replied in the
     Times Literary Supplement, October 13, 1972, pp. 1226-1227.
     Lionel Trilling also participated, Times Literary Supple-
     ment, October 20, 1972, p. 1257.

4   BERGSON, HENRI. Mélanges, edited by André Robinet. Paris:
     Presses Universitaires de France.
          Includes letters from and to James, many of Bergson's
     writings about James, and documents referring to James.

5   BISHOP, DONALD H. "William James and the Humanist Manifesto,"
     Religious Humanism, VI (Winter), 34-39.
          The Humanist Manifesto of 1933 declared that men must
     free themselves from religion and by themselves strive to
     improve the world. The roots of this manifesto lie in
     thinkers like James.

6   CADWALLADER, THOMAS C. and CADWALLADER, JOYCE V. "America's
     First Modern Psychologist: William James or Charles S.
     Peirce?", Proceedings of the 80th Annual Convention of the
     American Psychological Association, Contributed Papers and
     Symposia, VII, 773-774.
          Priority is established by interest in German psychophys-
     iology, book reviews, theoretical papers, experimental
     papers, and teaching. James can claim priority only in
     the last category.

7   DAVIS, STEPHEN T. "Wishful Thinking and 'The Will to Believe,'"
     Transactions of the Charles S. Peirce Society, VIII (Fall),
     231-245.

1972

(DAVIS, STEPHEN T.)
A defense of the will to believe against charges by D. S.
Miller and John Hick, Faith and Knowledge (Ithaca, N.Y.:
Cornell University Press, 1957). James does not violate,
he questions accepted standards of rationality.

8   DOOLEY, PATRICK K. "The Nature of Belief: The Proper Context
for James' 'The Will to Believe,'" Transactions of the
Charles S. Peirce Society, VIII (Summer), 141-151.
The will to believe must be placed in a larger context,
that of James's theory of belief and conception of human
nature.

9   FERM, DEANE WILLIAM. "William James: Moralism, the Will to
Believe, and Theism," Religion in Life, XLI (Autumn),
349-361.
For James, man's chief end is to improve the world by
cooperating with the divine power.

10 JOHNSON, ELLWOOD. "William James and the Art of Fiction,"
Journal of Aesthetics and Art Criticism, XXX (Spring),
285-296.
The Principles of Psychology mark a turning point in
American literature. James's denial of a substantial soul
and claim that the self exists "in the flux of experience,"
added a "new dimension to the art of characterization."

11 LAWN, BEVERLY. "From Temple to Streets: The Style of Pragmatism," The New England Quarterly, XLV (December), 526-540.
In Pragmatism, James chose to appeal to the "money-minded
and anti-intellectual" American. Pragmatism tells us to
look at consequences, but what would be the consequences
of reinforcing "the current obsession with money, technol-
ogy, and activity"?

12 RECK, ANDREW J. "Dualisms in William James's Principles of
Psychology," Tulane Studies in Philosophy, XXI, 23-38.
Two dualisms pervade The Principles of Psychology. A
psycho-physical dualism for which mind and body are pro-
cesses and an epistemological dualism which insists upon
a knower and known and considers them to be "irreducible."

13 SLACK, ROBERT C. "Willie Stark and William James" in In Honor
of Austin Wright. Edited by Joseph Bain and others.
Pittsburgh: Carnegie-Mellon University.
Examines hint by Robert Penn Warren that the character
of Willie Stark in All The King's Men is modeled after
James.

14   SPIEGELBERG, HERBERT. "What William James Knew About Edmund
      Husserl" in Life-World and Consciousness: Essays for Aron
      Gurwitsch. Edited by Lester E. Embree. Evanston, Ill.
      Northwestern University Press.
          Walter B. Pitkin in On My Own (New York: Charles
      Scribner's Sons, 1944) remarks that his translation of
      Husserl's Logische Untersuchungen was turned down by an
      American publisher on James's advice. A detailed analysis
      of James's whereabouts during this time shows that it is
      unlikely that James saw the manuscript of the translation.
      James could have known nothing of Husserl's phenomenology
      but only of Husserl's attacks on psychologism.

15   WERTZ, S. K. "On Wittgenstein and James," The New Scholasti-
      cism, XLVI (Autumn), 446-448.
          John Passmore (1966), p. 592, and Matthew Fairbanks
      (1966) have pointed out the importance of James for Ludwig
      Wittgenstein. James's influence goes further than either
      Passmore or Fairbanks had claimed.

16   WHITE, MORTON. Science and Sentiment in America. New York:
      Oxford University Press.
          In The Will to Believe, James gave sentiment a place in
      religious belief, in Pragmatism, in all beliefs. In A
      Pluralistic Universe, James espoused a form of irrational-
      ism in the tradition of "philosophical Romanticism." In
      Pragmatism, James came to adopt a holistic approach to
      truth.

1973 A BOOKS - NONE

1973 B SHORTER WRITINGS

 1   BAILEY, N. I. "Pragmatism in The Ambassadors," The Dalhousie
      Review, LIII (Spring), 143-148.
          The pragmatic theory of knowledge is followed by Henry
      James in the development of one of the characters.

 2   CARLSSON, P. ALLAN. "Jung and James on the Typology of World
      Views," The Journal of General Education, XXV (July),
      113-119.
          James's distinction between the tender-minded and the
      tough-minded was important in the development of Jung's
      theory of psychological types in Psychologische Typen
      (1921).

1973

3   EDIE, JAMES M. "The Genesis of a Phenomenological Theory of
      the Experience of Personal Identity: William James on
      Consciousness and the Self," Man and World, VI (September),
      322-340.
           Examines James's theory of the self from the point of
      view of phenomenology to throw light on the problem of
      personal identity. James did not work out a complete
      theory of the self. He provided the elements of a "phenom-
      enological elucidation."

4   FERM, DEANE WILLIAM. "Reality of the 'Divine,'" The Christian
      Century, XC (November 28), 1182.
           A rejoinder to Edward H. Sawyer (1973).

5   _____. "Taking God Seriously (With the Help of William James),"
      The Christian Century, XC (May 23), 596-600.
           Both secularism and pop-mysticism deny that a transcendent
      and personal God can be taken seriously. But theology
      must do so, and in this is greatly helped by James's work.
      Ferm emphasizes James's notion of a finite God.

6   GILMORE, R. M. "William James and Religious Language: Daugh-
      ters of Earth, Sons of Heaven?" Église et Théologie, IV
      (October), 359-390.
           An attempt, by reference to James's biography, to evoke
      James's state of mind while he was delivering the Gifford
      lectures at Edinburgh. Gilmore collects James's remarks
      on the status of reason and language.

7   GINI, A. R. "William James: Facts, Faith, and Promise," The
      Thomist, XXXVII (July), 489-509.
           Empiricists often restrict reality to the "immediate
      facts of experience." James is an exception. For James,
      facts are not enough and men can "out-strip" them through
      acts of faith. James is sensitive to the "ultimate goals"
      of men.

8   HOOK, SIDNEY. "William James and George Santayana," I Carb S
      (Southern Illinois University, Carbondale), vol. I, no. 1
      (Fall-Winter), 35-39.
           Santayana's initial reactions to James were favorable.
      In time, Santayana realized that a temperamental and philo-
      sophical gulf separated him from James. Included are fac-
      similes of a letter from James to Santayana on Santayana's
      review (1891) of The Principles of Psychology and of the
      presentation page of the copy of the Principles given in
      turn to Santayana, H. M. Kallen, and Sidney Hook, and now
      in the Morris Library at Southern Illinois.

9   MAURER, ARMAND A. "A Thomist Looks at William James's Notion
    of Truth," The Monist, LVII (April), 151-167.
        For St. Thomas, knowledge is entirely an empirical
    affair, while James in his own way makes the "transcenden-
    tal turn" and his modified Kantianism insists on the pres-
    ence of certain inborn forms which structure experience.
    For James, all knowledge has a practical cast. For a
    Thomist, this is a serious misconception of the nature of
    "speculative knowledge."

10 PARKER, GAIL THAIN. Mind Cure in New England. Hanover, N.H.:
    University Press of New England.
        James was one of several writers from whom the New
    Thought movement took its ideas. In James, there is a
    movement away from moralism. If earlier he associated
    moral effort with healthy-mindedness, later he attributed
    the same concerns to the sick soul.

11 PENDLETON, JAMES D. "The James Brothers and 'The Real Thing':
    A Study in Pragmatic Reality," South Atlantic Bulletin,
    XXXVIII (November), 3-10.
        Henry James's story "The Real Thing" (1893) shows that
    both for him and for James reality is "what stimulates the
    creative imagination and which works efficiently when put
    to use."

12 SAWYER, EDWARD H. "Ferm's Appeal to William James: Use or
    Misuse?" The Christian Century, XC (September 19),
    923-924.
        Comments on Ferm (1973). James can be used to support
    the notion of something greater than ourselves but not to
    support theism.

13 WHITE, MORTON. Pragmatism and the American Mind: Essays and
    Reviews in Philosophy and Intellectual History. New York:
    Oxford University Press.
        The first paper on James is a compilation of two pre-
    viously published reviews, a favorable review of Perry's
    The Thought and Character of William James: Briefer
    Version (1948) and a severely critical review of Allen's
    William James (1967). Allen attempts to relate James's
    life to his thought, but since he is entirely ignorant of
    philosophy, the results are embarrassing. The second
    paper, "Logical Positivism and the Pragmatism of William
    James," is a previously published review of Ayer's The
    Origins of Pragmatism (1968).

1974

<u>1974 A BOOKS</u>

1   DOOLEY, PATRICK KIARAN. <u>Pragmatism as Humanism: The Philoso-</u>
    <u>phy of William James</u>. Chicago: Nelson-Hall.
        James's theory of man provides us with a focus for a
    systematic understanding of him. Dooley surveys James's
    views on the scientific study of man in psychology, his
    approach to man in ethics and religion, and his humanistic
    epistemology and metaphysics. In all cases James sets up
    the "whole man" as his standard.

2   HOCKS, RICHARD A. <u>Henry James and Pragmatistic Thought: A</u>
    <u>Study in the Relationship Between the Philosophy of</u>
    <u>William James and the Literary Art of Henry James</u>. Chapel
    Hill: The University of North Carolina Press.
        Especially in his later works, Henry James "actualized"
    James's pragmatism. Henry James has "the very mode of
    thinking" which James expounds. Hocks does not attempt to
    study influences and is primarily interested in understand-
    ing Henry James.

3   STEVENS, RICHARD. <u>James and Husserl: The Foundations of</u>
    <u>Meaning</u>. Phaenomenologica, vol. LX. The Hague: Nijhoff.
        James's attempt to uncover the realm of pure experience
    is like Husserl's return to the "primordial evidence of
    the life-world." However, differences should not be
    ignored. James would have condemned Husserl's search for
    absolute certainty. James seeks for a direct description
    of what is given, Husserl always insists upon the "consti-
    tuting activity of consciousness."

<u>1974 B SHORTER WRITINGS</u>

1   BISHOP, DONALD H. "The Carus--James Controversy," <u>Journal</u>
    <u>of the History of Ideas</u>, XXXV (July-September), 509-520.
        Surveys Carus' criticism of James in <u>Truth on Trial</u>
    (1911). Carus opposed the notion of objective truth to
    James's utilitarianism. In metaphysics, central were the
    questions of relations and of monism. Carus also feared
    the consequences of James's views.

2   GINI, A. R. "Radical Subjectivism in the Thought of William
    James," <u>The New Scholasticism</u>, XLVIII (Autumn), 509-518.
        For James, "man is the locus of reality and the author
    and creator of history." Gini examines James's radical
    empiricism, theory of truth, and account of causality.

3   KAUBER, PETER. "Does James's Ethics of Belief Rest on a Mis-
    take?" <u>The Southern Journal of Philosophy</u>, XII (Summer),
    201-214.

James's attempt to develop an ethics of belief supposes
that belief is controlled by the will so that we may talk
about belief in terms of obligations. Contemporary analysis finds the notion of an ethics of belief meaningful.
James himself did not ignore difficulties. His analysis
is compatible with the modern one.

4   _____. "The Foundations of James's Ethics of Belief," Ethics,
     LXXXIV (January), 151–166.
        James's mature ethics of belief insists that we have a
     duty to follow the evidence when it is decisive. Where
     evidence is insufficient, we may either believe, disbelieve,
     or remain neutral. As a fact, in some cases we cannot
     remain neutral. The essay tries to find the origins of
     this ethics of belief in James's writings up to 1880.

5   _____, and HARE, R. M. "The Right and Duty to Will to Believe,"
     Canadian Journal of Philosophy, IV (December), 327–343.
        James's philosophy, in particular his voluntarism,
     implies a duty to will to believe, rather than simply a
     will to believe.

6   MARCELL, DAVID W. Progress and Pragmatism: James, Dewey,
     Beard, and the American Idea of Progress. Westport, Conn.:
     Greenwood Press.
        Pragmatism "bridges the gap" between the traditional
     American idea of progress and the more critical approach
     to experience "characterizing the twentieth century."
     James conceived progress as the result of the efforts of
     individuals trying to make their hopes come true.

7   MUYSKENS, JAMES L. "James' Defense of a Believing Attitude in
     Religion," Transactions of the Charles S. Peirce Society,
     X (Winter), 44–54.
        James's defense of belief is better construed as a
     defense of hope in the case of certain religious proposi-
     tions. Hope depends on evidential, moral, and pragmatic
     conditions, while belief, only on evidential.

8   PEARSON, FRED. "How the Energy Crisis Can Keep Us in Moral
     Fighting Trim," The Christian Century, XCI (March 6),
     256–259.
        Advice adapted from James.

9   SCHEFFLER, ISRAEL. Four Pragmatists: A Critical Introduction
     to Peirce, James, Mead, and Dewey. New York: Humanities
     Press.
        Contains sketches on a number of topics, emphasizing
     James's conception of truth.

1974

10 STRUG, CORDELL. "Seraph, Snake, and Saint: The Subconscious
Mind in James' Varieties," Journal of the American Academy
of Religion, XLII (September), 505-515.
James's notion of the "subconscious" is "fuzzy." Sometimes it simply means what is on the edges of consciousness
when I am paying attention to something else. At other
times, it indicates the "subliminal regions" of the mind,
a hypothesis about the ultimate nature of things. This
latter view is the "rotten apple" spoiling James's
conclusion.

11 ZEDLER, BEATRICE H. "Royce and James on Psychical Research,"
Transactions of the Charles S. Peirce Society, X (Fall),
235-252.
Survey's James's involvement with psychical research,
with some attempt to indicate James's conclusions. Contains a letter by Josiah Royce, written in 1900, defending
James against suggestions that James's ill health was due
to his interest in the occult.

Writings in Other Languages

1   AAKESSON, ELOF. "Begreppet 'medvetande' i William James'
    radikala empirism" in Gåva och krav: skrifter tillägnade
    Manfred Björkquist på hans femtioårsdag den 22 juni 1934.
    Uppsala: Almquist & Wiksells, 1934.

2   ALBEGGIANI, F. "Il prammatismo di W. James," Rivista di
    Filosofia, VI (1914), 200-219.

3   ALIOTTA, ANTONIO. Il problema di Dio e il nuovo pluralismo.
    Città di Castello: "Il Solco," 1924.
        Several sections treat James.

4   ALOYSIO, FRANCESCO DE. Da Dewey a James. Rome: Bulzoni,
    1972.
        A chapter, "Empirismo radicale, orientamenti
    spiritualistici e mondo della persona in James," appeared
    in Trimestre, V, 227-253.

5   ARANDA, LOUIS RODRIGUEZ. Introduction to Pragmatismo, trans-
    lated by Louis Rodriguez Aranda. Buenos Aires: Aguilar,
    1967.

6   ARDIGÒ, ROBERTO. Preface to La varie forme della coscienza
    religiosa, translated by G. C. Ferrari and M. Calderoni.
    Turin: Fratelli Bocca, 1904.

7   BARATONO, A. "Sviluppi della teoria Lange-James sulle
    emozioni," Quaderni di Psichiatria, XI (November-December
    1924), 201-209.

8   BASAVE FERNÁNDEZ DEL VALLE, AGUSTIN. "Significatión y sentido
    del pragmatismo norteamericano," Dianoia: Anuario de
    Filosofia, XVIII (1972), 251-272.

9   BERDIAEV, N. "O rasshirenie opyta," Voprosy Filosofii i
    Psikhologii, XXI (1910), 380-384.

Writings In Other Languages

10   BERTALAN, BIRÓ. A tudatalatti világ: William James
     lélektanában. Szeged, 1929.

11   BIRLIBA, D. M. "La Vérité et utilité chez selon W. James,"
     Analele Universitatii Bucuresti, serie filozofie, vol, XIX,
     no. 2, (1970), 145-149 (in Rumanian).

12   BOBOC, A. "Le Pragmatisme de William James," Analele
     Universitatii Bucuresti, serie filozofie, vol. XX, no. 2,
     (1971), 69-89 (in Rumanian).

13   BOSCO, NYNFA. "Due pragmatismi: Peirce e James," Filosofia
     (Turin), VIII (1957), 497-507.

14   BRUGMANS, HENRI JOHAN FRANS WILLEM. De waarheidstheorie van
     William James. Groningen: M. de Waal, 1913.

15   BUCZYŃSKA-GAREWICZ, HANNA. James. Warsaw: Wiedza Powszechna,
     1973.

16   CALÒ, GIOVANNI. Il problema della libertà nel pensiero
     contemporaneo. Milan: Remo Sandron, [1906].

17   CAPIZZI, ANTONIO. "Che cosa è la filosofia dell'opzione,"
     Giornale Critico della Filosofia Italiana, LII (4th series,
     vol. II) (April-June 1971), 179-207.

*18 CARPIO, ADOLFO P. Origen y desarrollo de la filosofía norte-
     americana. William James y el pragmatismo. Buenos Aires:
     Instituto Cultural Argentino-Norteamericano, 1952.
        Entry as given in the Handbook of Latin American Studies:
     1952, no. 18 (Gainesville: University of Florida Press,
     1955), p. 247.

19   CASTIGLIONI, GIULIO. James. Brescia: "La Scuola," 1945.

20   CELI, G. "La psicologia religiosa di William James," La
     Civiltà Cattolica, 63rd year, vol. III (September 21, 1912),
     654-665.

21   _____. "La santità secondo W. James," La Civiltà Cattolica,
     64th year, vol. I (February 1, 1913), 257-274.

22   _____. "William James e il pragmatismo," La Civiltà Cattolica,
     64th year, vol. II (April 19, 1913), 155-164.

23   _____. "William James e l'opera sua psicologica," La Civiltà
     Cattolica, 63rd year, vol. II (May 18, 1912), 401-413.

24   CHELPANOV, G. "Dzhams, kak psikholog," Voprosy Filosofii i
     Psikhologii," XXI (1910), 437-456.

25   CHIAPPELLI, ALESSANDRO. "William James e la sua opera di
     filosofo," Il Marzocco, vol. XV, no. 36 (September 4, 1910),
     1.

26   CHIOCCHETTI, E. Il pragmatismo. Milan: Edizione Athena,
     1926.

27   _____. "Saggio di esposizione sintetica del pragmatismo
     religioso di W. James e di F. C. S. Schiller," Rivista di
     Filosofia Neoscolastica, III (1911), 24-33; 212-231.

28   _____. "W. James e F. C. S. Schiller," Rivista di Filosofia
     Neoscolastica, II (1910), 142-158.

29   CUGINI, UMBERTO. L'empirismo radicale di W. James. Genoa:
     Società Anonima Editrice Francesco Perrella, 1925. Also
     published in Logos: Rivista Internazionale di Filosofia,
     VIII, (1925), 1-56.

30   DAZZI, NINO. Introduction to Saggi sull'empirismo radicale.
     Bari: Laterza, 1971.

31   DIJK, ISAAK VAN. Het pragmatisme van William James.
     Groningen: P. Noordhoff, 1911.

32   FARRE, LUIS. Unamuno, William James y Kierkegaard: y otros
     ensayos. Buenos Aires: La Aurora, ©1967.

33   FERNANDEZ, PELAYO HIPOLITO. Miguel de Unamuno y William
     James: un paralelo pragmatico. Salamanca, 1961.
        Discusses Unamuno's reading of James.

34   FERRARI, CARLO ALBERTO. "Giulio Cesare Ferrari nelle
     considerazioni di William James," Rivista di Psicologia,
     L (October-December 1956) (Fascicolo Giubilare), 27-32.

35   FERRARI, GIULIO CESARE. "Le emozioni e la vita del
     subcosciente," Rivista di Psicologia, VIII (1912),
     97-118.

36   _____. Review of Gli ideali della vita, 2nd edition, (Turin:
     Bocca, 1905), Rivista di Psicologia, I (1905), 421-422.

37   _____. "William James," Rivista di Psicologia, VI (1910),
     361-363.

Writings in Other Languages

38 GENTILE, GIOVANNI. "Religione e prammatismo nel James" in
    Il modernismo e i rapporti fra religione e filosofia.
    Bari: Laterza & Figli, 1909.

39 GIVONE, SERGIO. "Il problema della fede in Pascal e in
    James," Filosofia (Turin), XX (1969), 261-288.

40 HANSEN, VALDEMAR. William James og det religiose. Copenhagen:
    C. A. Reitzels Forlag, 1936.

41 _____. "William James og hans breve," Nordisk Tidskrift för
    Vetenskap, Konst Och Industri (1922), 176-184.

42 HÖFFDING, HARALD. Preface to Religiose Erfaringer, translated
    by E. Lehmann and C. Monster. Copenhagen: T. Branner,
    1906.

43 HOLK, L. J. VAN. "Van William James naar Henri Bergson,"
    Wijsgerig Perspectief op Maatschappij en Wetenschap, V
    (January 1965), 101-110.

44 KORTSEN, KORT K. "William James' Filosofi særlig med Hensyn
    til hans Opfattelse af det religiose," Teologisk
    Tidsskrift, 3rd series, vol. IX (1918), 177-209.

45 KOTLIAREVSKII, S. "Pragmatizm i problema terpimosti," Voprosy
    Filosofii i Psikhologii, XXI (1910), 368-379.

46 LAMANNA, E. P. Il prammatismo anglo-americano (James-Schiller-
    Dewey). Florence: Soc. Editrice Universitaria, 1952.
    Typewritten text of a course in the history of philosophy.
    Copy in the University of Michigan library.

47 LEVI, A. "La filosofia dell'intuizione indifferenziata (H.
    Bergson--W. James)," Rivista di Psicologia, VII (1911),
    47-75. Reprinted in La filosofia dell'esperienza, vol. II
    (Bologna: Stabilimento Poligrafico Emiliano, 1911).

48 LOSSKII, N. O. "Nedomolvki v teorii emotsii Dzhemsa," Voprosy
    Filosofii i Psikhologii, XII (1901), 99-134.

49 MANFERDINI, TINA. Studi sul pensiero americano. Bologna:
    Edizioni Alfa, [n.d.].
    Preface is dated 1960.

50 MANTOVANI, JUAN. Introduction to Los ideales de la vida.
    Buenos Aires: "El Ateneo," 1944.

51 MENDOZA, ANGELICA. Panorama de las ideas contemporáneas en
    Estados Unidos. Mexico, Buenos Aires: Fondo de Cultura
    Económica, ©1958.

52 MOLINA, ENRIQUE. Filosofía americana: ensayos. Paris:
    Garnier Harmanos, [1914].

53 _____. El pragmatismo o la filosofia practica de William
    James. Santiago de Chile, 1910.
        A pamphlet, in·the University of Wisconsin library,
    Madison, Wisc.

54 MORELLI, GABRIELE. La realta dello spirito nell'esperienza
    religiosa. Milan: Presso la Rivista Luce e Ombra, [n.d.].
        Pamphlet. The copy in the Widener Library at Harvard
    University is from James's library and was signed in 1905.

55 MORI, MASSIMO. "L'interpretazione attivistica di James negli
    scritti di Giovanni Papini," Rivista di Filosofia, LXIII
    (1972), 213-227.

56 MULLER, TOBIAS BALLOT. De kennisleer van het anglo-
    amerikaansch pragmatisme. The Hague: H. P. De Swart &
    Zoon, 1913.

57 PAPINI, GIOVANNI. Preface to Saggi pragmatisti. Lanciano:
    R. Carabba, 1910.

58 _____. Sul pragmatismo (saggi e ricerche). Milan: Libreria
    Editrice Milanese, 1913. 2nd edition, Pragmatismo: (1903-
    1911) (Florence: Vallecchi, 1920).
        A collection of articles on the pragmatic movement. Most
    of the articles were originally published in Leonardo.

59 _____. "William James," La Voce, vol. II, no. 39 (September 8,
    1910), p. 391.

60 PIANE, ARISTIDES L. DELLE. William James. Montevideo: A.
    Monteverde y Cia., 1943.

61 RAVAGNAN, LOUIS M. W. James. Buenos Aires: Centro Editor
    de America Latina, 1968.

62 RICONDA, GIUSEPPE. "L'empirismo radicale di William James,"
    Filosofia (Turin), XVI (April 1965), 291-332.

63 _____. "La filosofia della religione di W. James," Filosofia
    (Turin), XV (April 1964), 241-277.

Writings In Other Languages

64   RICONDA, GIUSEPPE. La filosofia di William James. Turin:
         Edizioni di "Filosofia," 1962.

65   _____. Un libro su James. Turin: Edizioni di "Filosofia,"
         [n.d.].
         Pamphlet. Review of Perry, In the Spirit of William
         James (1958).

66   _____. "William James: l'individualismo etico," Filosofia
         (Turin), XIV (April 1963), 367-386.

67   _____. "William James: la teoria pragmatistica della
         conoscenza," XIII (October 1962), 617-642.

68   ROGGERONE, GIUSEPPE AGOSTINO. James e la crisi della coscienza
         contemporanea. Milan: Marzorati, 1961. 2nd edition, with
         an added conclusion (Milan: Marzorati, ©1967).

69   RUIZ-FUNES, MARIANO. Introduction to Discursos a los maestros.
         Mexico, D. F.: Secretaria de Education Publica, [1948].

70   SÁNCHEZ BARBUDO, ANTONIO. "La intimidad religiosa de Unamuno:
         relación con Kierkegaard y W. James," Occidental, no. 7
         (September 1949), 10-13.

71   SANTUCCI, ANTONIO. "La filosofia del giovane James," Rivista
         di Filosofia, LV (1964), 13-53.

72   _____. Il pragmatismo in Italia. Bologna: Il Mulino, ©1963.

73   SARAILIEFF, IVAN V. Études sur le pragmatisme: le pragmatisme
         de William James. Sofia: Imprimerie de la Cour, 1934.
         Part of the Annuaire de l'Université de Sofia. Faculté
         Historico-Philologique, vol. XXX.
         A pamphlet, in Bulgarian, but on the title page the title
         is given both in Bulgarian and French.

74   SINI, CARLO. Il pragmatismo americano. Bari: Laterza, 1972.

75   SKRUPSKELIS, IGNAS K. "Tiesos samprata James'o pragmatizme,"
         Aidai, 1975, no. 3 (March), 115-119.

76   SPIRITO, UGO. Il pragmatismo nella filosofia contemporanea:
         saggio critico con appendice bibliografica. Florence:
         Vallecchi, 1921.

77   TAROZZI, GIUSEPPE. "Il pensiero di William James e il tempo
         nostro," introduction to Compendio dei principii di psico-
         logia di William James. Milan: Societa Editrice Libraria,
         1911.

78 TAROZZI, GUISEPPE. "William James," Nuova Antologia di
    Lettere, Scienze ed Arti, 5th Series, vol. CL (November 1),
    65-76.

79 TATÒ, FRANCESCO. "Possibilita e pluralismo nel processo
    temporale secondo James," Aut Aut, IV (1954), 144-161.

80 TEISEN, N. William James' laere om retten til at tro. Copen-
    hagen: J. Frimodts Forlag, 1911.

81 TISSI, SILVIO. James. Milan: Athena, 1924.

82 UBBINK, JOHAN GERHARD. Het pragmatisme van William James.
    Arnhem: A. Tamminga, 1912.

83 VAILATI, GIOVANNI. "'La concezione della coscienza' di
    William James," Rivista di Psicologia, I (1905), 242-246.

84 _____. Review of "Humanism and Truth" (1904), "A World of
    Pure Experience" (1904), "The Thing and its Relations"
    (1905), and "The Experience of Activity" (1905), Rivista di
    Psicologia, I (1905), 110-113.

85 _____. Review of Pragmatism, Rivista di Psicologia, III
    (1907), 284-286.

86 VAZ FERREIRA, CARLOS. Conocimiento y accion. Montevideo:
    Imprenta "El Siglo Ilustrado," 1920. Incorporated into
    Tres filosofos de la vida: Nietzsche, James, Unamuno
    (Buenos Aires: Editorial Losada, 1965).
       According to the preface, the three essays making up the
    original volume were originally published in 1908-1909.

87 VAZQUEZ, JUAN ADOLFO. La formacion del pensamiento de William
    James. Introduction to Problemas de la filosofia, trans-
    lated by Juan Adolfo Vazquez. Buenos Aires: Editorial
    Yerba Buena, 1944.
       Also published as a pamphlet.

88 VINOGRADOV, N. "Teoriia emotsii Dzhemsa-Lange," Voprosy
    Filosofii i Psikhologii, XIV (1903), 379-4 3.

89 WITWICKI, WLADYSLAW. "William James jako psycholog,"
    Przeglad filosoficnzy, vol. XVI, no. 1 (1913), 21-63.

90 ZINI, ZINO. Introduction to Principi di psicologia
    (estratti), Turin: G. B. Paravia & Co., 1928.

American Dissertations

Listed below are dissertations given in the Comprehensive Dissertation Index 1861-1972, vol. XXXII, and the supplements for 1973 and
1974. Names of persons and titles of books appear as given in the
index. Several dissertations which were published under the dissertation title and are included in the list of writings are not listed
below.

1 BAUM, MAURICE JAMES. Genetic Study of the Philosophies of
  William James and John Dewey. University of Chicago, 1928.

2 BAYLEY, JAMES E. Self and Personal Identity in William James's
  "Principles of Psychology." Columbia University, 1969.

3 BEARD, ROBERT WILLIAM. The Concept of Rationality in the
  Philosophy of William James. University of Michigan, 1962.

4 BENARD, EDMOND D. The Problem of Belief in the Writings of
  John Henry Newman, William James and St. Thomas Aquinas.
  Catholic University of America, 1950.

5 BLUESTONE, NATALIE SUZANNE HARRIS. Time and Consciousness in
  Jean-Paul Sartre and William James. Johns Hopkins
  University, 1963.

6 BRENNAN, BERNARD PATRICK. The Moral Implications of James's
  Pragmatism. Fordham University, 1961.

7 BUTTERFIELD, VICTOR L. The Ethical Theory of William James.
  Harvard University, 1936.

8 CHARRON, WILLIAM CLETUS. An Exposition and Analysis of William
  James's Views on the Nature of Man. Marquette University,
  1966.

9 CORELLO, ANTHONY V. Structures of the Field of Consciousness:
  A Study of Part-Whole Organization in William James'
  Epistemology. New School for Social Research, 1970.

191

American Dissertations

10   CWI, DAVID. William James's "Pure Experience" Philosophy:
     Genesis and Criticism. Johns Hopkins University, 1973.

11   CZERWIONKA, FELICIA EMILY. The Self in William James's Psychol-
     ogy. University of Notre Dame, 1974.

12   DAVID, KEITH RAYMOND. Percept and Concept in William James.
     Southern Illinois University, 1969.

13   DOOLEY, PATRICK KIARAN. Humanism in the Philosophy of William
     James. University of Notre Dame, 1969.

14   DUNCAN, FRANKLIN DAVIS. The Contribution of William James to
     the Psychology of Religion. Southern Baptist Theological
     Seminary, 1974.

15   EARLE, WILLIAM JAMES. James's Stream of Thought as a Point of
     Departure for Metaphysics. Columbia University, 1969.

16   FAUSER, JOHN JOSEPH. The Theory of Freedom in William James.
     Saint Louis University, 1967.

17   FORDERHASE, EARL DUANE. A Study of the Concept of a Finite
     God in the Philosophies of William James and Alfred North
     Whitehead. University of Oklahoma, 1973.

18   FRISBEE, JAY G. The Idea of a Limited God in James, Ward, and
     Tennant. Yale University, 1941.

19   GARRETT, RICHARD GEORGE. A Jamesian Metaphysics of Morals.
     Columbia University, 1971.

20   GAVIN, WILLIAM JOSEPH. An Aesthetic Approach to the Philosophy
     of William James. Fordham University, 1970.

21   GENDREAU, FRANCIS RICHARD. The Realism of William James.
     Boston College, 1974.

22   GILES, JAMES EARL. A Contemporary Interpretation of William
     James's Will-to-Believe Argument. Fordham University, 1971.

23   GOODWIN, JOHN BENJAMIN. Differences in the Meaning of Religion
     for Two American Pragmatists: William James and John
     Dewey. Temple University, 1970.

24   HAINES, WESLEY N. The Function of the Factor of God in the
     Philosophy of William James. Harvard University, 1949.

American Dissertations

25 HARRINGTON, JOHN BEATTIE. William James's Theory of Religious
    Knowledge. Princeton University, 1953.

26 KAPPY, ELLEN GAIL. Truth and the Justification of Belief: A
    Study in the Epistemology of William James. University of
    Wisconsin, 1972.

27 KAUBER, PETER GEORGE. William James's Ethics of Belief. State
    University of New York at Buffalo, 1972.

28 KESSLER, GARY EMERSON. Experience, Language, and Religion: A
    Study in the Significance of William James for the Analysis
    of Religious Discourse. Columbia University, 1970.

29 KOLLER, ALICE RUTH. The Concept of Emotion: A Study of the
    Analyses of James, Russell, and Ryle. Radcliffe College,
    1960.

30 KUNZ, ROBERT M. A Critical Examination of the Radical Empiri-
    cism of William James. State University of New York at
    Buffalo, 1953.

31 LESLIE, CHARLES WHITNEY. The Religious Philosophy of William
    James. Harvard University, 1945.

32 LONG, W. H. The Philosophy of Charles Renouvier and its Influ-
    ence on William James. Harvard University, 1927.

33 McCLUSKEY, MARILYN F. Faith and Human Life According to
    William James. Loyola University of Chicago, 1972.

34 McGEE, ELLEN FLANAGAN. An American Approach to the Problem of
    Evil: A Study of the History of Its Development and Its
    Articulation as a Philosophy by William James. Fordham
    University, 1969.

35 MacLEOD, WILLIAM J. Some Interrelations Between the Psychology
    and Philosophy of William James. Boston University, 1949.

36 MacMILLAN, DONALD. William James's Philosophy of Religion,
    With Specific Reference to His Philosophy of Mind. Univer-
    sity of Toronto, 1963.

37 MANICAS, PETER THEODORE. The Concept of the Individual in the
    Philosophies of William Graham Sumner, William James,
    Josiah Royce, and Lester Ward. State University of New
    York at Buffalo, 1963.

American Dissertations

38   MARSHALL, ERNEST CLARE. An Explication of William James'
     Neutral Monism and Some Applications to His Pragmatism.
     Ohio State University, 1970.

39   MATTHEWS, WILLIAM. An Evaluation of the Radical Empiricism of
     William James and Its Theological Significance for the
     Problem of Identity. University of Chicago, 1965.

40   MULLIN, RICHARD PATRICK, JR. The Place of Metaphysics in the
     Moral Universe of William James. Duquesne University,
     1973.

41   NEWHALL, JANNETTE ELTHINA. The Influence of William James on
     Georg Wobbermin's Psychology and Philosophy of Religion.
     Boston University, 1931.

42   NISULA, EINER SALO. Thought and Action in William James.
     Michigan State University, 1970.

43   PARKER, WILLIS ALLEN. Pluralism and Irrationalism in the
     Philosophy of William James. Harvard University, 1912.

44   PATTERSON, HERBERT PARSONS. An Extension of the Pure Experience
     Philosophy of William James. Yale University, 1913.

45   PETERSON, SVEN RICHARD. William James: The Formative Years,
     1842-1884. Columbia University, 1954.

46   PLATT, THOMAS WALTER. Spencer and James on Mental Categories:
     A Re-evaluation in Light of Modern Biology. University of
     Pennsylvania, 1966.

47   PROVINE, ROBERT CALHOUN. The Voluntarism of William James:
     An Historical and Critical Study. Brown University, 1933.

48   REILLY, WILLIAM FRANCIS, JR. The Pragmatism of William James
     as a Religious Philosophy. Fordham University, 1961.

49   ROELOFS, ROBERT T. William James' Views on Metaphysics: A
     Study in the Justification of Belief. University of
     Michigan, 1954.

50   ROSENBERGER, H. E. William James's Philosophy of Will. New
     York University, 1927.

51   ROTH, JOHN KING. An Appraisal of the Ethics of William James.
     Yale University, 1967.

American Dissertations

52 SCALES, ALBERT LOUIS. William James and John Dewey: An Interpretative and Critical Study. Yale University, 1917.

53 SEIGFRIED, CHARLENE HADDOCK. The Status of Relations in William James. Loyola University of Chicago, 1973.

54 STRUG, CORDELL THOMAS. William James and the Gods: A Peek at the Conceptual Underbelly of the "Varieties of Religious Experience." Purdue University, 1973.

55 TODD, QUINTIN ROBERT. James, Whitehead, and Radical Empiricism. Pennsylvania State University, 1969.

56 TRASK, IDA M. The Development of William James's Philosophy. University of Southern California, 1936.

57 TURNER, CHARLES CARLTON. The Meaning of God in the Philosophy of William James. Drew University, 1972.

58 VANDEN BURGT, ROBERT JOSEPH. Philosophical Roots of the Finite God Theories of William James and Edgar Sheffield Brightman. Marquette University, 1968.

59 VISGAK, CHARLES ANTHONY. The Physiological Theory of the Emotions as the Foundation for the Moral Judgment of the Individual According to William James. Duquesne University, 1972.

60 WAGENAAR, JOHN. Behaviorism and Religious Experience: An Investigation of B. F. Skinner Through William James. University of Chicago, 1973.

61 WATSON, SARAH MARTHA. James's Pragmatism and its Relation to Fascism. Ohio State University, 1942.

62 WILSHIRE, BRUCE WITHINGTON. Natural Science and Phenomenology: William James's "Principles of Psychology" as a Search for Reconciliation. New York University, 1966.

63 WINSTON, ALEXANDER P. The Concept of Human Freedom in Bergson and James. University of Washington, 1950.

James's Spirit Writings

Listed below are writings alleged to have been communicated by James through various mediums after his death. Such communications are plentiful and no effort to locate them was made.

1 BURKE, JANE REVERE. The Bundle of Life. New York:
   E. P. Dutton, ©1934.

2 _____. Let Us In. New York: E. P. Dutton, 1931.

3 _____. Messages on Healing. Privately printed, 1936.

4 _____. The One Way. New York: Privately printed, 1921.
   Reprinted, New York: E. P. Dutton, ©1922.

5 FRIEND, E. W. "From William James?", The Unpopular Review,
   IV (July 1915), 172-202.

6 SMITH, SUSY. The Book of James. New York: G. P. Putnam's
   Sons, 1974.

Index

In this index, no attempt was made to index in detail general works about James, such as R. B. Perry's The Thought and Character of William James (1935). It should be understood that Perry's book especially is a major source of information on almost all questions concerning James. William James himself is not treated as a subject; the user should consult specific topics, such as biography, bibliography, manuscripts, and the like, as well as titles of appropriate books and articles by James.

The letter F indicates a work listed in the section devoted to other languages; the letter D, the list of American dissertations; the letter S, James's spirit writings. Items falling into these categories were indexed by author and title, but not by subject.

"Pragmatisme anglo-américain et philosophie nouvelle" (J. Henry), 1912.B7

Pragmatisme chez Nietzsche et chez Poincaré (R. Bertholet), 1911.B8

"Pragmatisme contre le rationalisme, Le" (J. Bourdeau), 1909.B8

"Pragmatisme d'après Mm. W. James et Schiller, Le" (D. Parodi), 1908.B26

"Pragmatisme de William James, Le" (A. Boboc), F12

"Pragmatisme et humanisme" (F. A. Blanche), 1907.B13

"Pragmatisme et la vie religieuse, Le" (L. Boisse), 1914.B3

Pragmatisme et modernisme (J. Bourdeau), 1909.B8

"Pragmatisme et pragmaticisme" (A. Lalande), 1906.B4

Pragmatisme et sociologie (E. Durkheim), 1955.B3

"Pragmatisme pédagogique, Le" (L. Boisse), 1913.B1

Pragmatisme religieux chez William James et chez les catholiques modernistes (R. Berthelot), 1922.A1

"Pragmatism in Retrospect: The Legacy of James and Dewey" (C. Strout), 1967.B16

"Pragmatism in The Ambassadors" (N. I. Bailey), 1973.B1

Pragmatismo (L. R. Aranda, trans.), introduction to, F5

Pragmatismo (G. Papini), F58

Pragmatismo, Il (E. Chiocchetti), F26

Pragmatismo americano, Il (C. Sini), F74

"Pragmatism of William James, The" (J. F. McCormick), 1942.B26; (T. V. Moore), 1909.B16; (P. E. More), 1910.B51

Pragmatism of William James as a Religious Philosophy, The (W. F. Reilly, Jr.), D48

Pragmatismo in Italia, Il (A. Santucci), F72

Pragmatismo nella filosofia contemporanea: saggio critico con appendice bibliografica, Il (U. Spirito), F76

Pragmatismo o la filosofia practica de William James, El (E. Molina), F53

"Pragmatismus, Der" (C. Gutberlet), 1908.B11; (L. Stein), 1908.B32

Pragmatismus, Der (E. Baumgarten), 1938.A1

Pragmatismus: Eine neue Richtung der Philosophie (J. M. MacEachran), 1910.B44

"Pragmatismus von James und Dewey, Der" (G. Schrader), 1957.B5

Pragmatismus von James und Schiller, Der (W. Bloch), 1913.A1

"Pragmatism v. Absolutism" (R. F. A. Hoernlé), 1905.B4

"Pragmatism versus Science" (H. Nichols), 1907.B25

"Pragmatist Microbe, The" (Anon.), 1907.B9

"Pragmatist to Publisher: Letters of William James to W. T. Harris" (W. Nethery), 1968.B16

"Pragmatist View of Truth, The" (P. Carus), 1910.B20

"Pragmatizm i problema terpimosti" (S. Kotliarevskii), F45

Prammatismo anglo-americano, Il (E. P. Lamanna), F46

"Prammatismo di W. James, Il" (F. Albeggiani), F2

Pratt, Carnelia Atwood, 1900.B5

Pratt, James Bissett, 1907.B29; 1908.B27; 1909.B20; 1911.B32

Prayer, James on, 1912.A1

Précis de psychologie.
See Psychology

"Prerequisite to an Analysis of Behaviorism: The Conscious Automaton Theory from Spalding to William James" (P. H. Gray), 1968.B8

"Professor James on 'Nature'"
(J. A. Thomson), 1896.B7
"Professor James on Religious
Experience" (F. Sewall),
1903.B9
"Professor James on the Emotions"
(S. Bryant), 1896.B2
"Professor James' 'Pragmatism'"
(G. E. Moore), 1908.B23
"Professor James's 'Hole'"
(H. Nichols), 1906.B7
"Professor James's New 'Pluralis-
tic' Philosophy" (Anon.),
1909.B3
"Professor James's Pragmatism"
(Anon.), 1907.B10
"Professor James's Theory of
Knowledge" (A. K. Rogers),
1906.B10; review of, 1907.B14
"Professor Ladd's Criticism of
James's Psychology"
(J. P. Gordy), 1892.B3
"Professor Miller and Mr. Santayana"
(G. Santayana), 1921.B12
"Professor von Gizycki and Deter-
minism" (W. James), comments
on, 1888.B1
"Professor William James' Inter-
pretation of Religious Experi-
ence" (J. H. Leuba), 1904.B6
Progress, and pragmatism,
1970.B11; 1974.B6
Progress and Pragmatism
(D. W. Marcell), 1974.B6
Protagoras, and James, 1911.B9
"Protophenomenology in the Psy-
chology of William James"
(B. Wilshire), 1969.B23
Provine, Robert Calhoun, D47
Prüfung des "Pragmatismus" von
William James als Philosophie
(H. Drahn), 1910.A1
"Psicologia religiosa di William
James, La" (G. Celi), F20
"Psychiatrist's Comments on the
Importance of William James,
A" (W. Overholser), 1953.B12
Psychiatry, James and, 1968.B14
Psychical research, 1891.B5;
1896.B3; 1902.B10; 1904.B5;
1907.B31; 1910.B18, B42;

1911.B23; 1915.B5; 1924.B8;
1935.B1, B4; 1949.B4; 1957.B2;
1958.B6; 1960.A1; 1974.B11
Psychoanalysis, and James,
1942.B12
"Psychoanalytische Bemerkungen
zur James-Langeschen
Affektheorie" (Y. Kulovesi),
1931.B1
"Psychological Antecedents of
Social Theory in America:
William James and James Mark
Baldwin" (J. W. Petras),
1968.B18
Psychological laboratories,
1928.B1; 1949.B1; 1950.B5
Psychological Study of Religion,
A (J. H. Leuba), 1912.B15
Psychological Types (C. G. Jung),
1921.B7
"Psychological Types in Friedrich
Schiller and William James"
(P. Weigand), 1952.B9
Psychologie des sentiments, La
(T. Ribot), 1896.B6
"Psychologie de William James,
La" (L. Marillier), 1892.B5
Psychologie und Erziehung.
See Talks to Teachers, German
translation
Psychologische Typen (C. G. Jung),
1921.B7
"Psychologists' Letters and
Papers" (E. G. Boring),
1967.B2
Psychology, criticism of James's,
1894.B5; 1909.A2; controversy
over history of American,
1895.B2, B3; general estimates
of James's, 1907.B23;
1908.B33; 1910.A2; 1910.B43,
B47, B62; 1911.B1; 1921.B2;
1929.B1, B5; 1933.B2;
1934.B8; 1942.B7; 1943.B1,
B17; 1948.B7; 1953.B9;
1961.B1; 1963.B12; 1968.B24;
1969.A1; 1971.B21; 1972.B12;
method of, 1909.B6; experimental, 1912.B25; and James's
philosophy, 1913.B14;
1942.B8; 1968.B24; James's
influence on, 1936.B11,

Sabine, George H., 1905.B10;
1906.B4; 1912.B27
Sage, M., 1902.B10
"Saggio di esposizione sintetica
del pragmatismo religioso di
W. James e di F. C. S.
Schiller" (E. Chiocchetti),
F27
Saggi pragmatisti (G. Papini),
preface to, F57
Saggi sull'empirismo radicale.
See Essays in Radical Empir-
icism, Italian translation
Sainthood, 1929.A1
Salomon, Michel, 1920.B6
Salter, William Mackintire,
1881.B1; 1882.B1; 1908.B30
Salto mortale, 1947.B2
Sanborn, Herbert C., 1909.A1
Sánchez Barbudo, Antonio, F70
Sane Positivist: A Biography
of Edward L. Thorndike, The
(G. Joncich), 1968.B10
Sanford, Nevitt, 1969.B15
San Juan, E., Jr., 1964.B6
Santayana, George, 1891.B8;
1911.B37; 1920.B7; 1921.B12;
1953.B15; and James,
1921.B9; 1965.B4; 1973.B8;
James's influence on,
·1936.B15; ·letters to James,
1955.B1
"Santayana on James: A Conflict
of Views on Philosophy"
(J. J. Fisher), 1965.B4
"Santità secondo W. James, La"
(G. Celi), F21
Santucci, Antonio, F71, F72
Sarailieff, Ivan V., F73
Sawyer, Edward H., 1973.B12;
D. W. Ferm on, 1973.B4
Scales, Albert Louis, D52
Scenes & Silhouettes
(D. L. Murray), 1926.B5
Scheffler, Israel, 1974.B9
Schiller, Ferdinand Canning
Scott, 1897.B4; 1898.B2;
1902.B11; 1905.B11; 1907.B30;
1910.B63; 1911.B38; 1912.B28;
1913.B20; 1921.B13; 1927.B6,
B7; 1934.B7; his humanism,

1904.B3; and James, 1908.B26;
1910.B63; 1964.B9; controversy
with R. B. Perry, 1913.B20;
controversy with D. S. Miller,
1927.B5; letters about James,
1942.B17
Schiller, Friedrich, 1952.B9
Schinz, Albert, 1909.B23;
1911.B39; and pragmatism,
1912.B5
Schirmer, Daniel B., 1969.B20
Schmid, Karl Anton, 1951.B4
Schmidt, Hermann, 1959.A1
Schneider, Herbert W., 1926.B8;
1942.A2; 1942.B35; 1946.B4;
1964.B7
Schneider, Karl, 1909.B24
Scholz, Heinrich, 1917.B4
Schott, (unidentified person),
1908.B31
Schrader, George, 1957.B5
Schrag, Calvin O., 1969.B21
Schrickel, Klaus, 1957.B6
Schroeder, Theodore, 1916.B4
Schuetz, Alfred, 1941.B7
Schultze, Martin, 1913.A4
Science, and pragmatism,
1907.B25; James's conception
of, 1911.B14; 1932.B1;
1971.B27
Science and Sentiment in America
(M. White), 1972.B16
Science et religion dans la
philosophie contemporaine
(É. Boutroux), 1908.B6 B7
Scott, Frederick, J. D.,
1958.B8
Search for Truth, The
(E. T. Bell), 1934.B2
"Secret Life of William James"
(O. R. Lindsley), 1969.B9
"Seeking the Shade of William
James" (M. H. Hedges),
1915.B3
Seigfried, Charlene Haddock,
D53
Seillière, Ernest, 1913.B21
Selected Letters of William
James, The (E. Hardwick),
1961.A2

INDEX

("William James")
  (A. Keller), 1912.B11;
  (M. Knight), 1959.B7;
  (H. R. Marshall), 1910.B46;
  (D. S. Miller), 1946.B3;
  (D. L. Murray), 1926.B5;
  (L. Noël), 1911.B27;
  (G. H. Palmer), 1920.B5;
  (G. Papini), F59;
  (H. B. Parkes), 1941.B6;
  (R. B. Perry), 1910.B55;
  (J. J. Putnam), 1910.B58;
  (M. Salomon), 1920.B6;
  (F. C. S. Schiller),
  1921.B13; 1934.B7;
  (C. L. Slattery), 1918.B4;
  (Leo Stein), 1926.B9;
  (G. Tarozzi), F78;
  (E. L. Thorndike), 1910.B65
William James (G. W. Allen),
  1967.A1; 1970.A1; reviews
  of, 1967.B6, B8; 1973.B13
William James (É. Boutroux),
  1911.A2; reviews of, 1911.B28;
  1912.B18; 1913.B10;
  discussion of, 1913.B23
William James (B. P. Brennan),
  1968.A2; (G. H. Clark),
  1963.A1; (M. Knight),
  1950.A1; (E. C. Moore),
  1965.A2; (L. Morris),
  1950.A2; (A. L. delle
  Piane), F60
"William James, 1842-1910"
  (E. Nagel), 1942.B32
"William James, 1842-1942"
  (J. W. Buckham), 1942.B11;
  (I. Edman), 1942.B15
"William James: A Belated
  Acknowledgment" (Anon),
  1919.B1
"William James: A Portrait"
  (J. J. Chapman), 1910.B21
"William James: Builder of
  American Ideals"
  (E. Björkman), 1910.B11
"William James: Contributions to
  the Psychology of Religious
  Conversion" (W. H. Clark),
  1965.B2
"William James: Der Philosoph
  des Amerikanischen Lebens"

(E. Rosenstock-Hüssy),
  1950.B8
"William James, Dickinson Miller
  & C. J. Ducasse on the Ethics
  of Belief" (P. H. Hare and
  E. H. Madden), 1968.B9
William James: extraits de sa
  correspondance, (F. Delattre
  and M. Le Breton, eds.),
  1924.A1; 1924.B4; preface to
  1924.B2
"William James: Facts, Faith
  and Promise" (A. R. Gini),
  1973.B7
William James: His Marginalia,
  Personality and Contribution
  (A. A. Roback), 1942.A4;
  review of, 1943.B13
"William James, John Dewey, and
  the 'Death-of-God'"
  (J. K. Roth), 1971.B23
"William James: la teoria
  pragmatistica della conoscenza"
  (G. Riconda), F67
"William James: Leader in
  Philosophical Thought"
  (G. Hodges), 1902.B17
"William James: Leader of Amer-
  ican Psychology"
  (L. S. De Camp), 1958.B3
"William James: l'individualismo
  etico" (G. Riconda), F66
"William James, Lover of Life"
  (J. Erskine), 1921.B4
"William James, Man and Philo-
  sopher" (D. S. Miller),
  1942.B29
"William James, Man of Letters"
  (J. Macy), 1922.B7
"William James: Moralism, the
  Will to Believe, and Theism"
  (D. W. Ferm), 1972.B9
"William James, ou le manager de
  l'idéal" (H. Massis), 1914.B15
William James: Philosopher and
  Man (C. H. Compton), 1957.A1
"William James: Philosopher-
  Educator" (T. G. Madsen),
  1961.B3
"William James: Philosopher
  of Faith" (E. W. Lyman),
  1942.B25

"William James' Filosofi
særlig med Hensyn til hans
Opfattelse af det
religiose" (K. K. Kortsen),
F44
"William James' Humanism and
the Problem of Will"
(R. May), 1969.B15
"William James' Impact upon
American Education"
(H. A. Larrabee), 1961.B2
"William James in Brazil"
(C. S. Smith), 1951.B5
"William James in Nineteen
Twenty-Six" (J. Dewey),
1926.B3
"William James in the American
Tradition" (B. H. Bode),
1942.B5
"William James jako psycholog"
(W. Witwicki), F89
William James' lære om retten
til at tro (N. Teisen), F80
"William James' Morals and
Julien Benda's" (J. Dewey),
1948.B3
"William James nach seinen
Briefen: Leben, Charakter,
Lehre" (C. Stumpf), 1927.B8
William James of Albany, N. Y.
(1771-1832) and His Descen-
dants (K. Hastings),
1924.B5
William James og det religiose
(V. Hansen), F40
"William James og hans breve"
(V. Hansen), F41
"William James on Man's Cre-
ativity in the Religious
Universe" (R. Vanden Burgt),
1971.B29
"William James on Phantom
Limbs" (S. S. Olshansky),
1955.B6
William James on Psychical
Research (G. Murphy and
R. O. Ballou), 1949.B4;
1960.A1
"William James on Pure Being and
Pure Nothing (E. G. Reeve),
1970.B14

"William James on Religion"
(S. P. Parampanthi), 1955.B6
"William James on the Emotions"
(H. M. Feinstein), 1970.B6
"William James on the Will"
(G. Murphy), 1971.B16
"William James on Time Percep-
tion" (G. E. Myers), 1971.B17
"William James' Philosophy of
Higher Education" (M. Baum),
1934.B1
William James psychologue:
l'intérêt de son œuvre pour
des éducateurs (P. Bovet),
1910.B16
William James Reader, A
(G. W. Allen), introduction
to, 1972.B2
William James'
Religionsphilosophie,
begründet auf persönlicher
Erfahrung (W. Harberts),
1913.A2
"William James's Conception of
Truth" (B. Russell),
1908.B29
"William James's Contributions
to Education" (B. T. Baldwin),
1911.B6
"William James's Correspondence
with Daniel Coit Gilman,
1877-1881" (J. I. Cope),
1951.B2
"William James's Determined Free
Will" (G. W. Allen), 1964.B1
William James's Ethics of Belief
(P. G. Kauber), D27
"William James's Letters to a
Young Pragmatist"
(M. R. Kaufman), 1963.B4
William James's Philosophy of
Religion with Specific Refer-
ence to His Philosophy of
Mind (D. MacMillan), D36
William James's Philosophy of
Will (H. E. Rosenberger),
D50
"William James's Pluralistic
Metaphysics of Experience"
(V. Lowe), 1942.B24